Praise for *First In*

"A true-life adventure story . . . a superb case study of how efficiently the CIA works when things go right . . . a good fast read that details the CIA's seldom-discussed paramilitary capabilities."
—*The Washington Times*

"Compelling . . . a real-life ground-truth account of CIA human intelligence operations that were incredibly successful."
—BOB WOODWARD,
author of *Plan of Attack* and *State of Denial*

"*First In* adds a riveting account to the already rich martial history of Afghanistan and is destined to become a classic tale of CIA exploits in the war on terror."
—*Parameters* (U.S. Army War College Quarterly)

"[Gary Schroen offers] the kind of detail about life in the shadowy world of American espionage that used to remain secret."
—*The Christian Science Monitor*

"Gary Schroen tells his forceful story with the sharpened senses that come only from years of living in the long shadows of the Khyber Pass. . . . A terrific yarn about a sad and storied land."
—MILT BEARDEN, author of *The Black Tulip*
and co-author of *The Main Enemy*

"A timely account of the preliminary intelligence collection to combat Al Qaeda. The book was touted by the CIA Publications Review Board as 'the most detailed account of a CIA field operation told by an officer directly involved that has ever been cleared' for publication."
—*Seapower* (Navy League of the United States)

"[Schroen] vividly recounts how the seven-man team (code-named JAWBREAKER) helped the Northern Alliance defeat the hard-line Taliban regime."
—*U.S. News & World Report*

"I have read books by army officers who fought in wars past, but never one so true and thorough from a frontline intelligence officer, especially one involved in such an important episode in American history. This is really a grand achievement."
—STEVE COLL, author of *Ghost Wars*

"Riveting."
—CNN.com

Books published by The Random House Publishing Group
are available at quantity discounts on bulk purchases for
premium, educational, fund-raising, and special sales use.
For details, please call 1-800-733-3000.

FIRST IN

An Insider's Account of
How the CIA Spearheaded the War
on Terror in Afghanistan

Gary C. Schroen

BALLANTINE BOOKS • NEW YORK

2007 Presidio Press Mass Market Edition

Copyright © 2005 by Gary C. Schroen
Map copyright © 2005 by David Lindroth

Published in the United States by Presidio Press, an imprint of The Random House Publishing Group, a division of Random House, Inc., New York.

PRESIDIO PRESS and colophon are registered trademarks of Random House, Inc.

Originally published in hardcover in the United States by Presidio Press, an imprint of The Random House Publishing Group, a division of Random House, Inc., in 2005.

ISBN 978-0-345-49661-4

Cover design: Carl D. Galian

Printed in the United States of America

www.ballantinebooks.com

OPM   9   8   7   6   5   4   3   2   1

To my mother, Fern,
and my sister, Donna

To my three children,
Chris, Kate, and Jenny

And to Betsy,
whose love is the anchor of my life

ACKNOWLEDGMENTS

I must say thanks to "Rick," "Chris," "Stan," "Doc," "Murray," "Pappy," and "Brad," the JAWBREAKER Team members who shared this adventure with me. It was their skill and bravery that made the success of our mission possible. I also want to thank our aircrew, "Ed," "Greg," and "Buck," whose consummate professionalism ensured we flew safely in one of the most dangerous regions in the world for air operations. They are all truly unsung heroes, and I hope they feel that I have done justice to their story.

Thanks also to the soldiers of ODA-555 and all the other soldiers on the ODA teams that deployed to Afghanistan, who worked in seamless fashion with their CIA colleagues, putting their lives at risk to bring down the enemies of freedom and democracy who were taking sanctuary there.

I want to say a special thanks to all the men and women in the CIA, and all the U.S. military personnel, who daily continue to man the ramparts of freedom, fighting our enemies in Afghanistan, Iraq, and all the other dangerous places around the world where terrorists hide and plot. May we be worthy of their courage and their sacrifice.

My wife, Betsy, deserves a medal for her patience and understanding in putting up with me during the long process of bringing this story to print. Her encouragement was priceless. My daughter, Kate, did an outstanding job in providing editorial assistance during the early drafts of the manuscript, and is the only person who has read this work from front to back.

And a pat on the head for my dog, Otto; my deaf pug who sat at my feet every day that I worked on this story. His quiet companionship was welcomed.

CONTENTS

x   Contents

AUTHOR'S NOTE

One of the challenges facing every CIA officer who sits down to write anything for publication, regardless of the format or length, is the requirement to protect the secrecy of CIA sources and methods. This responsibility is spelled out in a formal secrecy agreement that each CIA officer signs as part of his initial employment processing. The agreement also includes a requirement that any and all materials written for publication must be submitted to the CIA's Publication Review Board (PRB), with the aim of editing out any classified information or any sensitive operational details that might jeopardize methods used in the field, identify specific foreign nationals serving as sources for the CIA, or identify CIA officers serving undercover.

I had no idea, however, that so many of the details that I included in the first draft of this manuscript would be considered sensitive and be marked for exclusion. The adjudication process was long and often tedious, with long exchanges over points such as why the actual nomenclature of the Russian helicopter that my team utilized on this mission could not be included in the text, or why the actual amount of money paid on a specific date could not be given. While painful, the process was fair and, in the end, virtually all the details highlighted for deletion were allowed to remain in the text.

What appears in the following pages is as clear, detailed, and accurate an account of the events and experiences of the JAWBREAKER Team (and the other CIA teams mentioned) as I can provide. The CIA Publication Review Board stated that it is the most detailed account of a CIA field operation told by an officer directly involved that has ever been cleared by the PRB for publication.

One area of review in which there was no question was the need to protect the names and identities of the CIA officers who appear in this story. I used two methods in writing about CIA officers. I created aliases for all the CIA officers who were part of the JAWBREAKER Team, or the other CIA teams working in other areas of Afghanistan. The CIA officers working at Headquarters, who appear in the text, I identified by their true first names and initials of their last names. This was the same process used to identify all U.S. Special Forces soldiers. Afghan personalities are identified with full true names.

I have used the term "Northern Alliance" to describe the coalition of commanders affiliated with Ahmad Shah Masood, primarily because that is the most common name used in the media when discussing Masood's organization. Engineer Aref explained to me early in my dealings with him that he preferred that I use the term "United Islamic Front for the Salvation of Afghanistan" (UIFSA), the name adopted by Masood after his break with Professor Rabbani in 1996. Another name commonly used by Masood's followers is "Shura Nazar" (Council of the North), a term coined by Masood in the late 1980s to describe the coalition of Mujahedin commanders who had pledged cooperation with Masood. According to Aref, the term Northern Alliance was created by Pakistan's intelligence agency to highlight the point that Masood's coalition was made up of northern, non-Pashtun tribal leaders, as opposed to the collection of Pashtun commanders in the southern regions of Afghanistan. It was just another way for the Pakistanis to try to isolate Masood and his Alliance.

Another difficulty was clarifying complicated terminology that the U.S. military uses in describing its various units. There is the official designation of the unit, such as the U.S. Army Special Forces, operational detachment ALPHA. The formal acronym for these units is SF/ODA. This is routinely shortened by soldiers to ODA. Each ODA has an identifying number, such as ODA-555, featured in this story. This team, because of its unique number, is nicknamed "Triple Nickel." These two designations are used interchangeably by army personnel in discussing the team. In addition, when deployed in the field, each ODA team is assigned a radio-call sign. In Afghanistan, all the call signs for the ODA teams were in a series that began with the word "Texas." ODA-555 might be Texas 10, another one Texas 12. Soldiers also used a team's call sign when talking about that team. I hope that I have managed to keep all this straight in the text.

Finally, I have included accounts of events in which I was not directly involved. In all cases, I gathered the details for these portions of the manuscript by personal conversations with the participants, and from a review of the written accounts of those activities submitted in the immediate aftermath of the events. In some cases, I have taken liberties with dates and have consolidated events to provide a tighter narrative. But in all cases, I have strived to keep these accounts as true to the individual reflections and memories of the participants as possible. I also tried very hard to present these episodes in the style and manner that the participants used in their conversations when retelling these events. While some of the events recounted here may differ slightly from what actually took place on a given date and time, I believe I have captured in an honest and accurate manner the events and actions of the brave officers involved. Any inaccuracies in detail are mine; but let no one doubt the heroism and bravery of the men described in this story.

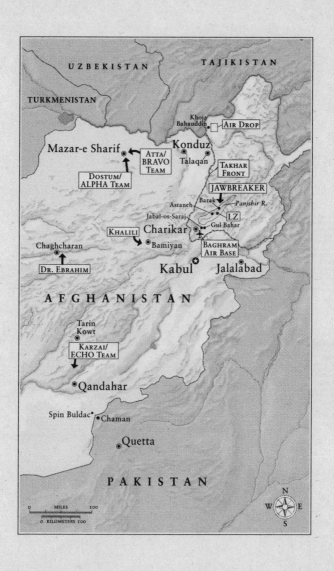

UZBEKISTAN

TAJIKISTAN

TURKMENISTAN

Khoja
Bahauddin   **Air Drop**

Mazar-e Sharif   **Atta/
BRAVO
Team**   Konduz

Talaqan

**Dostum/
ALPHA Team**   **Takhar
Front**

JAWBREAKER

Barak   *Panjshir R.*

Astaneh

Jabal-os-Saraj   **LZ**

Chaghcharan   **Khalili**   Charikar   Gul Bahar

Bamiyan   **Baghram
Air Base**

Dr. Ebrahim   Kabul ✪   Jalalabad

A F G H A N I S T A N

Tarin
Kowt

**Karzai/
ECHO Team**

Qandahar

Spin Buldac   Chaman

Quetta

P A K I S T A N

MILES   100

KILOMETERS 100

N
W   E
S

PROLOGUE

9 September 2001

The small travel alarm chirped Khalili awake. It was 6:00 a.m., and he had fallen asleep less than four hours earlier. The night before, Ahmad Shah Masood, the Commander, as Khalili always called him, had wanted to talk, and when the formal meeting broke up he kept Khalili behind. They discussed the future—the Commander was worried. The Taliban had pressed back Masood's Shura Nazar (Northern Alliance) slowly but steadily over the past five years until they controlled barely 10 percent of the country—the mountainous northeast corner of Afghanistan, centered on the Panjshir Valley.

"Time is on the side of the enemy," the Commander said. With the Taliban receiving assistance from the Pakistanis and Usama bin Ladin, they would gain strength over time. The Shura Nazar stood alone, with only a bare minimum of assistance being provided by Iran, India, and the Russians. The future looked grim.

The Central Intelligence Agency (CIA) wanted the Commander to help capture bin Ladin. He would be happy to do it but could not because his force was bottled up behind their defensive lines here in northern Afghanistan. Khalili reminded the Commander that the CIA did not make policy for the U.S. government; their job was to provide intelligence that helped shape policy. But one day the United States would change its policy toward Afghanistan and the Shura Nazar. It would have to, with bin Ladin becoming more and more of a problem. The Commander was not completely convinced, but he agreed that the relationship with the CIA was important. He just needed to find a way to press them for a significant increase in assistance.

Khalili hurried out of bed and dressed. The Commander would already be sitting down to a light breakfast. Khalili wished he had time to shower, but the Commander had insisted that he join him for morning tea. During this brief visit—the two days in Dushanbe, then yesterday here in the Panjshir—the Commander had been unusually attentive, wanting to be with Khalili, to sit and talk together. It was somewhat unusual, for although they were close friends, the Commander was usually so focused on business that their time one-on-one was rare.

As Khalili slipped into his jacket, there was a knock at the door and then it opened. The Commander stood there smiling. "I thought I would find you still sleeping. Come on. Let's talk over tea. There is much to discuss before we fly to Dushanbe." He walked into the room and stood a few feet from Khalili.

"You never sleep, Commander. How can I keep up with you?" Khalili smiled at him. The Commander looked worn, and he had aged these past few years.

As Khalili picked up his personal items from the dresser top and put them into his pockets, the Commander reached for Khalili's passport. "Here," he said, thrusting it at Khalili, "don't forget this."

Khalili waved his hand. "No, thanks, I'll just leave it here for the moment."

"No, no," said the Commander, stepping closer. "You'll forget it for sure. Here," he said, reaching forward and slipping it into the outer left breast pocket on Khalili's jacket, "keep this safe." He pushed it into the pocket and patted it lightly with his fingertips. Then he turned and walked toward the door, with Khalili following and shaking his head in wonder at the Commander's strange behavior.

As they talked over tea, they were joined by Engineer Aref, the head of Masood's intelligence organization, and one or two others, including Dr. Abdullah, who handled foreign affairs for the Shura Nazar. The talk was of overnight developments, news from abroad, and plans for the day. Khalili paid little attention to the flow of the discussions, which were typical of many mornings over the past twenty-odd years. There was a brief discussion about two Arab journalists who had been waiting in the Panjshir for several weeks to interview the Commander. Would the Commander see them this morning? There was a one-hour window of time before they were to depart. The Commander asked exactly which organization the reporters represented. Aref explained that the two had letters of introduction from an Islamic organization in London, and Professor Sayyaf had arranged for their visit to the valley. The Commander thought for a few moments, then agreed to the interview. As the group began to break up, Khalili turned to the Commander. "I will take my shower now and meet you after the interview."

"No, no, Khalili. Stay with me. Besides, you are good with the press."

"Sir, I am a civilized man. I must be clean," said Khalili jokingly.

"Yes," the Commander replied, "too civilized. You've spent too much time in the West, too much time in air-conditioning. You are forgetting your Mujahedin roots." He paused, smiling. "Please, I want you close by." Khalili nodded a yes and moved to follow the Commander as he headed for the meeting room.

The room was large, comfortable, and decorated in Western fashion. There was a small two-seat sofa and several chairs around a large square wooden coffee table. The Commander sat on the sofa and invited Khalili to sit to his right. Other chairs were pulled up for Aref, Dr. Abdullah, and several of Masood's close staff. As the men were getting settled, the Arab journalists were escorted into the room.

They were dressed in Pakistani style, with long shirts draped over baggy pants, and each wore a black sleeveless vest. Both were clean-shaven, with dark complexions, of medium height, and fit-looking. One carried a metal tripod in one hand and a heavy commercial video camera in the other, with a battery pack, cables, and other pieces of equipment suspended from straps hanging from his shoulders. There was confusion as they approached, with one man moving forward toward the Commander and the cameraman shuffling his equipment into the other's way. Finally they both stood before the Commander and each in turn shook his hand, bowing, speaking greetings in Arabic. Khalili asked if they could speak English and they both nodded yes. Khalili said to the Commander, "I will translate for these two."

The one who seemed to be the reporter and the senior of the two asked if they could move the coffee table out of the way so they could better arrange the camera. While this was taking place, with more confusion as the others in the room moved their chairs back to allow the table to be shifted, the Commander turned to Khalili and asked jokingly, "Are they going to wrestle us? Neither looks much like a reporter to me. Perhaps they are wrestlers."

Finally, arrangements were completed. The senior Arab pulled a chair close to the Commander while the cameraman set up the tripod and attached the camera to it. Khalili noticed that the camera was set low, with the lens about chest high to the Commander and himself. The cameraman held an electrical cable and a battery cable connection in his hands and stepped back several feet from the camera. It seemed strange; these two were hardly the polished journalists with whom the Commander normally dealt. Khalili asked, "Which news organization do you represent?"

"Oh, sir, we are not with a news group. We work for the Islamic Observation Center in London," the seated Arab said. "We travel the Islamic world reporting on the status of Islam in each country."

Khalili translated this for the Commander.

"They aren't really journalists?" the Commander replied. "Well, then, what questions do they have for us?" Khalili repeated the Commander's question to the seated Arab.

"We want to know why Commander Masood said that

Usama bin Ladin was a murderer and should be sent from
Afghanistan," the Arab replied. "And many more questions."

Khalili could see that the answer upset the Commander,
whose head drooped forward, his chin on his chest—a sure
sign he was angry. Khalili asked him, "Should we continue?
We could send them away."

"No, no," said the Commander with a slight wave of his
hand. "Let's get on with this. We will make the time short,
though."

Khalili noticed that the Arab sensed the Commander's
tone and was beginning to frown. "Please, let us have your
questions," Khalili said, smiling to ease the tension. The
Arab relaxed a little and looked at the small notebook he had
in his hands. Khalili shifted in his seat, turning slightly more
toward the Commander, crossing his right leg over his left
and placing his hands together on his right knee. This will
not take long, he thought. We've done this a thousand times.

The Arab looked up from his notebook, turned his head
back toward the cameraman, and said, "We begin." The
cameraman took several more steps back from the camera,
and a small red light on the front of the camera came on.
Khalili had a quick thought that the cameraman would soon
topple the camera if he got any farther away from it.

The Arab looked at the Commander and asked, "Sir, what
is the state of Islam in Afghanistan?" Khalili turned his head
slightly toward the Commander to translate when he was hit
with a soundless blue wave of fire and pressure that slammed
into him harder than any blow he had ever experienced. He
could feel his body being thrown back, the sofa moving, his
flesh burning, and a sudden explosion of pain sweeping from
head to foot. Then there was blackness.

The camera detonated with incredible force, disintegrating into thousands of tiny metal fragments. The explosion
was directed primarily toward the three men at whom it was
pointed. The Commander and Khalili caught the brunt of the
blast and were slammed backward, the sofa overturning and
tumbling the two men several feet farther back. The blast
shredded the Arab seated before the Commander, blowing

him off his chair and tossing him toward the sofa. The others in the room were knocked off their chairs and slammed, bruised, and hit by shrapnel from the explosion.

There was silence for some seconds. Then there was a slow stirring as the wounded gathered their wits and tried to clear their senses. Khalili returned to consciousness almost immediately, his mind surprisingly clear. That was a bomb, he thought. I didn't hear anything, but the smoke, the gunpowder smell—it had to have been a bomb. Then he felt a thud and a slight pressure on his left breast. He knew it was the Commander's hand before he looked. He turned his head and saw the Commander lying next to him, terribly wounded, his face ripped and torn. He's dying, Khalili thought, and so am I. He raised his left hand to try to touch the Commander and saw that the back of his hand was burned across the knuckles, the flesh cut and bleeding.

There was a scurry of activity as a few in the room shook off the effects of the blast and began to move to assist the Commander. Khalili was beginning to hear sounds now, but his ears were ringing and things sounded as if coming from far away. He was vaguely aware of others pushing into the room, then a struggle taking place as the men grabbed at the second Arab. They were pulling him bleeding and torn from the floor, jerking and pummeling him as they dragged him from the room.

Khalili looked again at the Commander and saw that someone was kneeling behind him, partially lifting his head and supporting it on their knees. The Commander rolled his head toward Khalili and made a slight jerk with his hand. "Take care of Khalili first, please," he said, his eyes locking on Khalili's. Then the Commander slumped, went limp, his eyes closing. Unconscious, thought Khalili, or dead. Allah be merciful, he thought, or maybe he said it out loud; he wasn't sure. Then he too slipped into the blackness drawing him under.

Sometime later, Khalili drifted up from the darkness to find himself on a cold metal floor and engulfed in noise. He was racked with pain, as if his entire body was on fire. He could see only with his left eye. It surprised him how clear his mind was at that moment. I'm in a helicopter, he realized, and they are flying us out of the valley. He twisted his head, wincing with the pain that the movement brought, and saw the face of the Commander close to his own. They have cleaned away most of the blood, Khalili thought. The Commander's face was pale and slack, his eyes were closed, and his mouth was hanging open loosely. He's dead, thought Khalili, and a wave of incredible sadness swept over him. His tears felt warm on his cheeks, and he reached out with his left hand to touch the Commander's arm. Thankfully, the darkness came back again and drew him under.

PART ONE

WASHINGTON, DC
11–19 September 2001

CHAPTER ONE

In northern Virginia, the morning of 11 September 2001 was beautiful, with clear blue skies and mild temperatures that gave just a hint of fall. That morning I left my home in Alexandria, Virginia, an hour later than my past routine had called for, having entered into the CIA's ninety-day Retirement Transition Program just eleven days earlier. I had spent the time since then cleaning up loose ends at the office, preparing a resume covering my thirty-five-year career in the most exciting, challenging, and—not infrequently—dangerous job within the CIA. Retirement was going to be a dramatic shift for me, and, quite frankly, it was a stretch to say that I was looking forward to it. The Retirement Transition Program is designed to help ease employees into retirement and alleviate, as much as possible, the inevitable career-change angst. The three-month period I would spend in the transition program with others facing their own retirement—many with excited anticipation, I'm sure—would help us in our respective searches for "life after the CIA." Although I was interested in exploring employment opportunities in the private sector, I had no idea exactly what I wanted to do. I was hopeful that the transition program would provide the time and the insights to allow me to develop a clear plan for the next several years.

I was anxious to reach the office, because I had received bad news late the previous day that Ahmad Shah Masood, the charismatic Tajik leader of the Afghan Northern Alliance, with whom I had a long professional relationship, had been killed in a suicide bomb attack at his headquarters in the Panjshir Valley. Worse for me was the news that Masood's senior political adviser, Masood Khalili, had been seriously injured in the blast and might not survive. Khalili and I were professional colleagues and close personal friends. I felt saddened and helpless at the news of his condition. The assassins were identified as two "Arab journalists" representing some, as yet, unidentified Islamic organization based in Europe. This was disturbing news. The Arab angle immediately pointed to the possibility that Usama bin Ladin and his al-Qa'ida organization were responsible for the attack. Bin Ladin, hosted by Mullah Omar, leader of the Taliban, was hiding in Afghanistan, and the U.S. government was applying all the pressure it could muster to force the Taliban to remove bin Ladin from their country.

The Taliban had grown from a handful of refugee Afghan religious students in the radical madrasses (religious schools) of northern Pakistan in early 1994 to a force now controlling three-fourths of Afghanistan. The only serious military opposition to the Taliban rested in Ahmad Shah Masood and his Northern Alliance forces, which controlled the rugged, mountainous northeast corner of Afghanistan. Masood's absence would seriously weaken the Northern Alliance, a shaky collection of regional warlords held together primarily by their charismatic leader. Killing Mullah Omar's last major opponent seemed a sure way for bin Ladin to gain continued acceptance as the Taliban leader's favored guest.

When I arrived at the CIA compound in Langley, Virginia, I drove past the Old Headquarters Building, passing my former parking spot located just fifty yards from the front entrance of the building. The spots in the immediate front of the building are reserved for senior officers in management positions; as deputy chief of the Near East and South Asia Division of the Directorate of Operations (DO), I had been part of that rather small group. Now I was relegated to parking in the West Parking Lot, the lot farthest from the building, and I would join the morning scramble to park there, then face the ten- to twelve-minute walk back to the building. A little thing, to be sure, but it was a clear daily reminder of my changed status.

I was in the Near East Division (NE) front office suite, down the hall from where I had sat for the last two years. It was a comfortable office, and I was near my friends and colleagues, at least for a few more days. Once I finished the remaining administrative tasks facing me, I would stop coming into the office on a daily basis. I reached the office this morning only to find that there was no further news from Afghanistan concerning the fate of Khalili or the status of the Northern Alliance leadership in the aftermath of what should have been a serious, perhaps crippling blow to them. I slipped into my morning routine of getting on the secure computer system, checking e-mail, and reviewing the work I would focus on that day; then I wandered toward the area in front of the division chief's office to get a cup of coffee.

At least five or six people were standing there, including Chief NE, Jim H., and the television set was on. This was unusual, because the morning is a busy time at the DO. Our stations overseas are open while Washington sleeps, and when we arrive in the morning we have a full dump of incoming traffic from the field to review, organize, and respond to. I joined the group and I too stood transfixed by the images on the television screen. The first tower of the World Trade Center poured a billowing cloud of black smoke from its wounded side, staining the clear blue September sky.

There was confusion within the group watching the TV, and people spoke softly with an ear to the commentary. A small plane had hit the building. No, it was an airliner. How could this have happened? How badly was the tower damaged? I recalled that a B-25 bomber had struck the Empire State Building on a foggy morning in late 1944, and although there had been extensive damage, the building itself withstood the explosion and fire. Surely the World Trade Center buildings were equally well constructed. Someone reminded the group that one of the towers had withstood a terrorist attack in the early 1990s when a truck filled with explosives was detonated in its underground parking garage.

Then, as we watched, a second aircraft flashed into the picture and penetrated the second tower. The scene rocked the room. We all recognized that this was no tragic accident unfolding before us; it was a deliberate, planned attack. Word soon came from friends in the Counterterrorist Center (CTC) that perhaps as many as six commercial airliners had been hijacked that morning. More attacks were to come. The group standing before the television set grew and changed as people joined the crowd and others wandered off, dazed and shaken. Then we watched the screen—as did millions of Americans—in disbelief and horror as the first tower collapsed.

I am not sure of the sequence of events after that. I was too shocked by the unbelievable scenes playing out in real time before us. There was a telephone call at my secretary's desk, and she picked up and listened carefully. I recall a hush beginning to settle on the group around her, and she looked up and said, "The Pentagon was just struck by an airliner. It crashed right into the building, at the side just next to Route 395."

I was reeling. My son, Christopher, worked at the Pentagon. Was he hurt? Was he dead? What was going on? I could not recall what area of the Pentagon he worked in, and I prayed that he was safe. I called my daughter Jenny, who is a State Department officer in the East Asia Bureau. She came on the phone choked with emotion, having also heard the news about the Pentagon. She had immediately tried to call Chris on his cell phone, but the cell network was overloaded with calls and she could not get through. I asked about Kate, my other daughter, and Jenny said she had gotten through to her at her office in Rosslyn, Virginia, and she was fine. Kate said she'd remain at her office until she knew what was going on. I said good-bye to Jenny with a large lump in my throat; it seemed to me that the State Department complex would be an attractive target.

Jim came out of his office and called for attention. He had just been contacted by our Seventh Floor (senior CIA management resides there) and was told that the decision had been made to evacuate CIA Headquarters save for a small, key skeleton staff. There were reports that at least one other hijacked plane was in the air and heading for Washington. The attack on the Pentagon was taken as confirmation that key government installations in the DC area were targets, and all were to be evacuated. All CIA personnel were to close up their offices and immediately depart the compound.

It was an eerie experience trudging down the stairwell from the sixth floor with friends and colleagues, leaving when there was a crisis under way. It ran contrary to all my years of experience as a CIA operations officer. A time of crisis was when we dug in and worked the hardest. This evacuation seemed too much like running away. Insult was added to injury when we exited the building and saw the massive traffic jam that had already begun, as thousands of employees tried to exit the compound at the same time. I was angry and frightened, and I thought of my wife and children. I had tried to reach my daughter Kate before leaving my office, but the phone lines were still jammed. I hoped she really would stay in her office until the attacks were over and the streets clear. And I thought of my wife, Betsy, now in Beirut, Lebanon, on a temporary duty assignment with the State Department. Who knew what impact these events would have overseas. Beirut had become much safer in the past few years, but I hated to think of her there at a time like this.

Later that evening the news was better. Christopher was safe, having delayed going in to work after a late night in the office on 10 September. He had just arrived at the metro station at the Pentagon when the plane struck, and the exits up to the street level and the Pentagon itself had quickly been closed. Passengers in the station were safe and were able to exit the station on following trains. Jenny and Kate were back home, shaken but also safe. Later that night I got a call from Betsy. By then we knew that all air traffic into the United States from Europe was canceled for at least several days; so although she was stuck in Beirut until that situation was resolved, at least she was safe.

* * *

For me, the next several days were a blur. Although I was relieved of the worry about my family, the saturation of media coverage of the events playing around the clock made it hard to focus on anything but the tragedy. I returned to the office the next day and somehow managed to halfheartedly resume the final tasks left undone from the day before, and by the thirteenth I finished the last of my administrative requirements. With no real job on which to focus my energy, and rather than feel like a fifth wheel by hanging around the office, I decided to take several days off and think about my future. I was adrift and, like everyone in the country, I was angry, dazed, and frustrated at the inability to do anything to punish those who had perpetrated this horror on so many innocent people. Betsy's arrival home late that night helped bring some focus back into my life.

Late in the evening of 13 September, I received a call at home asking me to meet with Cofer Black, chief of the CTC, early the next morning at his office. I had no idea what Cofer wanted with me, and while I drove to the compound I mused over the possibilities of what he would want to discuss. Cofer is a large man, well over six feet tall, always well dressed and imposing. He greeted me warmly and seated me at the small conference table that he used for meetings. He came straight to the point. "Gary, I want you to take a small team of CIA officers into Afghanistan. You will link up with the Northern Alliance in the Panjshir Valley, and your job is to convince them to cooperate fully with the CIA and the U.S. military as we go after bin Ladin and the al-Qa'ida. You will also evaluate their military capabilities and recommend steps we can take to bring the Northern Alliance forces to a state of readiness so they can effectively take on the Taliban forces, opening the way for our efforts against UBL." Cofer leaned forward and spoke quietly. "Gary, this is an incredibly risky assignment, but it is also incredibly important. You are, frankly, the best-qualified officer to lead this team."

I responded without a pause. "Of course I'll take the team in. I'm honored and grateful to be asked."

Cofer thanked me, saying that anything I needed—people, materiel, money—would be made available. He asked that I meet immediately with Rod S., chief of the Special Activities Division (SAD), to get SAD's input into the planning. That thought had already occurred to me. I telephoned Rod from Cofer's office, and he said he was waiting to meet with me.

Rod greeted me outside his office door. He is a former marine and has maintained that fit and solid image, with hair still closely cut. I was sure he never, ever observed "casual Fridays." Rod repeated Cofer's assurances of providing whatever assistance I might need. He had one request, however—that I consider taking one of his senior officers as my deputy on the team, and he named Rick as his choice. I agreed immediately. Although I had met Rick on several occasions, I knew him more by his excellent reputation as one of the youngest Senior Intelligence Service (SIS) officers in the CIA, and one of the best officers working in the paramilitary area of operations. Rick was standing by, and while we waited for him to come to the office, Rod expressed his concerns about the upcoming mission.

He explained that the decision to field a team to Afghanistan had been made the day before by CIA's director, George Tenet, who ordered Cofer and the CTC to take the lead in pulling together a team for the mission. With a shake of his head, Rod said that the CTC had placed Murray, a former CIA technical operations officer, in charge of making the initial arrangements for the mission, until Cofer could meet with me to offer me the assignment. Rod went on to say that Murray had hit the ground like a tornado, creating, in his opinion, almost as much confusion as progress.

I knew Murray from the 1991 Gulf War and Riyadh, where he had worked for me on a paramilitary program to develop intelligence collection capabilities inside Iraqi-occupied Kuwait. Murray had done an excellent job in that program, but he clearly chafed under bureaucratic restraints, and he had trouble working for officers he did not respect. He had resigned from the CIA following the end of the Gulf

War, although he had eventually come back to work for the
CTC on contract. I knew I could work effectively with Murray, and the fact that part of his background included a number of years as a navy SEAL team member made him an attractive candidate for our team.

Rick arrived and we exchanged greetings, recounting quickly where we had previously met. I then welcomed him as my deputy. Our operational backgrounds and experiences complemented each other: I had been involved in Afghan affairs on and off since 1978 and had personally dealt with many of the senior Northern Alliance commanders during the 1988–90 time frame; Rick was a former Special Forces A-Team member and he had years of field experience in CIA paramilitary operations. I said I thought the matchup was perfect. We left Rod to meet with Murray and review the status of his efforts.

Rick and I spent several hours with Murray, and indeed he was a whirlwind of activity. He had contacted various offices to arrange for equipment we would need. He had been in touch with SAD to discuss possible flight arrangements to get the team into central Asia, where we would have to stage before moving into Afghanistan. Murray also "recruited" a young CTC officer for our team. Neither Rick nor I said much, simply taking notes on the things Murray had under way. He had made an excellent start, but it was clear that bureaucratic toes had been stepped on and that Murray had too many balls in the air for one man to possibly handle.

I listed several factors that we should consider in our planning. The team should be small—six or seven officers maximum. We would need a professional communications officer with extensive field experience, and we should have a medic accompany us. With Rick, Murray, and me, that made five officers. (I had already decided that Murray's recruit would not come along; he had no CIA field experience and lacked area knowledge of Afghanistan.) The other two officers should be operations officers, and I mentioned I had a strong candidate in mind for one of those positions. Rick said he had a Special Activities officer in mind for the other slot.

I noted that our mission was open-ended and that we might be required to stay in Afghanistan for months. Resupply would eventually be worked out, but we should take with us as much essential material as we could safely manage. I suggested to Rick that he and I take the night to think through the myriad administrative and logistical details facing us, then regroup early the next morning to pull together the team and the necessary equipment.

As we headed our separate ways, all I could think of was that I had just been given an opportunity to take the first real steps to strike back at bin Ladin and the al-Qa'ida. The images of the Twin Towers collapsing, the Pentagon in flames, and that blackened crater in Pennsylvania were etched in my memory. I knew that the only way to effectively get at bin Ladin was to go after him in Afghanistan, and the only way to effectively chase him in that country was to eliminate the Taliban forces protecting him. The only way to do that was by using the only military force in Afghanistan that was organized and capable of taking on the Taliban in the field— Masood's Northern Alliance. My only fear was that Masood's death might have so shaken the confidence of the remaining leadership of the Alliance that they would be too demoralized to carry on the fight.

My immediate concern, however, was the upcoming struggle I would face when I arrived home and informed Betsy of my new assignment. My wife is a State Department officer, and we had shared a number of dangerous assignments during our twelve years of marriage. We were together in Riyadh during the Gulf War, and we had sat in our living room there with Iraqi SCUD missiles exploding in the skies overhead. She took in stride the threat of chemical or biological weapons, the massive explosions of conventional SCUD warheads nearby, and the real threat of Iraqi terrorist attacks in Riyadh. We did a three-and-a-half-year assignment in Islamabad after that, again dealing with the constant threat of terrorist attacks. She was evacuated from Pakistan following the al-Qa'ida bomb attacks against U.S. embassies in Africa in August 1998, but she returned to finish out her assignment in Islamabad the following spring. Dangerous places and dangerous assignments were not new to her. And over the years she had come to accept the fact that my CIA work put me at far greater risk than that taken by officers from other government agencies serving abroad.

But this was the most dangerous assignment of my career. She and I had already discussed the situation on the ground in Afghanistan, and how shaky the Northern Alliance was following Masood's assassination. I had to tell her that the team would be isolated, and we would be on our own should the situation deteriorate and the Northern Alliance break. We were going deep into harm's way, and I could not lie to her by saying that help would be anywhere nearby. I knew she would be angry with me for taking on this risk so late in my career. Our lives had been on a smooth path, and we had plans for retirement. We were looking forward to sharing a new life outside U.S. government service. Now all of that was in jeopardy.

We sat up late into the night discussing the mission, and there were tears and anger, as I had anticipated. In the end she knew that my mind was made up. As she got ready for bed, she said, "I know you're going to do this. I don't really understand why you want to put yourself at such risk. I'll try to be supportive, but just don't expect me to pretend to be happy about it." I knew that not being able to share this danger with me was one of the hardest things for her to accept about the situation.

CHAPTER TWO

The meeting the next morning went smoothly. I opened with a statement to clarify the chain of command, more for Murray's sake than anything else. I was in charge; Rick was the deputy, and he and I would make all decisions on the structure and organization of the team. It was 15 September, and I wanted to leave the United States on the twenty-first, giving us six full days to complete preparations. Not a lot of time for all we needed to do, but soon enough, I hoped, to satisfy the Seventh Floor.

Rick would concentrate on coordination with SAD. His last assignment at Headquarters had been as a senior officer in charge of one of the largest components within the Special Activities Division, giving him encyclopedic knowledge of SAD's capabilities and exactly who to call to get things done. I did not know until that morning that Rick had been in language training for the past two months in preparation for a command job overseas. He volunteered for this new mission as soon as he learned about it, putting his long-planned assignment on hold.

During Rick's years in SAD, he had developed an extensive network of contacts within the U.S. military Special Operations community, and he made use of those contacts to ensure we were in touch with the various military entities we might be working with in Afghanistan. I agreed with Rick's idea that we should invite the U.S. military to send a Special Operations representative as part of our team.

Murray was on logistics. We needed weapons, handguns and long guns, ammunition, MREs (meals ready to eat), water purification kits, laptop computers and associated hardware, and on and on. We also needed space at Headquarters for a temporary office for our team, as well as the ability to send and receive cable traffic ourselves and to directly coordinate arrangements for our actual deployment.

Rick had already contacted Pappy, a field communications officer with whom he had worked in Bosnia. Pappy was simply the best, most experienced field communications officer in the business, and he was working here at Headquarters. Rick tracked him down the previous evening, and Pappy immediately agreed to join the team. Given the Seventh Floor's interest in this mission, there was no question of Pappy not being allowed to participate. Once Pappy was on board, he would pull together the necessary communications equipment.

Rick suggested we ask Doc to serve as our medic. I agreed immediately. I knew Doc well; he had worked for me in Riyadh on the same paramilitary project as Murray. He was a former Special Forces medic with extensive combat experience in Vietnam and other hot spots. Following his retirement from the army, Doc joined the CIA's Office of Medical Services. He has served in the most challenging, hostile field environments and still found time to obtain a physician's assistant degree and write several excellent military history books. Rick and I both knew that Doc would accept the assignment without a second thought, despite his recent months away from home on an extended field assignment overseas for the CTC.

Rick learned last night from the CTC that Doc was stranded in Gandor, Newfoundland, a passenger on one of the many international flights from Europe that were diverted there on 11 September. He was returning from his extended assignment overseas. This started a discussion as to where we should have Doc join up with the team. Getting Doc from Gandor might take days, given the limited facilities and the number of aircraft on the ground there.

SAD informed Rick that a Russian-built CIA helicopter, positioned at a location in central Asia, would serve as our primary transportation into Afghanistan. Efforts were under way to identify a convenient location where we could receive it. We would have to test the helicopter, check our equipment, and make last-minute contact with the local Northern Alliance (NA) representatives to ensure that our flight route and travel arrangements were approved by our Afghan hosts and the appropriate local governments.

Tashkent, in Uzbekistan, or Dushanbe, in Tajikistan, were the most likely locations for staging areas. Rick suggested that we have Doc travel to Tashkent and wait there to join our team. Tashkent seemed the most logical choice—the U.S. government had good relations with the Uzbek government, and the Uzbeks seemed anxious to see those relations improve. Even if Tashkent was not selected as our staging area, Doc would still be relatively close at hand. At fifty-seven, Doc would be the second-oldest team member; I was fifty-nine.

Chris was the operations officer whom I had in mind to join the team. He was simply the best case officer with whom I had ever worked, and in the summer of 2001 he had completed four years working the Taliban/terrorist target in Pakistan. He knew the area, knew Afghans, spoke excellent Dari (the language spoken by the northern tribes of Afghanistan), and was an excellent outdoorsman, having camped and hiked all over Pakistan. But it would be a sacrifice for him to come along with the team because he had already been separated from his family for a year.

Finally, Rick requested that Stan join the team as the seventh man. Stan was one of the new breed of cross-trained officers being recruited by SAD. A former marine with excellent paramilitary skills, he was fully trained as a CIA operations officer. Stan would add depth to the paramilitary end of the team and would beef up our intelligence collection and production capabilities. Pending the possible addition of a U.S. military Special Operations representative, our team was complete.

One last thing was required—the team needed a name. I suggested that we call ourselves the Northern Afghanistan Liaison Team (NALT), which was the formal NE Division name for earlier teams dispatched into northern Afghanistan. However, our code name would be JAWBREAKER. This was a small but symbolically important concession: NE Division owned the turf on which we would be operating—Afghanistan—but CTC owned the problem we would be working on—terrorism. There had been some friction between NE and the CTC in the past when previous teams had been sent to northern Afghanistan, and I wanted to ensure that interdivisional rivalries would be kept to a minimum.

Pappy showed up later that morning, and Rick and I quickly brought him up to speed on the mission. Pappy began to develop a checklist of the communications equipment we would need. He said he would start pulling things together by early that afternoon. I told him that if he ran into problems to let me know immediately, and if I could not resolve the problem, I would contact Cofer Black to break any logjams that developed. I grew to like Pappy. He had an engaging personality and was down-to-earth and straightforward, and his competence was as clearly evident as his enthusiasm for his work was infectious.

Stan arrived a little later, also full of enthusiasm. He had a young-looking face that belied his nearly forty or so years, and I learned later that he preferred a soft cotton plaid shirt and a tan Orvis corduroy sport coat with leather sleeve patches to the rest of the team's scruffy, outdoorsy look. He said that his Russian was excellent, and I thought that was fine but didn't expect it to be of much use to us in the Panjshir Valley. Later, I was proved to be very wrong on that point.

Rick came back after lunch with the support chief for SAD, who informed us that we would have the use of one of their conference rooms as our temporary office space. The support chief showed us the room, and we discussed furniture and the number of computer drops we needed. We would be placed on the SAD cable database, which would allow us to send and receive cable traffic as well as have access to all other traffic being generated on our mission. By 16 September, the conference room was fully converted into the JAWBREAKER Team room, with six computers up and running.

Rick performed another miracle later that afternoon when he recruited Cofer Black's wife to work as our office manager while we prepared for deployment. Mrs. Black proved to be incredibly competent, efficient, and hardworking, and her unspoken but well-known connection to the CTC chief helped smooth over any reluctance to cooperate that other offices might have had when called requesting support.

Murray arranged with the CTC for our team to receive a cash advance to cover the purchase of field clothing and equipment, and he came around late that afternoon with $1,200 for each of the five team members at Headquarters. (Eventually we opted to purchase some clothing and equipment for Chris and Doc and take it with us when we deployed. Although our color or pattern selections for them were not perfect, we did fairly well in equipping them.) Murray and I arranged to meet that evening at an REI outdoor-equipment store, where we would purchase the clothing and equipment needed for the mission.

Choosing the items to take along was not as simple as it might seem. We did not know what our living conditions would be. Outdoor camping or unheated mud huts? Would local food be available? What about potable water? It seemed unlikely that bottled water would be available once the supply we were taking along ran out. What kind of weather would we encounter? We knew that the weather in the valley was now warm, and there had been no rain in months. But we also knew that winter weather usually began in mid-October, with snow starting to fall in the high mountains even earlier than that. Would we have snow to contend with in the valley? What about winter rains? Also, because we would be traveling into Afghanistan by helicopter, space for our personal gear would be at a premium. Extra fuel, generators, weapons, communications gear, and so forth would dictate how much additional weight in personal items we could bring along. Therefore, the mix of clothing, appropriate footwear, camping-type food items, water purification kits, entrenching tools, knives, compasses, and the like was important. What if we could take only half of our personal gear into Afghanistan, having to leave the rest behind at our staging point? How would we divide the equipment for that possibility? A mistake at this end could have unpleasant consequences at the other. Murray and I were in the store for three hours that night, and we were popular customers when we finally went through the checkout.

CHAPTER THREE

On the morning of 17 September, we sat down with senior SAD officers to review transportation arrangements for the deployment. Given the nature of our mission and the odd nature of the equipment we would be taking with us, we relied on a mix of U.S. military and leased aircraft for our transport. The officer coordinating this aspect of the operation explained that the best option for the first leg of our travel was to use a regularly scheduled U.S. military C-5A aircraft to ferry the team and our equipment from Dover Air Force Base in Delaware to Frankfurt, Germany. We would stage out of Frankfurt, using a U.S. military–controlled support facility. From there we would use a chartered L-100 aircraft (the civilian version of the C-130 military cargo transport) for the flight to Tashkent, Uzbekistan.

The timing of our flight from Frankfurt would depend on our obtaining appropriate flight clearances from the Uzbek government. CIA officers in Tashkent were working hard to smooth the bureaucratic obstacles that the Uzbeks were erecting in regard to our use of their country as a staging area for the insertion of CIA personnel into Afghanistan. Although U.S. government relations with the Uzbeks were excellent, the political sensitivities of allowing the CIA to utilize Uzbekistan for this mission had to be recognized and resolved. Here we would most likely need the help of the Russians, who continue to exert enormous influence over the Uzbek government. We had been assured that, if necessary, the CIA would request that President Bush contact Russian leader Putin to ask that he intervene.

We learned more about the helicopter we would be using on this mission. It was a Russian-manufactured heavy-duty troop/cargo helicopter that had been purchased by the CIA several years earlier to ferry CIA personnel into northern Afghanistan to meet with Ahmad Shah Masood. Although the helicopter was not new, it had undergone extensive reconditioning and upgrades to its avionics. With those upgrades, it was undoubtedly the best helicopter of its type in the region. We also learned that two CIA helicopter pilots were on their way to Tashkent and a seasoned mechanic/crew chief was en route separately to link up with the pilots. The helicopter would be ready and flight-tested by 20 or 21 September.

Our officers in Tashkent were confident that the Uzbeks would agree to our using their facilities to stage for the deployment, but no one was sure what stand the neighboring government of Tajikistan would take. The best, or at least the safest, route for us to use for insertion was to travel directly east from Tashkent across the mountains into Dushanbe, Tajikistan. We could refuel there, then fly directly south into Afghanistan. That way we would be entering Afghan airspace over what was Northern Alliance–controlled territory, minimizing the risks of being fired on by Taliban antiaircraft defenses. The Taliban had a large number of shoulder-fired antiaircraft missiles of all types, and a slow-moving helicopter was a relatively easy target, even for an inexperienced gunner.

Unfortunately, our relations with the Tajiks were not the best. Over the past several years, CIA efforts to develop close, professional contacts in Tajikistan had foundered, because the level of lawlessness and street violence in Dushanbe was simply too great to allow our officers to visit there for more than a day or two at a time. However, we did have a basic working relationship with the Tajik government, and a senior CIA officer assigned in the region traveled to Dushanbe about once a month for several days of meetings with their intelligence service, just to keep that door open. That officer would travel to Dushanbe to be in place to assist in our transit through there and, more important, to add whatever personal pressure he could manage to help persuade the Tajiks to cooperate.

If we were not able to use Tajik airspace for our entry, we would be forced to fly directly south from Tashkent and enter Afghan airspace over Taliban-held territory, then fly several hundred miles east over areas known to have a number of Taliban antiaircraft defenses in place. Few if any of those positions would have radar systems operating, making our ability to spot them electronically, and thus avoid them, almost impossible. Not a comforting thought.

Finally, our officers in Tashkent had been in touch with Northern Alliance (NA) representatives in Tashkent and Dushanbe. The CIA had had fairly regular contact with them for several years, and they in turn were in contact with their Northern Alliance leadership in the Panjshir Valley. We were assured that the team was welcome and that the NA leadership was anxious to have the team in the Panjshir.

As a bonus, an experienced Northern Alliance helicopter pilot would be available to join the team in Tashkent or Dushanbe to provide flight assistance and route advice to our pilots. We would continue to coordinate arrangements via these NA representatives, to ensure that we kept the Northern Alliance leadership well in the loop.

Things were coming together. Pappy came by in the late morning with two carts piled with boxes of equipment. This equipment was the heart of our communications link back to Headquarters and would allow full secure data exchange between the team and all CIA stations. Secure voice transmissions would be possible with Headquarters and a few other CIA locations. Pappy got busy opening each box and carefully examining the contents. Although all the equipment had been checked and serviced prior to issue to Pappy, this was gear that had been used previously on numerous field

deployments. After each deployment the gear was reconditioned, checked, and repaired as necessary, but Pappy had to
make sure that each unit was complete, and that no obvious
problems had been overlooked. Once we were inside Afghanistan, spare parts and replacement units would be difficult or impossible to obtain.

Pappy also requested several types of satellite telephone
systems, which would be delivered the following day. One
system was a briefcase-size phone that transmitted via a
high-orbit, geostationary satellite network. Those satellites
are, in effect, fixed in locations above the Earth, providing
a reliable communication channel once a phone signal is
locked onto a satellite. The other, a commercial phone system, used the low-orbit satellite network of the now-defunct
Iridium Corporation. The low orbits of those satellites cause
them to move across the sky rather quickly. In a mountainous
area such as northern Afghanistan, the signal link to these
satellites would be lost frequently. However, Pappy was confident that, between these systems, we would be able to
maintain nonsecure voice contact with the outside world.

Other tasks exhausted hours of this long day. We had a
session with an officer who briefed us on procedures and
techniques should we find ourselves needing rescue by the
U.S. military. Without these procedures, a rescue helicopter
crew could not know whether the individual seeking rescue
was really the American they expected or a hostile enemy
luring them in. There is a simple but effective protocol for this
situation, and we went over it carefully, because our lives could
depend on getting this correct. All and all it was a sobering
reminder of the dangerous nature of our upcoming mission.

Another hour was spent on the phone getting the necessary approvals to bring money for the Northern Alliance.
Money is the lubricant that makes things happen in Afghanistan. I discussed the issue with Ben B., one of Cofer's key
deputies, and we tossed out numbers. We settled on three
million dollars. That amount would provide me with sufficient reserves to carry our team through the first three to four
weeks, and it was about the maximum amount of cash we

could manage to carry easily. I knew from past experience that a million dollars is bulky and heavy and does not fit into one of those small metal briefcases carried by the bad guys in the movies. I called a senior CTC finance officer and explained my requirements for cash. I stressed the urgency of the request— since we were planning to depart within a few days. I was told he would forward the appropriate paperwork to Ben, and he assured me that, if the request was approved, the money would be ready for me by the morning of 19 September.

Stan, who had taken on some of the logistical duties from Murray, reported that the weapons had been approved and were being flown in from a warehouse facility managed by SAD. That facility stores equipment for use in SAD's paramilitary operations worldwide. We would receive ten AK-47s with folding stocks along with ten Browning 9mm Hi-Power automatic pistols. There would be ammunition for each type of weapon, with four thirty-round magazines for the AK-47s and three magazines each for the Brownings. Holsters, ammo pouches, cleaning kits, and military equipment web gear and belts would be included in the shipment. Stan had also arranged for individual GPS (global positioning system) sets and top-of-the-line compasses for the team, and he agreed to provide GPS training as time allowed.

A surprise for me were the multipurpose U.S. Air Force survival maps that Stan had somehow managed to procure for each member of the team. These large-scale maps covered the area in which we would be operating. Each map sheet was made of a special waterproof material and could be used as a survival blanket, a ground cloth, a water catch, and even a bandage. In addition to the normal map information, each sheet had numerous survival tips printed along the borders, including instructions on starting a fire without matches, finding water, land navigation without a compass, and first aid. The map rolled into a thin, compact tube, which occupied a special place in each of our backpacks.

As Stan was finishing his review of the items he had obtained, Murray arrived with a box containing knives for the team. There were Ken Kershaw folding knives with belt clips featuring a razor-sharp, spring-loaded three-inch blade, with an interior lock to keep the blade in place. A flick of the thumb opened the blade with an impressive snap. There was also a variety of longer belt knives. I selected a Japanese-made knife with a five-inch Tanto-style blade. We were impressed with Murray's selection and his initiative, because none of us had mentioned a need for knives. Murray also purchased for each of us a Camelbak water system, which can be worn as part of a backpack, with a drinking tube that fits over a shoulder so you can drink with minimum effort even while moving. Another excellent choice by Murray.

The shock of the day came at about six that evening, when Rod called from the SAD front office. He had just come from a meeting with the director of Central Intelligence (DCI) and Cofer, and the decision had been made to move our departure date forward two days; we would be deploying on 19 September instead of the twenty-first. Our original departure date barely left us enough time to complete all the arrangements and pull together all the materials we would need to take along. Rod said there was no wiggle room on this, because the U.S. president had pressed the DCI for this earlier departure date and the DCI promised the president he would make it happen.

We quickly took stock of the state of our preparations. We had the basic equipment and personal gear we would need. The things we did not have could possibly be obtained en route or be flown in to us eventually.

However, we realized that each of us still had a long list of personal tasks to attend to prior to departure. Our finances had to be put in order, and we needed to ensure that our wills were up-to-date. We had to know that, in our absence, our spouses could carry on the responsibilities of home and children. We didn't know when—or even if—we would return from our mission.

We broke off to head home and work on those essential tasks. It was another busy, late night.

CHAPTER FOUR

The evening before our departure found me at the local supermarket. I was looking for condiments and special items to add some zip to our menu of dehydrated packaged meals, dried fruit, and PowerBars obtained from REI. Peanut butter seemed like a good idea, as did instant coffee. Two large jars of each went into the cart. Powdered Gatorade, salt, pepper, Tabasco sauce, soy sauce, processed cheese spread, and a box of saltine crackers all helped round out what I would be taking with me.

Then I made a stop in the drugstore area to put together a selection of over-the-counter medicines. With winter coming soon to northern Afghanistan, I wanted aspirin, ibuprofen, Band-Aids, antiseptic cream, antibiotic hand soap and wipes, and cold, cough, and flu medicine. When the cart was nearly full, I finally stopped, realizing that there was a limit to what I could take along. I was going to war—not on a camping trip. I went back through my cart and returned a number of nice-to-have items to the shelves.

Betsy and I had a light meal that night. Neither of us felt much like eating. My hectic efforts to pull my gear together over the past several nights had added to Betsy's stress. My news over dinner that my departure date had been pushed forward added more fuel to the fire. There were tears but no anger this time, and she said in frustration, "Why are you putting yourself in such danger? You've served this country for more than thirty years. Why are you going to Afghanistan?"

I struggled to answer in a way that did not seem corny or smack of bravado. There was a *Washington Post* newspaper on the kitchen counter, and the front page had a photo of a New York City fireman in dress uniform, saluting, with tears streaming down his cheeks. I picked up the paper and pointed to the photo. "Honey, this is why I'm going. We all feel the pain of those deaths. Everyone wants to strike back at those bastards who did this to America. I've been given a chance to do just that. But even more than wanting personal satisfaction, I'm the right man to lead this team. I can make a real contribution." I paused, looking at her and trying to smile. "Besides, if I turned down this assignment, I wouldn't be the man you fell in love with, or the man I've worked all my life to be. I simply have to go." It was the best explanation I could come up with for my motivation, then or now.

As we were cleaning up the dinner dishes, we brushed against each other at the kitchen sink, and turned and embraced and kissed. There was nothing to say except "I love you," and that was said several times over the next hour.

I put thoughts of the previous night behind me as I entered the office that last full day at Headquarters. It proved to be as hectic as any day I can remember. Pappy was running around hunting down critical communications equipment, so we could link with the CIA network. He had also obtained ten handheld high-frequency (HF) radios, which would allow secure communications between team members as we moved around the valley.

Murray had a contact in CTC Logistics and was working directly with him to bypass the normally slow procurement procedures. He announced that morning that he had succeeded in arranging for the purchase of six Sony laptops with all the bells and whistles. These would be in addition to the computers that Pappy was bringing along as part of his communications system. Murray also arranged to buy four high-end digital cameras, computer photo software, and two printers that could handle photo-quality print work. The CTC Logistics officer would deliver them later in the morning, and all this needed to be packed for shipment.

Rick was working on transportation arrangements with

SAD. We would depart from Dover, Delaware, on an air force C-5A at 7:00 p.m. the following evening, 19 September. Murray, Pappy, and Stan would be transported to Dover by truck with our personal gear. They would leave here late that morning to be sure to be there on time. Rick and I would fly to Dover on a chartered aircraft later in the afternoon to allow time for us to meet with several senior officers, including Cofer Black, for a final review of our mission. The bulk of our equipment—all the communications gear, weapons, food, and general team items—would be flown to Germany that night.

As soon as his office opened for business, I called the senior CTC finance officer I had spoken to earlier and notified him of the change in our departure date. I was assured that the money would be ready for pickup by 11:00 a.m. on the nineteenth. We would carry the money as part of our personal gear.

We learned that Chris had arranged for his own travel to Frankfurt and was scheduled to arrive there late on 19 September. He would meet us on the twentieth at the U.S. military facility where we would be staging. Doc was already in Tashkent and would wait for us there. We also received notification from the CTC front office that the Uzbek government had given approval for our flight into their country. There was still no word on approval to travel onward to Afghanistan, but at least we had the green light to move into Uzbekistan.

Although the memory of many events leading up to the nineteenth remains a blur, one thing that remains clear in my mind was the issue of having a U.S. military Special Operations (SpecOps) officer accompany the team. Rick had been working the phones steadily for two days, talking with his Delta Force contacts at Fort Bragg in North Carolina, with Special Operations Command and U.S. Central Command (CENTCOM) at Tampa, Florida, reviewing our mission and stressing the importance of having a clear, transparent link back to the U.S. military Special Operations community. To our surprise, however, although Rick's contacts were enthusiastic and more than willing to participate, no one he spoke with knew what the mix of SpecOps forces would be in Afghanistan, and it turned out that there was debate over what the appropriate mission should be. Should the military stage Delta Force or SEAL personnel in the Panjshir for raids behind Taliban lines? Position SpecOps helicopters in the valley for search and rescue (SAR) operations in support of the coming bombing campaign? Assign army Special Forces to work with Northern Alliance troops on the front lines to laser-designate Taliban targets for our bombers?

There was also the serious issue of SAR coverage for any troops that might deploy into the valley, because there were no U.S. military helicopters anywhere in the region that could provide backup SAR support in the valley. Unless the deployed U.S. forces brought their own helicopter support, they would be isolated without hope of rescue should the Taliban break through Northern Alliance lines.

The bottom line was that no SpecOps personnel would accompany JAWBREAKER into Afghanistan. The official reason given was that without SAR capability, the mission was considered "too dangerous" for U.S. military personnel.

That evening was a long one. I repacked my personal gear for the third time, compressing the volume and getting rid of some things that were clearly excess or would not survive the long journey (saltine crackers and glass jars). I repacked the instant coffee into light plastic bowls and put everything else that might break open and spill into Ziploc plastic bags. Clothing was sorted again and refolded. I worked on this while Betsy watched television, just to be near her. But finally, at 11:00 p.m., she gave up and went to bed.

Then I went to the computer room in the basement and sat down to draft my will. It was another of those sobering tasks that brought into sharper focus the danger I would be facing. There was a good possibility that I would not come back from this mission. We had no idea what we would find when we landed in the valley. The Taliban must have realized the impact that Masood's loss was having on the Northern Alliance. Would the NA be able to resist a strong attack by the Taliban?

Also, accidents were the rule rather than the exception in Afghanistan. Land mines buried throughout the country claimed hundreds of lives each year. Rough, war-ravaged roads, twisting through high, rugged mountains, combined with inexperienced drivers, made traffic fatalities a major cause of death.

So a new will was necessary. I sat there for an hour or more, trying to put my wishes for my family into appropriate legal language. In addition to the division of my estate, I wrote personal notes to Betsy, the children, my mother, and my sister Donna, trying to express how much I loved each of them. I printed the document, signed and dated it, put it in an envelope and sealed it, and wrote "To be opened only in the event of my death" on the front. I told Betsy the next morning that the will was in the top drawer of my dresser.

CHAPTER FIVE

The next morning, 19 September, I was up at 5:00 a.m. once again looking over my gear, reviewing in my mind what was in my three bags. Most of my clothing was in a large, metal-framed backpack; my food and other equipment were in two medium-size soft-sided bags. It seemed like a lot to be bringing, and lugging this much baggage would be awkward, but I reminded myself that we might be gone for months, and re-supply would be difficult.

Betsy was getting ready for work, and I was trying to relax, reading the newspaper and drinking coffee. I had arranged with my daughter Jenny to drive me in to work so I would not have to leave my car parked at the CIA. Betsy came down, ready to leave for the office, and we said our final good-byes. There was not a lot more to say other than how much we loved each other and how much we wanted each other to be safe and careful while we were apart.

We stood there for a long, hard embrace, and I could feel her tears on my cheek. Holding her was good, and the thought that it could be months before we were together again made the embrace even more meaningful. We kissed, and I told her I would be back, safe and sound. She nodded and tried to speak but her voice choked, then she half smiled, turned, and walked out the door.

Jenny made a point of being upbeat as we drove toward the CIA that morning. I explained that I would get out at the front gate guardhouse and would be met by a CTC Logistics officer. He would take the bags, then move them to the pickup point (still to be determined) around noon. I know it was hard for Jenny to keep up a positive, happy face, but she did a good job of it. She assured me that she and Kate would keep in close touch with Betsy while I was gone. I told Jenny that I thought I might be able to call them on one of our satellite phone systems once we got established in the valley.

The drive to the Agency seemed quick, and I directed Jenny to pull into the visitors' lane at the front gate. I spoke into the video camera to tell them I was an employee being dropped off, and we pulled ahead and parked near the Reception Building. I unloaded the bags and we began our good-byes. We hugged tightly. I kissed her cheek, and I could see tears forming in her eyes. She turned, opened the car door, looked back, smiled, and said, "I love you, and I am so proud of you. You come back to us." She ducked into the car and pulled away. I watched her drive off, standing there until she turned out of view. It was only then that I felt the tears on my face.

The piles of equipment we had accumulated in our makeshift office were gone, having been moved out, as promised, by the CTC and SAD support staffs for shipment to Frankfurt the night before. The team gathered with several senior SAD officers and a representative from CTC Support for a meeting to iron out transportation details. The final schedule called for Murray, Stan, and Pappy to depart the compound at 11:00 a.m. We would all need to be at the pickup point with our personal baggage by 10:45 a.m. Because Rick and I were scheduled for a series of meetings after that, we would stay behind; our final meeting was with Cofer Black at 1:00 p.m. Following that, we would be driven to a small public airport and would board a chartered commercial Learjet for the short flight to Dover Air Force Base. We would meet up with the other team members in the departure area of the passenger terminal.

One unexpected issue was that our C-5A flight did not terminate at Rhine-Main Air Base in Frankfurt but rather at Ramstein Air Base, about 170 miles south of Frankfurt. Arrangements had been made for a commercial bus to meet us upon arrival and take us on to Frankfurt. Beyond that, there were no obvious loose ends that any of us could see, and we set off to take care of whatever personal business we had left to address.

I went down to the CTC at 10:30 a.m. and took charge of three cardboard boxes containing $3 million. The money was in hundred-dollar bills, all used and none in sequence, and packaged in bundles of $10,000. Ten of those bundles were plastic-wrapped into bricks of $100,000 each. Ten bricks were packed in each box. There were no markings on the boxes, and each was strongly sealed with heavy-duty tape. Each box weighed about fifteen pounds, but their size made them awkward to carry. I borrowed a small cart to move the money to the pickup point. It was clear that it would be a chore to lug around these three boxes.

At 10:45 a.m., I joined the other team members standing around the mound of baggage piled on the sidewalk in a parking area just outside the New Headquarters Building. There was much joking among the team members, and I relaxed as I joined the company of these professionals. This was routine business for these guys, all of whom had de-

ployed to dangerous field locations many times before. It
was like standing around with a group of guys just before the
shift starts at the factory, laughing and joking with one another. The fact that we were off to Afghanistan and would be
the first and for many weeks the only Americans there, working with an untested ally inside well-drawn battle lines, surrounded by thousands of Taliban and Arab fighters, was not
lost on the group, but it was not something that really mat-
tered. We all knew the risks, and we all had volunteered for the
mission. Simply put, it was our job, and we were setting out to
accomplish that job without a lot of worry or introspection.

I entrusted the three boxes of money to Stan to be transported with the rest of our personal baggage. There were the
expected jokes about diverting the truck to Dulles airport
and having the team travel first class on United to Frankfurt
rather than on a C-5A. The Chevy Suburban pulled up, and
we loaded the baggage and the money into the rear. Murray,
Stan, and Pappy got in, and the vehicle pulled away. Rick and
I started our round of meetings.

As we walked the halls, we were stopped repeatedly by officers we knew who had heard of our mission. There were
handshakes, good wishes, and always "I wish I was going
along with you guys." I ran into my longtime friend Chase
Brandon, who worked in our Public Affairs Office. We stood
and talked for a few minutes. It was a quiet, serious conversation about the upcoming mission, the risks, and being
careful. He too said he wished he was going with me. I mentioned my children, all of whom Chase knew from our time
together as instructors at the Farm, the CIA Training Center,
in the early 1980s. I think seeing Chase, talking to him and
discussing my children, sobered me and again brought home
the reality that I might not come back from this mission.

Rick and I arrived at Cofer Black's office right on time.
Cofer was alone and greeted us as we entered. We sat around
his conference table and exchanged pleasantries, then we recounted our state of readiness and provided him with a brief
outline of our travel plans.

Cofer leaned forward, both arms resting on the table, and

looked back and forth between Rick and me. "Gentlemen, I want to give you your marching orders, and I want to make them very clear. I have discussed this with the president, and he is in full agreement. You are to convince the Northern Alliance to work with us and to accept U.S. military forces into the Panjshir Valley so we can utilize that area as a base for our operations. But beyond that, your mission is to exert all efforts to find Usama bin Ladin and his senior lieutenants and to kill them." He paused to let what he had just said sink in, then continued. "I don't want bin Ladin and his thugs captured, I want them dead. Alive and in prison here in the United States, they'll become a symbol, a rallying point for other terrorists. They have planned and carried out the murder of thousands of our citizens. They must be killed. I want to see photos of their heads on pikes. I want bin Ladin's head shipped back in a box filled with dry ice. I want to be able to show bin Ladin's head to the president. I promised him I would do that." Cofer paused again, then asked, "Have I made myself clear?"

Rick and I glanced at each other and smiled, and I said, "Perfectly clear, Cofer. I don't know where we'll find dry ice out there in Afghanistan, but I think we can certainly manufacture pikes in the field."

It was the first time in my thirty-year CIA career that I had ever heard an order to kill someone rather than to effect their capture and rendition to justice. We stood and shook hands, and he wished us luck.

As I walked out of the office, I thought that for sheer bravado and showmanship, Cofer's speech matched—no, beat—Alan Wolfe's speech to us in Islamabad in August 1978, when he announced that the CIA was going to overthrow the Afghan communist regime, and the effort would start that day in that room. Four of us had been sitting around the table that day with Wolfe, and I had looked around and thought that the plan was pretty ambitious for the four of us to accomplish. I had a similar feeling walking out of Cofer's office. Our seven-member JAWBREAKER Team had our work cut out for us.

PART TWO

HISTORY

CHAPTER SIX

The C-5A was dimly lit and the seat was remarkably comfortable. The generous legroom allowed me to stretch out, and I tried to relax. My mind was busy, though, and I found myself reviewing the CIA's involvement with Afghanistan from the Soviet invasion in December 1979 to the present, and how my own career was woven into that long history. Sitting there in the half-light, lulled by the drone of jet engines, I could see, in hindsight, that I had played a pivotal role at most of the key junctures in the CIA's involvement with the Afghan Mujahedin.

The events that led to the CIA's involvement in Afghanistan really began in 1973, when Mohammed Daoud, a cousin of King Zahir Shah, leading a coalition of Muslim radicals and some communists, succeeded in forcing King Zahir Shah off the throne and into exile in Rome. For the Soviet Union, this was a golden opportunity to extend its influence into Afghanistan, another step in the centuries-long "Great Game"—the struggle by the Soviets to push their influence and control deeper into the old British Indian Empire.

Few within Afghanistan even cared that the king had been ousted. He had proven to be an ineffective ruler, and the majority of the population outside Kabul lived in abject poverty, without the knowledge or any real concern about who was actually running the country. In fact, many of the Muslim leaders who later gained prominence, such as Professor Rabbani, Gulbuddin Hekmatyar, and Ahmad Shah Masood, welcomed the change in national leadership, hoping for the chance to play a more significant political role under the new regime. Those hopes were dashed a year later when Daoud cracked down on the Islamic groups, forcing their leadership to flee to Pakistan. The Pakistanis, worried about the growing communist influence within the Daoud government, welcomed the Islamists, offering them sanctuary and assistance. Islamist efforts in 1975 to stage a coup to oust the Daoud regime failed, leading to splits within the Islamists' ranks. This failure also helped to strengthen the growing communist party.

Daoud also proved to be an ineffective leader as he tried to play the Soviets, the Americans, and the Pakistanis against one another. The Afghan communists, with support from the Soviet Union, grew stronger. In 1978, disgusted with Daoud and hungry for power, the communists staged a coup that removed Daoud from power. However, the Afghan communists were themselves split into two major factions, the Parcham and the Khalq parties. Although they maintained control of the country for nearly the next two years, there was a constant back-and-forth struggle within the communist ranks over which faction was to dominate the government, with the leadership of the country frequently changing hands between the two parties.

Despite a heavy flow of aid from the Soviets, the struggle caused a steady spiral downward for the country, and a growing dissatisfaction with and opposition to communist rule among Afghanistan's general population. Small groups around the country began open, armed resistance against the communist regime. This opposition was fragmented, disorganized, and poorly equipped, and they struggled on with no real recognition and no support from the outside.

In September 1979, Hafizullah Amin seized power within the then ruling Khalq Party. Popular unrest was peaking, and Amin was disliked and distrusted by the Soviets. By December 1979, the Soviets had had enough of Amin, and on Christmas Eve a strong force of Soviet troops invaded the country. Landing in the darkness at Kabul airport and pouring over the northern border in massive force, the Soviets

moved quickly to assassinate Amin and most of his government, and placed Barbak Karmal and the Parcham Party in
power. Over the following weeks, Soviet troops flowed into
Afghanistan by road and air, moving rapidly into all areas of
the country.

The reaction to the Soviet invasion was especially strong
within the ranks of students at Kabul University, and many
student activists fled to Pakistan to avoid arrest. A young
Tajik leader, Ahmad Shah Masood, joined the flood of
refugees in Peshawar. In early 1980, he declared Jihad (holy
war) against the communists and took a number of his fellow
Tajik students back with him into Afghanistan, to the sanctuary of their Panjshir Valley homeland, to begin the fight to
remove the communists from power.

Other groups from around the country also declared formal opposition to the Soviets, but without assistance from
outside the country they were doomed to remain fragmented,
disorganized, and poorly equipped, desperately overmatched
in their efforts to challenge the might of the Soviet army.

The CIA's role in this story began about eighteen months
earlier, in late 1978, when the ruling Khalq regime unknow-
ingly made a small but serious mistake—they instituted a
new national flag for the country. A photo of the flag appeared a few days later in the *Washington Post*. Within a
week, an agitated and angry Alan Wolfe flew to Islamabad.
Wolfe was then chief of the CIA's Near East and South Asia
Division, which had operational responsibility for Afghanistan and Pakistan. Wolfe was a legend within the CIA, and
he had devoted a number of years of his career to South Asia,
having served in an early tour as chief in Lahore (where he
somehow managed to have the pleasure of entertaining Ava
Gardner each summer afternoon at his residence during the
filming of the *Rains of Ranchipur* on location there). Some
years later he served as our chief in Kabul, then as the chief
in Islamabad; he was an acknowledged expert on the history
of the region. His wife too was a well-recognized scholar on
Afghan tribal history and customs.

I arrived in Islamabad in the summer of 1978, accompanied by my first wife, Patricia, and our three small children. I was the most junior of four officers there. The announcement that Wolfe was coming was a surprise to us all, for at that time senior officers rarely traveled from Headquarters, and certainly not to visit small offices that were considered backwaters. Like most officers within the Near East Division, I was in awe of Wolfe and it was clear that our chief, John R., was as nervous as a cat as he prepared for Wolfe's visit.

Upon his arrival at the embassy, Wolfe, always the actor, always on stage, immediately gathered the chief and us three junior officers into the embassy's secure briefing room, known as the "bubble" because of its clear plastic walls, floor, and ceiling. Wolfe sat at the head of the green felt-covered table and looked at each of us slowly and carefully. Then he began to speak. "I was sitting on the patio after work last week with my wife. We were having our evening martini and I was looking at the *Washington Post*. I couldn't believe it. There was a photo of the new Afghan flag on the front page. I turned to my wife and said, 'Honey, those communist bastards are not going to screw with our Afghanistan like this. I'm going to overthrow that damn regime.'

"Now, gentlemen, I'm here to get things started. Our people in Kabul can't do much, hemmed in by the regime as they are. But the Mujahedin, they have representatives here in Pakistan, in Peshawar, and here in Islamabad. This is where our fight will begin. You will recruit assets in every Mujahedin group. I want to know what they are doing, how their fight is going. I want to know what they need, how we can help them. I want action. I want results!"

I could feel the electricity in the room. It was pure theater, an incredible performance. Even then I wished to myself that I'd been able to record the whole thing on tape. I knew I had just witnessed history in the making.

By mid-1979, following Wolfe's dramatic orders, we had recruited assets in all of the seven major Mujahedin groups. In addition, driven by Wolfe's efforts back in Washington, the U.S. government, with the cooperation of the Pakistani government, had established a small covert effort to provide humanitarian assistance to the Mujahedin.

On 21 November 1979, however, an event occurred that turned our world in Islamabad topsy-turvy. A mob of Pakistanis that eventually grew to 15,000 stormed the walls surrounding the U.S. Embassy compound and set fire to the buildings inside. Two Americans and two Pakistani employees of the embassy were killed in the rioting, and 138 people, me included, were trapped for five hours inside the inferno of the burning Chancellery Building. We managed to escape with our lives, but we found ourselves preoccupied, dazed, and shocked following the event.

In the aftermath there was clear evidence that the Pakistani government of General Zia ul-Haq had simply stood by and let the buildings burn. Several senior Pakistani army officers flew a helicopter reconnaissance of the embassy compound at the height of the rioting and mistakenly concluded that no one could be alive in the burning Chancellery Building. They advised President Zia that it was better to allow the rioters to vent their anger and eventually disperse than to use force to break up the mob just to retrieve the bodies of dead Americans.

From there, relations with the Pakistani government were strained to the breaking point, and our small covert program of assistance to the Afghan Mujahedin was in danger of being abandoned. Then the Soviets invaded Afghanistan.

The Soviet miscalculation in December 1979 changed the course of events in the region in ways far beyond what the masters of the Kremlin could have foreseen. It brought the full weight of the U.S. government behind the Afghan Mujahedin and energized the Islamic world to support the Afghans in their struggle for freedom. Within days of the Soviet invasion, at President Carter's direction, a massive program was started that would last twelve years and pump billions of dollars in cash, military equipment, and humanitarian assistance into the hands of the Mujahedin. Pakistan would take on the role of distributing these assets to the Mujahedin.

As the effort to support the Mujahedin grew during the first few years of the 1980s, it became clear that although the Pakistanis shared our common goal of seeing the Soviets driven from Afghanistan, they had their own agenda for dealing with the various Mujahedin groups and even individual Afghan commanders.

From the start, Pakistan saw this covert effort as a means of achieving its own long-term political goals in Afghanistan, which can be distilled into a simple concept: work to help Afghanistan be controlled by a Pashtun-centered, fundamentalist religious party that will be malleable to manipulation by Pakistan; focus its energy on internal issues, allowing Pakistan trade access to Afghanistan as well as to oil and trade with the Islamic Republics of the former Soviet Union; and provide Pakistan with a secure western border.

This objective expressed itself in favoring some Mujahedin commanders over others. For instance, whereas Gulbuddin Hekmatyar and his Hezb-e Islami party were given large amounts of cash and materiel, other commanders— such as Ahmad Shah Masood, the finest tactical commander on either side of the fighting—were blatantly shortchanged. Hekmatyar's fundamentalist beliefs fit perfectly into Pakistan's strategic goals for Afghanistan. Masood and his Tajiks had a broader vision for a post-Jihad Afghanistan that did not fit into Pakistani plans.

To counter this shortsighted bias, the CIA developed a program to deal unilaterally with key commanders who were effective on the battlefield but were given short shrift by the Pakistani government. We knew who these commanders were, and it was not hard to identify their representatives. All the senior Afghan commanders had such personnel assigned in Pakistan to coordinate deliveries of assistance.

Once we established unilateral contact with each representative, we arranged a meeting in Pakistan with the commander himself. That direct meeting was essential so we could be sure that we were actually dealing with the commander, and he approved and agreed to what we offered.

It was a simple, straightforward arrangement. We would provide the commander a monthly cash payment (sometimes as much as $50,000 a month for senior commanders, and usually around $5,000 a month for lesser commanders). In return, the commander would provide us with monthly reports that documented his combat operations and listed the amounts of cash and materiel provided him by the Pakistanis. No commander I know of ever turned us down. They were not recruited assets, and when the fighting in that area stopped or the Jihad was eventually won, our relationships would end. Not only did this system allow us to get cash into the hands of effective commanders who were out of favor with the Pakistanis, it gave us a mechanism to confirm what the Pakistanis were telling us about how they distributed the cash and weapons.

By the summer of 1988, the Soviets were beaten, and it seemed clear that they would withdraw from Afghanistan sooner rather than later. Ours was one of the few Western embassies still open in Kabul, which gave the few personnel we maintained there the ability to gain firsthand knowledge of conditions on the ground. There was, however, a growing consensus within the ranks of senior policy makers in Washington to draw down U.S. personnel and eventually close the embassy. The consensus was that this would make a powerful statement to the Soviets and the Afghan communist regime.

As station chief in Kabul, but waiting in Washington for a final decision on the status of the embassy, I struggled to convince Frank Anderson, then the chief of the CIA's Afghan program, to keep CIA personnel there, but I failed. The embassy was to close. Anderson, along with many senior officers in Washington, was convinced that the Soviet departure from Afghanistan would have a serious impact on the Afghan communist regime, and closing our embassy would somehow hasten the collapse of that regime. Since May

1986, the Afghan regime had been headed by Muhammad Najibullah, whose reign as head of the KHAD, the KGB-trained Afghan intelligence service, proved him to be a brutal killer. His record of bloodshed in his previous position would earn him only death should he fall into Mujahedin hands, and I saw little reason why he would not go down fighting. Moreover, Najibullah's military forces were strong, at least compared to the Mujahedin, and they controlled strategic, well-fortified defensive positions around the country. I argued that the fighting would continue well into the future. Having the embassy open and having me there, active and moving around the city, would provide us with a real advantage in monitoring events in a post-Soviet Afghanistan.

Anderson dismissed my analysis with a wave of his hand, saying that Najibullah would be gone in a couple of months and the embassy would reopen by early 1989. With that he unceremoniously threw me out of his office. Being a good soldier, I headed off to Islamabad to wait until Najibullah and his gang of thugs were defeated.

That analysis by Anderson and the rest of the senior intelligence community was only just a little off. The Najibullah regime finally collapsed in early 1992, three years after the Soviet withdrawal. The U.S. Embassy in Kabul wasn't reopened until 15 December 2001, one month after the defeat of the Taliban.

CHAPTER SEVEN

In late 1988, I returned to Islamabad. Milt Bearden was as gracious as he could be in welcoming me to his station. He made it clear, however, that there was only one chief in Islamabad, and it was him. There was no question in my mind about that, for at that juncture Milt was a larger-than-life figure at the peak of his career. I quietly became the senior case officer within the group of officers handling the Afghan intelligence collection program—the group dealing unilaterally with the Mujahedin commanders. In the long run, this was an excellent opportunity for me, for it was then that I began my relationship with Ahmad Shah Masood.

Back in 1980, when Masood left Peshawar to return to the Panjshir, one of the young Tajiks who accompanied him on that historic move was one of Masood's closest friends and advisers, Masood Khalili. It soon became clear that Khalili, a gifted writer and poet, a brilliant public speaker fluent in three languages, was better suited for political work than for carrying an AK-47 up and down the mountains of northern Afghanistan. Khalili was appointed one of Masood's key representatives in Pakistan, and eventually came to serve as a senior political adviser to Dr. Burrudin Rabbani and his Tajik-based Hezb-e Islami political party, based in Peshawar. At some point in the mid-1980s, CIA officers met Khalili and established a cooperative relationship with him. He was in no sense a recruited agent; he saw his cooperation with the CIA as a way to further his own personal vision of what the political landscape of a post-communist Afghanistan should look like.

Shortly after my return to Islamabad in late 1988, I was introduced to Khalili, and I began to meet with him whenever he was in Islamabad on business. My interest in Khalili was not in his close relationship with Masood. We were already in direct unilateral contact with Masood via one of his younger brothers, Ahmad Zia. Rather, my interest in Khalili rested in his wide range of contacts throughout the entire spectrum of Mujahedin groups, and his willingness and ability to broker direct access to key commanders in whom we were interested.

Over the weeks that followed our introduction, we came to know each other well and a personal friendship developed. Our discussions let me gain insight into what motivated

Khalili to cooperate with the CIA. He firmly believed that the Mujahedin, with the help of the CIA-managed assistance program, would eventually succeed in defeating the Soviets and driving them from Afghanistan. He was equally convinced that the Pakistanis viewed this CIA program as an opportunity to expand their own influence among the Pashtun Mujahedin groups, especially those with strong conservative religious beliefs. Khalili was convinced that when the communists were defeated, the Pakistanis would work to help their Pashtun favorites gain control of the new Afghan government, keeping the Tajiks and other ethnic minorities in their traditional second-class status. Cooperating with the CIA allowed Khalili to help ensure that the victory he so fervently believed in would be achieved as quickly as possible. By introducing CIA officers to good commanders whom the Pakistanis disliked, he would ensure that those commanders would be better equipped to resist Pashtun-Pakistani pressures in the post-communist political arena.

Khalili's range of contacts within the ranks of Mujahedin commanders was extraordinary. Through him we were able to deal with commanders from all over Afghanistan, and from all the ethnic groups: Uzbeks from the north, Pashtuns from the provinces along the Pak-Afghan border south of Jalalabad, and even Afghan Shi'a groups from the area just west of Kabul. Khalili was (and is) a true Afghan patriot, and has demonstrated that fact by his commitment and sacrifice for his country for more than twenty-four years.

Khalili made two trips a year into Afghanistan to visit Masood, riding on horseback over the high mountain passes from Chitral in Pakistan down into the Panjshir Valley. It was a long, dangerous trek, taking eight days or more to navigate the trails. The Soviets had air-dropped thousands of small land mines into this region, and it was common to lose a horse or a mule on each trip, or for a man to lose a leg if he wandered off the narrow, well-worn trail they used.

I wanted desperately to make one of those trips with Khalili, to meet Masood face-to-face, but I could never get Headquarters to agree to the proposal; it was always "too dangerous to risk." But on those trips in, as I learned years later, Khalili spoke to Masood at length about me. The goodwill, trust, and confidence that Khalili had for me was transferred to Masood, something that would serve me, and the CIA, well in the future.

In January 1990, I accepted a posting as deputy chief in Riyadh, Saudi Arabia, to begin in August of that year. Parting with Khalili was a sad occasion and the hardest part of my leaving Pakistan. He was a true friend, and the situation in Afghanistan looked gloomy, with Najibullah's forces holding on stubbornly. There were growing tensions between Masood's Northern Alliance and the forces of Gulbuddin Hekmatyar and other Pashtun fundamentalist groups. The euphoria of the Soviet departure from Afghanistan, and the high expectations of a quick victory over the communist regime, had all melted away. It was equally clear that the U.S. government wanted to disengage from Afghanistan, and there were serious negotiations under way with the Russians on how to cut off aid and assistance to both warring sides.

   To have come so close to winning what so many had sacrificed so much for and then see it slipping away was hard to deal with. I think my departure symbolized for Khalili the pullback that the CIA was making from the program of support to the Mujahedin—a program to which Khalili had devoted himself for the past seven years. I had no idea if or when I would see Khalili again. I certainly did not realize that my relationship with him would continue over the next six years, and that our relationship would again be of great significance.

CHAPTER EIGHT

At the end of my assignment in Riyadh, in August 1992, I returned to Langley to take command of what soon became the Iran Task Force (ITF), with responsibility for the conduct of Iranian operations worldwide. In April 1992, Kabul fell to Masood's Tajik forces, bringing final victory over the Najibullah regime. There was no large-scale retribution by the victorious Mujahedin against the communists, as many had predicted. In fact, Najibullah took refuge with the United Nations and was housed in one of their compounds in Kabul. He remained there under informal house arrest for the next four years as the new Mujahedin interim government struggled to decide what to do with him. (When the Taliban forces took Kabul under their control in late September 1996, one of their first acts was to force their way into the UN compound where Najibullah was staying and drag him into the street for swift and brutal punishment. The photo on the cover of *Time* magazine of Najibullah hanging from a Kabul lamppost, his body viciously mutilated, should have given the West a clear picture of what to expect from the Taliban as they established control over more and more of the country.)

The victorious Mujahedin quickly established an interim government, with Hezb-e Islami leader Burrudin Rabbani as president. Ahmad Shah Masood was appointed minister of defense. Khalili found himself still in Pakistan, serving as the ambassador to Pakistan for the new Afghan government.

As the Mujahedin consolidated power in Kabul, the CIA was ordered to formally close down the U.S. government's twelve-year program of support to the Afghan Mujahedin.

By that point, little remained of the structure of the original program. Closing things down basically consisted of contacting the Mujahedin commanders with whom we had dealt and telling them we were saying good-bye.

For the Pakistanis, the political situation in Kabul offered an opportunity to push forward with their political agenda for Afghanistan. The Pakistanis continued to provide support to Gulbuddin Hekmatyar, who was serving as foreign minister of the new Afghan government, and to other Pashtun fundamentalist leaders, pushing them to oppose Tajik and other non-Pashtun participation in the new government. Rabbani, Ahmad Shah Masood, and other northern ethnic leaders were totally out of favor with the Pakistanis. Under those conditions, civil war was inevitable, and serious fighting erupted in mid-1992 as Hekmatyar and Masood began to slug it out in the streets in the western area of Kabul. The fighting went on for months, and the destruction to the city was devastating. Block upon block of western Kabul was reduced to rubble, and most of that destruction remains unrepaired to this day. Pakistani support to Hekmatyar and the fundamentalists was blatant, and Ambassador Khalili was active in keeping that support in the public eye in Pakistan and the rest of the world.

The Pakistanis soon grew weary of Khalili, and he was arrested and held for some days; his home was ransacked and his family was harassed. He was eventually released but given forty-eight hours to leave Pakistan. With his U.S. Green Card Resident Alien status, Khalili was able to bring his family to northern Virginia.

When I learned of Khalili's arrival in the United States, I quickly renewed our contact. I informed the appropriate office within the CIA, but there was no official aspect to our relationship; it was just two friends meeting socially. I met with Khalili on a monthly basis, usually for lunch in a local restaurant. He was actively lobbying for the Afghan government, working Capitol Hill tirelessly, and building contacts within the media, occasionally even getting someone interested enough to listen to what he had to say about affairs in his country. The events in Afghanistan in the mid-1990s were back-page news at best, just another civil war among squabbling warlords in a country so devastated and backward that there was little or nothing to fight over. It was a frustrating time for Khalili, and he, like many other Afghans, deeply resented the fact that the U.S. government and the CIA, after having done so much to help the Mujahedin achieve victory, now stood on the sidelines and refused to become involved in his country's tragedy.

Despite his frustrations, our personal relationship remained warm and friendly. There was little I could do for him except offer sympathy and encouragement. We had no embassy in Afghanistan. No CIA personnel were there—I certainly could attest to that. Islamabad did a little reporting on Afghan issues but primarily focused on narcotics-related affairs.

In the summer of 1994, I was given command of our European-based Iranian operations effort, and once again Khalili and I parted ways. Betsy was assigned as a general services officer (GSO) for housing at the post, a big job for her, and we were both happy to be going to Europe for an assignment.

Later, Khalili was appointed the Afghan ambassador to India, a key assignment and one for which Khalili was well suited. Although it seemed unlikely at the time, that assignment ensured that our paths would cross again.

I expected to remain in Europe for three to four years, but in October 1995 there were unanticipated shifts among senior CIA personnel, with the then-chief in Islamabad being transferred back to Headquarters to assume a senior-level command. I was asked to take his place.

It was an offer I found hard to refuse; I had always wanted that assignment. Betsy and I discussed the offer carefully. Although another separation would be hard, the job was too good to turn down. I headed off for Pakistan in January 1996.

In early August 1996, after six months in Islamabad, I

stepped back and took stock of the operational situation in the Pak-Afghan region. At that time, Islamabad was primarily focused on traditional internal objectives. All political developments were monitored, but the focus was on Pakistani relations with India. Pakistan's "clandestine" support to Pakistani and Kashmiri militant groups fighting the Indian armed forces in occupied Kashmir ensured that relations between the two nations were tense, and the threat of nuclear war between the two nations was very real.

Pakistan's deteriorating economy and the massive corruption by whichever political party was in power was slowly but surely pulling the country into a downward, depressing cycle from which there seemed no exit. The two main political parties—the Muslim League, headed by Nawaz Sharif, and the Pakistan Peoples Party, headed by Benazir Bhutto— were indistinguishable once either was in power. Both parties concentrated on looting the country and filling their foreign bank accounts with as much cash as they could grab when it was their turn at the trough.

The 1994 defeat of Hekmatyar and the Afghan fundamentalist Mujahedin parties by Masood and his Northern Alliance disappointed the Pakistanis, who now came to view these parties as a lost cause. In mid-1994, Pakistan began to focus attention on the nascent Taliban movement, headed by Mullah Omar.

The Taliban movement was born in the fundamentalist madrassas [religious schools] in the Pakistani provinces of Baluchistan and the Northwest Frontier. There were hundreds of these small madrassas offering shelter, food, and a religious education to homeless Afghan young men and poor Pakistani youth. These schools were primarily supported by the more fundamentalist religious political parties in Pakistan and by private contributions from wealthy Saudis made through several of the large, Saudi-based Islamic charitable organizations. These schools taught a narrow, strict, almost mindless version of Islam.

Mullah Omar was a Mujahedin veteran who was seriously wounded in the Jihad and had a war record that greatly outshone his knowledge of the Koran. By early 1994, Omar had shifted his base of operations to Qandahar and slowly began to oppose the corruption and lawlessness of the local warlords in the area. His early successes were welcomed by the common people, tired of years of war and of being subject to the rapacious attacks of petty warlords commanding small groups of armed criminals. Omar gathered followers, and they called themselves Talibs (defenders).

The Pakistanis quickly came to see the Taliban as a possible answer to achieving their strategic political vision for Afghanistan, and shifted their full support accordingly. With that assistance, the Taliban, growing in military strength and popular support, moved steadily to increase their control of the southern region of Afghanistan. By mid-1996, the Taliban had succeeded in taking control of nearly two-thirds of the country. Taliban military forces, strengthened by Arab and Pakistani volunteers, stood poised on the outskirts of Kabul, threatening the fragile hold that the Afghan Interim Government had on the rest of the nation.

Yet in August 1996, the U.S. government was not concerned with the political developments in Afghanistan. There were only a couple of areas involving Afghanistan in which the U.S. government had even a small interest. One was the serious level of narcotics production in Afghanistan and the trafficking of those narcotics out of the region into Europe. There was also a growing realization that Afghanistan was becoming a major sanctuary for international terrorists.

At that time, however, there was one unique operational effort under way in Islamabad that peripherally touched on Afghanistan, and that was the hunt for Mir Amal Kasi. Kasi was a Pakistani Balouch tribesman who murdered two CIA employees and wounded three others at the main entrance to CIA Headquarters on Route 123, in McLean, Virginia, on the morning of 23 January 1993.

Kasi succeeded in escaping to Pakistan, and despite the best efforts of the CIA and the FBI, he was successful in evading arrest. He was thought to be supported by his fellow

Balouch tribesmen and hiding in the border area of Pakistan and Afghanistan, moving in the area between Quetta in Pakistan and Qandahar in Afghanistan.

Islamabad had organized a team of Afghanis to hunt down Kasi. The team's activities produced intelligence of interest to a few CIA analysts on local Taliban activities and personalities, so we in Islamabad began to gain a working knowledge of the Taliban and the situation on the ground in Afghanistan. (Although the efforts of our Afghan team in the hunt for Kasi did not pay off, I did have the pleasure of co-leading with the FBI the operation that resulted in Kasi's capture in June 1997. It is a story worth telling, if for no other reason than to set the record straight on the CIA's key role in that operation.)

It was clear to me that one day soon the U.S. government would have to wake up to the fact that the Taliban were poised to take control of Afghanistan, and once fully in power, the Taliban would turn Afghanistan into a unique haven for international terrorism. That realization would certainly be quickly followed by a hue and cry from Congress demanding to know why the CIA had ignored the situation. We needed to begin reporting on political developments in Afghanistan. The question was how to get around Washington's current shortsighted lack of interest in the country.

As we considered how to begin such an effort, several factors stood out. In the Pashtun south, the Taliban and their program to disarm the warlords had initially been popular with the average Afghan, weary of violence after almost twenty years of war. That popularity was wearing thin, however, as the Taliban gained control over more and more of the country. The Taliban's twisted view of Islam resulted in harsh, repressive laws that added pain and misery to the lives of the average Afghan under their control. Across the southern regions of the country, resentment of Taliban rule was slowly surfacing, and it was clear that many Pashtun tribal leaders chafed under the heavy-handed repression of the Taliban. Many of these leaders had fought valiantly against the Soviets, then against the Afghan communist regime, and I was sure that they would cooperate with the CIA against the Taliban if the circumstances were right. However, given the Taliban's tight control over the population in the south of Afghanistan, establishing such contacts there would be difficult.

In the north, however, the military forces of the ethnic populations were locked in combat with the Taliban, although without outside support and assistance, they were slowly being pushed back and defeated in piecemeal fashion. It would take some effort to recontact those commanders in the north, but I was sure we would find many willing to renew their relationship with the CIA.

Following this logic, I felt that the place to start was with Ahmad Shah Masood, minister of defense of the Afghan Interim Government, and still the single most powerful military figure in the country. He had effective contacts with the leaders of all the ethnic groups in the north, and he had long-established relationships with many non-Tajik commanders around the country. He was leading the fight against the Taliban, and his Northern Alliance forces provided the bulwark of defense against the advancing Taliban military units.

I needed a valid operational reason to justify reestablishing contact with Masood. Although in Washington there was no real interest yet in the Taliban, there was the growing concern over Afghanistan's serving as a sanctuary for Usama bin Ladin and his terrorist followers.

In May 1996, bin Ladin, under intense U.S. pressure, had been forced to shift his base of operations from Sudan. Bin Ladin's previous activities in Afghanistan made it the logical choice for his next sanctuary. Upon arrival in the country he was initially hosted by such fundamentalist Mujahedin leaders as Professor Sayyaf and Yunis Khalis. It was not long, however, before bin Ladin's Jihad credentials, his anti-Western stance, and his large checkbook attracted the interest of Mullah Omar, who soon welcomed bin Ladin as an honored guest.

Also, as early as 1990, the Pakistanis had begun to send Kashmiri militant fighters to Afghanistan for training, utilizing the many Mujahedin training camps located inside Afghanistan along the border area near Waziristan, Pakistan. This move made sense for the Pakistanis, given the increasing pressure that the United States and the rest of the international community were exerting on the Pakistani government to halt the training of Kashmiri "Freedom Fighters" inside Pakistan. The Arab volunteers flowing into Afghanistan, many of whom were terrorists on the run from their own countries, were welcomed into those same training camps as the Kashmiri and Pakistani volunteers. The close relationships among these odd elements that can be seen today in Pakistan began at this time.

In mid-1996, as the shadowy structure of this terrorist network began to emerge, bin Ladin became the CIA's primary target. His presence in Afghanistan seemed the perfect justification for my visiting Kabul to meet Masood, so we could explore his willingness and ability to assist the CIA in working against bin Ladin and the foreign terrorist elements in Afghanistan. I also knew that my old friend Khalili, still the Afghan ambassador in New Delhi, was the key to having a successful, positive meeting with Masood. I wrote a cable outlining this proposal and the Counterterrorist Center gave its blessing for the trip and agreed to provide the funding.

CHAPTER NINE

Khalili was delighted at the proposal. Even I was surprised at the speed at which he moved forward to make arrangements for the visit. Within a day of receiving my proposal, Khalili had contacted Masood and won his approval to proceed. I thought there might be some resistance on Khalili's part to renewing contact with the CIA, given his long-standing resentment of the U.S. government's 1992 termination of support for the Mujahedin. Khalili, however, had always had a pragmatic view of U.S. involvement in Afghan affairs, and in our encounters over the years he had always told me that he was convinced that the United States would eventually be forced by events to renew its role in Afghanistan.

Khalili proposed dates for our meeting in New Delhi and for our onward travel to Kabul. I coordinated the arrangements with Headquarters and New Delhi, and Khalili and I had our reunion there in late September 1996. I knew that Masood would be hoping for financial assistance and political support for his fight against the Taliban, but I told Khalili that no one in Washington wanted to address that at this time. However, assistance in tracking down bin Ladin and his key lieutenants could prove profitable for Masood, because the U.S. government, under State Department auspices, had posted large cash rewards for the arrest of bin Ladin and those in his inner circle.

Khalili and I flew together into Kabul on Ariana's only serviceable Boeing 727. The flight was all I expected. It was an old aircraft, poorly maintained, and had only about thirty seats in the main cabin, all clustered toward the front of the aircraft. The rest of the main cabin was used for cargo, with boxes of all sizes, wooden crates, bags wrapped in burlap and bound with colored plastic rope piled helter-skelter into a long line in the middle of the aircraft, secured to the deck with aging canvas netting. The seat belts were worn and ragged. When I questioned Khalili on the wisdom of flying on the aircraft, his only comment was "Don't worry, Gary, it makes it safely every time," and he settled into his seat. I shut up and buckled my seat belt.

Despite some occasional strange noises and loud groans of metal, the flight into Baghram Air Base proved uneventful. Baghram is a military airfield about thirty miles north of Kabul. It was one of the key airfields used by the Soviets, then by the Najibullah regime. It had been fought over, shelled, rocketed, and bombed, which was plain to see as we stood on the corrugated metal runway waiting for our driver to arrive. No repairs had been made to the air base in the intervening years. I alternated watching the Ariana ground crew as they clumsily rolled the heavy boxes and crates down the passenger stairs to the runway, with long looks around at the devastated air base.

There were deep holes blasted into the metal strips near where we stood. Several hangars had collapsed roofs and shattered walls, and in the distance were a number of destroyed Soviet military aircraft scattered randomly, smashed and abandoned. (They were still there in 2001, and caused JAWBREAKER some problems when the U.S. Air Force decided they should bomb those "Russian aircraft parked all over the air base"!)

While we waited, one of Masood's MiG-27 fighters, painted a drab brown with red markings and carrying a single 250-pound bomb, took off and headed east toward Jalalabad. It was a stark reminder that the Taliban forces were pushing from Jalalabad toward Kabul, as well as pressing the outer defensive lines of the city from the south and west. The situation on the ground was stable for the moment, but the Taliban appeared confident and were making steady progress, especially from the east. Sorubi, a small town midway between Kabul and Jalalabad, controlled the major roadway into Kabul from that direction. The power station that provided electricity to Kabul was on the river at Sorubi, and it was a natural target for the Taliban, as it had been for the Mujahedin during the Jihad.

Kabul was struck by rockets and bombed by the Taliban on an almost daily basis that September, but Khalili assured me it was safe. "We are a small target, you and me, and the city is large. Besides, the Taliban can't shoot straight anyway." (My team would hear that same statement again in September 2001.) With that assurance, I relaxed and waited for our driver to arrive.

Our driver Mumtaz finally arrived and drove us to Khalili's family home in Kabul to wait for the meeting with Masood, which was to happen "soon." There is a rhythm to how things move in Afghanistan. Plans are made, meetings are set, but the time for these things is always a little vague. I suspect that when two Afghans arrange to meet, a time is not even discussed; only a vague "morning" or "afternoon" might be mentioned. But when dealing with foreigners, an Afghan will set a time for the meeting. Although the time agreed upon has no relation to when the meeting will actually take place, it makes the foreigner feel good—for a while. Over the years I came to call this phenomenon "Afghan time," and I suspected that the "soon" mentioned for our meeting with Masood fell into that category.

It was about four in the afternoon when we arrived at Khalili's residence, and after touring the small house and grounds, which were originally owned by Khalili's father and were in desperate need of repair, we settled down to talk and wait. At 7:00 p.m., with no word from Masood, Khalili's small staff served us a dinner of beef stew and rice, with a delicious fresh melon for dessert. Afterward, Khalili busied himself with his daily journal entry and I tried to read. At almost midnight, in a sudden flurry of frantic activity, we were summoned to meet Masood.

Two Toyota Land Cruisers arrived, one for Khalili and me and the other for the four armed guards that apparently were to accompany us. We were ushered into the first vehicle, which then drove off at top speed, bouncing and banging through the totally dark streets of the city. That was bad enough, but worse were the checkpoints we encountered at the numerous traffic circles. The young, heavily armed, somewhat nervous Mujahedin manning these checkpoints would surround our vehicles with AK-47s ready while one of them approached the driver's window to exchange that night's passwords in guarded whispers. There was a real fear that Taliban sympathizers might be out and about to conduct sabotage, and the guards took the exchange of passwords seriously. I had the impression that it would take little for the nervous young guards to start firing.

I knew that this meeting with Masood was critical. Khalili assured me that Masood remained grateful for the CIA's assistance during the Jihad years and was anxious to explore reopening that relationship. At the same time, I knew that Masood resented the fact that the U.S. government had abandoned the Mujahedin in 1992 and was undoubtedly wary of our motives in recontacting him.

I had little to offer Masood. I had no funds to provide and no authority to promise him future support. But I could assure him that the CIA was very interested in exploring areas where we might assist each other, especially in eliminating Usama bin Ladin and pushing his Arab volunteers out of Afghanistan, which I knew Masood dearly wanted to see happen. My goal was to reestablish a relationship with Masood and hold out the possibility that successful cooperation might bring him "positive benefits."

Beyond what Masood and his forces might be able to do against bin Ladin, Masood was the premier military figure in Afghanistan, and his prestige and influence stretched into all areas of the country. He could facilitate contact with a number of former Mujahedin commanders for us. If I failed to convince Masood that there was real value in reestablishing his relationship with the CIA, it would make our efforts to renew contacts with other Mujahedin commanders that much more difficult. Also, should Masood refuse to cooperate, it would dampen interest at Headquarters in trying to deal with the lesser commanders. I had to make this work.

Masood was waiting for us in a comfortable room at what turned out to be the former Austrian Embassy, now serving as a guesthouse for Masood and the Rabbani government. Masood was dressed, as always, in Western-style khaki pants, a matching shirt, and vest, with his flat-topped Chitrali hat set back rakishly on his head. He was slim and olive-skinned with a narrow face and a short, wispy beard and mustache. His presence commanded attention, and even in repose, relaxed in his chair, he drew my eyes to him. He rose to greet me. His handshake was firm, and he looked directly into my eyes. We started the conversation in Dari. Although I can speak the language fairly well, I was rusty and recommended that Khalili serve as our translator.

I wanted to establish rapport with Masood quickly. I knew that Khalili had spoken to him about me in the past, and that Masood knew who I was and what my role was during the Jihad years. But I wanted to open the conversation with personal topics and remembrances of times past rather than get bogged down in the long, formal opening exchanges that are usual in such meetings. I explained to Masood that in the 1988–90 time frame I had been the officer responsible for contacting him through his brother, Ahmad Zia, in Islamabad. I spoke of the financial assistance that the CIA had provided to Masood during that two-year period, including the large onetime payment of funds I made in May 1989 for reconstruction projects in the Panjshir Valley—the first and only money paid to any Mujahedin group for reconstruction efforts during the Jihad years. I knew I would hear about the mistake that the U.S. government made in walking away from the Mujahedin in 1992, but I emphasized the positive by stressing the extent of the CIA's assistance to Masood over those long years of struggle.

Masood launched into a tight, articulate review of the history of the fight against the Soviets, then the Afghan communist Najibullah regime. His recitation was clear, concise, and thoughtful, and he spoke without emotion, just a simple recounting of the factual history of the times. He touched on the U.S. government's break with the Mujahedin once final victory was achieved, and how that left the new Mujahedin government without the funding and support needed to consolidate power. That had opened the doors for the Pakistanis to create civil war by their support of Hekmatyar and other religious fundamentalists. Those elements had been defeated, but at great cost to the country, and had left Masood and the commanders who had fought against the Hekmatyar coalition in a weakened state. Now, Pakistan was backing the Taliban with materiel and financial support. Masood said he was receiving only token support from the Iranians and had to pay in cash for whatever equipment and ammunition he received from the Russians. The Afghan Interim Government, headed by Dr. Rabbani, was the legitimate government of Afghanistan. But without support from the United States and other Western governments, the fight would be difficult if not impossible to win. The Taliban were likely to end up controlling most of the country.

We talked well into the night, and I stressed my main theme: cooperation now with the CIA on the issue of bin Ladin and the Arab terrorists would earn Masood the goodwill and appreciation of the U.S. government. Success against bin Ladin and the Arabs would directly benefit Masood on the battlefield, because the Arab volunteers fought hard and proved to be a real thorn in Masood's side whenever he encountered them. I also told him that the U.S. government was already beginning to revive interest in Afghanistan, and eventually there would be pressure from senior Washington leadership to reengage in Afghan affairs. Cooperation now would position Masood to be the first to receive the aid that the renewed engagement would bring.

Masood clearly recognized the benefits he could gain from cooperating. He had little to risk, and should things go as I was suggesting, the potential gains could prove enormous. He agreed to cooperate to the full extent of his ability, but he noted that he was engaged in a bitter struggle with the Taliban and was hemmed in by drawn battle lines. Going directly after bin Ladin would be difficult for his forces, positioned as they were. I acknowledged his points but stressed that there was still much that could be done. We explored possible scenarios where we might cooperate, and we discussed former commanders in other areas of the country whom Masood could call on for assistance or to persuade them to cooperate with the CIA in this effort.

As we concluded our discussions at almost four in the morning, I felt I had accomplished all I had hoped for. Masood agreed to provide whatever information became available to him on bin Ladin and his movements and activities. Masood considered bin Ladin a personal enemy, and the Arab fighters whom bin Ladin was sponsoring were a serious factor in the fighting now under way around Kabul. The elimination of bin Ladin would be a positive step forward in

Masood's struggle to defeat the Taliban. Masood agreed to future meetings with me in Kabul, and with any other CIA representatives we wished.

In hindsight, this was an extraordinarily significant meeting. The door to future cooperation with Masood and the Northern Alliance was again open, and the CIA's efforts over the next five years would keep that door open. This proved critical in making it possible for my team to enter Afghanistan on 26 September 2001 to a warm, friendly welcome from the Northern Alliance leadership.

This meeting was also timely, because just two days after it, the Taliban bribed their way through Masood's defenses at Sorubi and pushed to the gates of Kabul. Rather than inflicting more destruction on the city, Masood opted to retreat without fighting. The Taliban quickly occupied the city, and Masood established his new defensive lines to the north, including a large portion of Baghram Air Base. Those lines were still in place in September 2001.

The bond of trust I established with Masood that late night in Kabul grew and strengthened over the next five years. That relationship and trust were the key elements in allowing the U.S. government to have the strategic base and the strong local allies necessary to bring down maximum force onto the main body of Taliban and al-Qa'ida fighters, at exactly the correct place and time, resulting in a rapid, decisive victory on the battlefield and in ridding Afghanistan of Taliban suppression.

PART THREE

ON THE MOVE FROM GERMANY TO UZBEKISTAN

19–25 September 2001

CHAPTER TEN

Our portion of the team arrived in Ramstein right on schedule. We passed through the Ramstein entry process with ease and retrieved our bags. We had gotten permission from the flight crew to keep the three cardboard boxes of money with us, relieving me of the worry about them being "lost in transit." There was, however, the anticipated confusion of our locating the bus that was to take us to Frankfurt. It was cold, with a misty rain falling, and we had to lug our baggage a long way out past the new security barricades that had obviously been hastily erected around the terminal building in the aftermath of 9/11.

Once we found the bus, we were surprised to learn that we had to pay for our travel ourselves. The driver insisted that we use deutsche marks if we were paying in cash; he would take dollars if we used a credit card but would have to verify each card and ensure that credit was available. I opted to put the entire bill on my U.S. government travel card, but we still had to wait forty minutes while the driver went back and forth with his office on his cell phone trying to verify that I could credit $235 to the card. I was sitting on $3 million, and we were stuck over a $235 bus ride. Finally we were on our way, on a gloomy, rain-slicked autobahn to Frankfurt.

Our reception at the facility where the temporary CIA support office had been established was not what we expected. We were not looking for a red carpet, but we thought there would be a sense of anticipation and excitement by the staff. Here we were, the first CIA officers heading out after 9/11 to strike at the al-Qa'ida, and this staff in this little office was part of that effort. Instead, our arrival seemed to be a pain in the butt to them. Apparently, the staff assumed that they were there to support a large-scale deployment of personnel that would not start until sometime well into the future. Only one or two people in the office knew what we were up to, and it took a while for them to figure out that we were connected to the large pile of cargo that had arrived late the previous afternoon. Someone knew that an American named Chris was in town, but no one had any idea where he might be staying or when he might show up at the office.

Finally we were put in touch with the officer who was coordinating our onward travel, and he told us we would be leaving for Tashkent early the next morning on a chartered L-100. That was good news, but it also meant that we had to inspect our two pallets of cargo and do some more work to reduce the total weight and overall size of our shipment; although the L-100 could easily handle the cargo, we were concerned about the helicopter waiting for us in Uzbekistan. The total weight of the cargo and passengers would be an important issue, but equally important would be the actual space available on the helicopter for those items. The helicopter was outfitted with a large auxiliary fuel tank, which took up a good amount of the cargo area, and the fuel in that tank would reduce the amount of weight available for cargo and passengers. Weight was critical, because this flight would be made over one of the highest passes in the Hindu Kush Mountains.

Chris arrived at about half past two that afternoon—later than we expected; he had some difficulty gaining access to the facility because of the heightened security procedures in place since 9/11. He also had been snowed in during his transit out of Istanbul airport, and his flight was hours late in leaving there for Frankfurt. He feared he would miss us on our brief stopover in Frankfurt. Chris had already been shopping for winter clothing, and after a short meeting we sent him off to the closest U.S. military post exchange to finish outfitting himself for Afghanistan over and above the items we had brought along for him.

*   *   *

We were up early the next morning and left the hotel at 5:15 a.m. Although our support folks might not have been enthusiastic about our arrival, they did an excellent job of moving us and our cargo to planeside. The L-100 was waiting with its tail ramp down, and we met the crew and boarded as the two cargo pallets were loaded. This was certainly a no-frills mode of travel. Red canvas benches were suspended from either side of the plane at the front of the cargo area, and our personal baggage and boxes of food and water were stacked in a row between them. There was a small cleared area at the front bulkhead with a urine tube and a small chemical toilet for our use, both out in the open. We selected seats, and as the canvas sagged against the metal tube frame I could only think that this was going to be a long, uncomfortable flight. The fact that the crew chief distributed rubber earplugs only reinforced my suspicions about the comfort level we were to experience for the next six hours.

As spartan as the accommodations were, the flight proved surprisingly comfortable. We could stretch out across the canvas seats, and even climb up on the cargo to sleep. It was too noisy to talk much, but there was a microwave oven, and the crew chief had stocked the plane with various easy-to-heat food and soft drinks. We passed the time reading and sleeping, and landed in Tashkent at 8:30 p.m.

CIA officers met us at the plane along with several employees of a contract Uzbek travel firm that the U.S. Embassy used. It had connections among the customs and immigration staff at the airport. There was some confusion over our lack of Uzbek visas, but the Uzbek immigration officers finally agreed to allow us into the country. The aircraft was quickly unloaded, and we followed a large Russian truck with our cargo to the U.S. Embassy. While the cargo was offloaded into a newly constructed warehouse in the embassy compound, I went into the embassy building to meet the CIA officer in charge and catch up on where plans stood as to our deployment. Even at 11:00 p.m. things were busy, and the chief, a young officer whom I had known for some years, performed his duties well. He had arrived in Tashkent expecting it to be a quiet time in a backwater central Asian country and now found himself in the center of a storm of activity, with high-level interest from Headquarters. I called Headquarters, touching base with the CTC, NE, and SAD, and followed up the phone calls with a formal cable announcing our safe arrival.

We reached the Sheraton Hotel at midnight, tired but excited. We were pleasantly surprised to see that the entire front desk reception staff was made up of young, attractive women, each wearing an extremely short miniskirt. Rick commented that it was too bad the hotel could not afford to buy them each a whole skirt, but no one in the group complained. We confirmed that Doc was checked in at the hotel, and Murray immediately called him in his room to tell him we were meeting for breakfast at 8:00 a.m. There was a round of banter between the two, who were close friends. That bantering and joking would continue between them for the entire trip.

We learned that our helicopter was still being refurbished but would be ready in a day or two at the latest. The two pilots who would fly the helicopter were en route and would be here in two days. There also was the issue of waiting for bureaucratic red tape to be untangled and for the Uzbek and Tajik governments to grant approval for us to overfly their airspace on our way to Afghanistan. This was the subject of high-level diplomacy, which directly involved the U.S. secretary of state. There was nothing we could do to influence those negotiations, so we would focus on being fully ready to go as soon as our travel was approved. We spent the next four days in busy anticipation of receiving the green light to proceed.

Pappy broke out all his communications equipment and checked it thoroughly. The two satellite phone systems were tested and all the associated batteries were charged. Our portable generators were gassed and tested. We broke out the weapons and checked each one, then spent several hours loading the thirty-round magazines for the AK-47s and putting them into the ammunition web gear we would carry once we were on the ground in Afghanistan. We checked the handheld GPS system, and Stan trained each of us to use the equipment. We shopped in town, buying cases of bottled water and several pairs of small Russian binoculars, which seemed well made and remarkably inexpensive.

We also purchased a large, heavy black plastic suitcase and managed to shoehorn all the money into it, although it was a tight fit. The suitcase was heavy, but it was a much more convenient way to carry the funds. Besides I liked having only one big suitcase to watch rather than three smaller boxes. The seemingly endless, but nevertheless necessary, need to shift and move the cargo made me uncomfortable about keeping track of the money.

Over the next several days, diplomatic negotiations with the Uzbek government seemed to be progressing, and we were told we could expect to receive their approval for our flight. The Tajiks, however, remained doubtful. The Russians had influence with the Tajiks, and we were told that Washington was pressuring the Russians to convince the Tajiks to agree. If that failed, we would be forced to consider the more dangerous route of darting south out of Uzbekistan into Afghan airspace, then hugging the border and flying east over Taliban-controlled territory. Once we reached Northern Alliance territory, we could turn south and head over the Hindu Kush Mountains into the Panjshir.

There was resistance to the latter plan back in Washington and from the Uzbek government, because we would be at great risk as we flew over several hundred miles of Taliban territory. We would have no air support to suppress enemy antiaircraft positions, nor would any air rescue assets be available. If we were forced down in Taliban-controlled territory, we would be totally on our own. For several days it appeared that if we did not gain Tajik government flight approval, our mission would be in jeopardy.

Chris was busy establishing contacts with Afghan resistance commanders through our Tashkent hosts. These commanders were affiliated with Masood's Northern Alliance, and their forces would be fighting in concert with the NA forces based in the Panjshir Valley. We wanted JAW-BREAKER to have the ability to establish direct contact with those commanders or their representatives once we were inside. I actually broke out the first of the cash, giving Chris $50,000 to pass to a senior Hazara Shi'a commander who happened to be visiting Tashkent. We had dealt with this commander for years during the Jihad against the Soviets, and he and his forces had been extremely effective in and around Kabul.

Our pilots, Ed and Greg, arrived on 23 September and immediately set to work with Buck, our crew chief/mechanic, putting the final touches on our helicopter. The next day at noon they pronounced the helicopter fully airworthy and ready to fly. Ed and Greg were both highly experienced former U.S. military Special Operations pilots with thousands of flight hours between them in every type of helicopter imaginable. Buck was equally experienced, having been trained in the U.S. military, and could fix anything mechanical, from a jet turbine helicopter engine to a portable generator to the engine of a Russian jeep.

On the morning of 25 September, we received official confirmation that both the Uzbek and Tajik governments had agreed to our use of their airspace. We could deploy the following day. The flight plan was quickly pulled together. We would load the helicopter at 6:00 a.m. and fly to Dushanbe, land there and refuel, then pick up two Afghan Northern Alliance personnel—one the NA representative from Dushanbe and the other an experienced helicopter pilot who would provide advice and guidance to our pilots on the flight in. Then it would be up and over the Hindu Kush, crossing the mountains via the Anjuman Pass, which, according to our pilots, is at 14,500 feet.

There was a scramble to get the communications equipment repacked and to ensure that the boxes were properly sealed, stacked, and counted. Laundry was done, cables were sent to Headquarters, and coordination was made with the

Tashkent support officer for the next morning's transfer to the airport. We were almost more concerned about the departure arrangements from Tashkent than any other aspect of our planning, because the young support officer assigned to Tashkent had proved to be difficult. His attitude from our arrival at the embassy was that dealing with our team irritated him. I should not have worried, though; the move to the airport went smoothly. I suspect the young support officer was happy to see us go.

We headed back to the Sheraton late that afternoon with plans for a 3:50 a.m. wake-up call. All of us were excited. It had been a hectic eleven days since we were told we would deploy, days filled with hard work, long hours, frustration with bureaucratic delays, and emotional good-byes to our loved ones. The wait was over. Tomorrow morning, the real adventure would begin.

CHAPTER ELEVEN

Our Russian-made workhorse of a helicopter shuddered to maintain altitude as we climbed steadily toward the 14,500-foot-high Anjuman Pass, which would take us over the Hindu Kush Mountains and down into the Panjshir Valley. Even though our helicopter had been extensively reconditioned and upgraded by expert mechanics, this flight over the pass was straining the limits of the aircraft.

Our load was heavy, with several thousand pounds of equipment and supplies jammed into every nook and cranny of the cargo area. Besides the pilots and Buck, the crew chief/mechanic, there were nine passengers on board, all with several heavy bags of personal items. The heaviest sin-

gle cargo item was the large wooden case containing our
weapons and ammunition. The single most important item of
cargo, the large black plastic suitcase containing the money,
was within my sight and secured with metal packing straps.
The supplies, personal gear, extra fuel, and the twelve of us
on board put the load at the maximum this helicopter could
handle at this altitude.

I was sitting on the cold metal floor of the helicopter leaning against my backpack. I was jammed into the corner at the
front of the small passenger area between the bulkhead and
the metal-framed canvas seats. Increasingly cold air was hitting me from an open vent somewhere behind me, and I
pulled my jacket tighter to fend off the arctic blast. The other
six members of my team were either pressed close together
in the few canvas seats or sitting on various items of cargo.

Chris was leaning against a low stack of MRE boxes piled
against the hull opposite me. He was looking out one of the
few windows and watching the snowcapped mountains slipping past us, their peaks rising above our straining helicopter. He turned and looked at me and smiled, putting up
his right glove-covered thumb, a grin spreading across his
face. Nearly thirty-seven years old, with a full blond beard,
he was, like the rest of us, dressed in heavy camping clothing, with a wool watch cap and gloves to ward off the cold as
we struggled up the pass.

The aircraft shuddered again, and the pitch of the rotor
blades changed—for a few seconds taking on a higher,
shriller sound. I looked over at Buck, who was sitting next to
Chris. Buck's white plastic earphones connected him to the
cockpit, and I could see him listening carefully. After a few
seconds he turned to the rest of us and raised his right hand
and made an upside-down U-shaped movement in the air—
hand rising, going straight, then downward. His thumb
popped up. We were over the Anjuman Pass! It was only
then—when all of us were smiling and pumping our fists
yes!—that I realized I had been holding my breath. There
was still dangerous flying ahead, but the worst was now behind us.

Movie scenes to the contrary, it is too loud to hold a real conversation in a military helicopter; besides, we were wearing soft rubber earplugs or plastic earphone-type noise suppressors. I leaned back, relaxing a little, and began to review the situation. At that point, our destination was about forty-five minutes' flying time south to a helicopter landing field used by our hosts-to-be, the Afghan Northern Alliance. Beyond that, we knew little about what we would find when we landed.

Masood's tragic death in the 9 September 2001 suicide bombing had removed him from the equation. I could only speculate on the impact of Masood's death on the NA leadership. We knew that in the immediate aftermath of the assassination, the leadership group had pulled together, contacting their senior commanders throughout the north, assuring them that the Alliance held and the fight against the Taliban would continue. But we did not know just how the reins of power had been divided, or if there was a struggle under way within Masood's inner circle for control. I knew that our welcome would be friendly, but the uncertainty as to who was actually in charge and in what shape we would find this new leadership worried me.

I felt a nudge against my shoulder and glanced up at Rick. He nodded toward Mumtaz, our primary contact with the NA, one of the two Afghans we had picked up that morning at our refueling stop in Dushanbe. I was pleasantly surprised to recognize Mumtaz as the young driver who had met Khalili and me at Baghram Air Base back in September 1996 on my visit with Masood. Mumtaz had obviously risen in the world since then. He was huddled deep into his heavy jacket, hood up, his white-and-black-patterned Panjshiri neck scarf covering most of his face. His eyes were closed. Rick leaned closer to my ear and, lifting his noise suppressor off one ear, said, "Our buddy looks a little spooked."

I returned the nod and leaned toward his ear. "Yeah, but do you blame him? He's tied to us for the duration. Who knows what we'll find when we land?" I smiled.

"I wouldn't be too happy either." Rick nodded, smiling, and we both leaned back into our thoughts.

Mumtaz had been one of the key NA representatives in Dushanbe for a number of years, working for Amrullah Saleh, one of Masood's most trusted young officers. The CIA was in regular contact with Saleh and his NA staff for at least the past two years. We knew that at twenty-eight or so, Mumtaz was a talented linguist, speaking excellent English and fair Russian. He was born and raised in the Panjshir and was reported to have been a favorite of Masood's. The Dushanbe assignment was considered a plum one, and only a trusted protégé of Masood's would have been given the job. Mumtaz told us as he boarded that Saleh had assigned him to our team for as long as we were in Afghanistan.

The second Afghan on board was Nasir, a Russian-trained helicopter pilot, who had joined the Northern Alliance when the Afghan communist regime was finally defeated in April 1992. Nasir had flown for the Soviets until they left Afghanistan in February 1989, then had flown for the communist Najibullah regime, actually flying combat missions against Masood's forces. When Najibullah was defeated and hung from a lamppost in Kabul, Nasir joined the victorious Northern Alliance. That might seem strange to us, but changing sides in Afghanistan has never been unusual. Nasir was now trusted, and he had even flown Masood on many occasions. He was considered one of the best helicopter pilots in the NA. Nasir was stationed on the third seat in the cockpit, behind and between our two pilots. He had been providing them guidance on the best route to fly since we had crossed into Afghanistan airspace and been negotiating the treacherous twists and turns into the Panjshir.

About an hour after takeoff, Nasir pointed out a group of men dug into a defensive position on a hilltop, noting that they were Taliban troops. As Ed pulled the helicopter away from the hilltop, Nasir had laughed and said, "We are flying too fast for them, and they can't shoot accurately anyway. Don't worry." If the men on the ground had time to notice, they might have wondered who we were—our aircraft was painted a neutral tan with red trim. That would be changed once we were established in the Panjshir Valley.

Murray was standing next to Chris and leaning back against the mound of cargo, looking relaxed; he was an old hand at this. An impressive figure, he was well over six feet tall, with broad shoulders and a narrow waist. He had a short-cropped beard and wore a black baseball cap. He was the kind of man you would want at your side if you were going into combat.

After boarding the helicopter, Doc had disappeared over the cargo into the rear of the aircraft. Lean, slightly built, with white hair, he would be easy to underestimate. Besides his years of military experience and his numerous CIA para-military deployments, he was an expert in psychological operations (psyops).

Stan was sitting on a jump seat set against the bulkhead near the door, opposite me. At forty, his youthful face, glasses, and well-trimmed blond hair belied his years of extensive military experience in the Marine Corps. His preference for tan corduroy sport coats with leather elbow patches helped give him a professorial look. But I knew from watching him work these past few days that besides being brilliant (with a master's degree from Harvard), he was in excellent physical condition and strong as an ox.

Pappy was sitting next to Buck and was bent over working the radio set bolted beneath his canvas seat. He was about five feet ten inches tall, with a solid build and curly black hair just beginning to be peppered with gray. I was impressed with Pappy; it was clear that he was an expert in his field, with an enormous capacity for work. His sense of humor was infectious, and he and Rick had already started their back-and-forth impressions of the Marx Brothers, quoting long lines of film dialogue to each other.

Buck suddenly began waving for our attention. He raised both hands and extended all fingers—ten minutes to touchdown. Our nearly five-hour flight was almost over. There was a steady change in pressure as we descended into the valley, and I had been clearing my ears almost absentmindedly. The temperature inside the helicopter began to rise, and we were now almost warm. The mountains outside the window behind Chris were no longer snowy but brown and rocky.

I was also beginning to feel the first signs of a headache, with a small, sharp pain building behind my eyes. Doc had warned us that the nearly one-hour climb up and over the Anjuman without oxygen support would probably cause some of us problems—headaches, dehydration, and tiredness. Those symptoms would be exacerbated by our living above six thousand feet in the Panjshir. I had a wry thought that, with my luck, I'd have all three symptoms and probably then some. Unfortunately, I was right about that.

With Buck's signal, there was a flurry of activity as we pulled together our personal gear, tightened straps, and stowed gloves and scarves and other loose items. Then we settled down, waiting out the last few minutes of the flight. The long days since we started planning this mission were almost over, and we were now just minutes away from landing. That was a sobering thought, as we ten Americans were now deep inside Afghanistan with only Masood's Northern Alliance forces to protect us. The helicopter we were in would be our only real lifeline to the outside world, and the closest American forces were in Uzbekistan, too far away to be of any assistance if we got into trouble. Even if that was not the case, those forces did not yet have the authority to act.

The helicopter slowed and began to hover, seeming only to inch forward. I looked at my watch—it was 2:40 p.m. Buck, standing at the exit door, was watching our forward movement, and he turned just as there was a gentle bump. The helicopter rocked slightly, then steadied, and Buck grinned and again raised his hand, his thumb popping up. We had landed!

Buck opened the door and worked the metal steps into place. The rotors were blowing up reddish dust, and Buck held on to his baseball cap as he stepped to the ground and circled toward the front of the aircraft, doing his visual safety check. Then, at his signal, the pilots cut the engine. All of us inside were now standing, peering through the small windows, trying to catch a glimpse of what was happening outside. The rotor blades began to slow with a diminishing whine. Murray pushed forward and moved down the steps, anxious to be the first of the team on the ground. Rick and I exchanged glances and shook our heads simultaneously, laughing.

I followed Murray, stepping gingerly onto the small metal steps, my legs suddenly a little unsteady from the flight. The bright sun made me blink. The sky was a clear, cloudless blue, and the air was warm. I jumped down onto the bare reddish-brown dirt of the landing field and moved away from the helicopter to make room for the rest to exit. Mumtaz followed me, then hurried off to greet the group of Afghans standing some yards away, outside the sweep of the rotor blades. As we collected ourselves, we began to notice that we were surrounded by Afghans, all anxious to shake our hands and greet us. It was 2:45 p.m. on 26 September 2001, and we were deep in the Panjshir Valley in northeast Afghanistan.

CHAPTER TWELVE

Our reception was as friendly and positive as we had anticipated. Our hosts were clearly happy to have us there. Mumtaz took over the activities at the landing field, directing the loading of our personal gear into the back of several Toyota Hilux double-cab pickup trucks and assigning the team members places in those trucks or in the several Russian jeeps standing by for the ride to our compound. I stayed by the helicopter until the heavy black suitcase with our money was unloaded, and I carefully secured it in the cargo area of the jeep in which I was to ride. The flight crew, along with

Murray, remained behind to oversee the unloading of the equipment and to secure and close up the helicopter. With everyone else accounted for, the small convoy pulled out.

The area around the landing field, named Astaneh, was on the east side of the Panjshir River, which at that point was about a hundred yards wide and flowing fairly swiftly. A metal suspension bridge crossed the river next to the landing field. We all assumed we would drive across the river on that bridge. I was in the jeep with Rick and Chris, which was the lead vehicle in the convoy. As we lurched forward, the driver headed downstream away from the bridge, angling toward the river.

I twisted around to look back at the others, meeting confused looks and shoulder shrugs. "Do you think we're going to ford the river?" I asked. Before anyone could reply, the driver stopped with a jerk and clumsily began grinding gears. He finally managed to shift into four-wheel drive.

"I think the answer is yes," said Chris. And with another lurch the driver popped the clutch and drove the jeep off the riverbank, sending up a spray of water that splattered the windshield. Immediately the water rose above the level of the floorboards, splashing hard against the jeep, although we did not seem to be taking on water. The river was relatively shallow, and the riverbed was covered with smooth, basketball-size rocks. There appeared to be a well-worn path across the river bottom, and the jeep was making good headway, bouncing, lurching, and jerking as the driver fought to keep us on the correct heading. Chris asked between bounces, "What happens if we stall out?" As if on cue, the jeep's engine sputtered, then died. Sitting in the front passenger seat, I watched the current begin to pile water against my door.

The driver seemed unmoved by the impending drama. Ignoring our agitated comments, he simply began to grind the starter over and over again. The other vehicles behind us started to pass, raising waves, but they offered no assistance. This is great, I thought. The driver will flood the engine, then the jeep will flood with water, and we'll drown minutes after our arrival. I turned to the rear, laughing at the situation, and asked, "Should we hike across or what?" At that moment the engine caught, sputtered, then held, the driver grinning and revving the engine hard. With a screech of the gears and a hard lurch, we started again, and in a couple of minutes the jeep scrambled out of the river and up the opposite bank. We were bounced and shaken but, amazingly, dry.

We learned later that the suspension bridge was just an elaborate footbridge. It looked sturdy but would have collapsed under the weight of any vehicle. For a vehicle, fording the river was the only way across. We made the trip to and from the landing field many times over the next forty days, and we never got wet and never again stalled out.

We headed north, back up the valley over ground we had flown above coming in. Our route barely qualified as a road. It was unpaved, one and a half lanes wide, and so heavily potholed that the jeep bounced and jerked constantly, regardless of how slow the driver went. Within the first few minutes I was bounced off my seat and banged my head hard against the unpadded roof. A few seconds later I was tossed to the right, smacking my head on the door window. The blows did nothing to help ease the headache I was nursing. I quickly learned to brace myself, legs stiff, feet planted firmly in the corners of the fire wall, right hand clutching the handgrip above the window, and keeping my butt slightly off the seat to better ride with the bounces and sudden shifts. It turned out that we were only a little over a mile from the village of Barak, where we would stay, but it took us more than fifteen bruising minutes to get there.

Barak proved to be a collection of stone-walled houses set on either side of the road, with other buildings spreading out randomly behind those. Some of the houses had traditional mud covering on the walls. One or two larger compounds were scattered among the smaller buildings. We drove on, raising a cloud of gray-brown dust. The driver worked the horn to alert the occasional small groups of children and adults standing along either side of the road, usually in front of what appeared to be open storefronts with small counters displaying fruit and vegetables. The road veered to the right as we left the village, but we turned left off the road into a rutted, bare field. On our right was a major Northern Alliance ammunition depot. The complex was surrounded by a high barbed-wire fence with one mud-covered building inside. The rest of the area was filled with large wooden crates of artillery rounds and what appeared to be uncovered 122mm rockets, some of which were haphazardly piled inside the fenced area. About fifty yards directly behind the ammo dump was a large stone-walled compound. The jeep headed directly toward the front of the complex—clearly our destination. "Oh, great," said Rick from the backseat. "We're going to live right next to an ammo dump. If that thing ever blows, we'll all just be dust." On that cheery note the jeep jerked to a stop behind the other vehicles from the convoy, and with dust billowing around us, we stiffly climbed out.

Mumtaz was in charge of our reception committee, which was already hard at work moving the gear out of the other vehicles. In the midst of barking orders to the lower-ranking individuals, Mumtaz brought over Jan Mohammad, a tall, heavyset, white-haired Afghan, who was introduced as the manager of the compound. He would be in charge of our support during our stay there. The Afghan staff, mostly young men in their late teens, with a few grizzled war veterans mixed in, hustled our gear out of the jeep. I watched with some trepidation as one young man struggled with the heavy money case. Stan said he would monitor its delivery and keep an eye on it until things settled down. Once we were joined by the rest of the team, Jan Mohammad directed us around the compound.

The compound was built on a hillside, with two main buildings, one set uphill from the other. We explored the lower building first; it was on the same level as the entry gate. It was a long building, and although it had a roof, the interior was only half completed. Construction materials—bricks, tools, bare tree trunks, and mounds of rock and sand—were scattered in the courtyard about halfway along one side of the building. There were two large rooms and a long hallway in the front of the completed portion. Behind a doorway in the hall was a second area of three or four smaller rooms. We would occupy the front end of the building, with one room serving as my sleeping quarters and the other for Mumtaz. Our Afghan hosts would utilize the smaller collection of rooms as living quarters. The hallway would serve to store the bulk of our equipment and supplies.

I initially resisted taking the large room as my sleeping quarters, but Jan Mohammad insisted, having been told by Chris that I was a general, a very senior officer. I immediately became "Agha General"—Mr. General—to Jan Mohammad and all the Afghans with whom I would deal. Nothing would do but a private room of my own. I was somewhat embarrassed when I saw the limited space available for the rest of the team; but given the nasty health problems I would encounter, I was grateful many times over for the privacy.

The other building was completed but was only about half the length of the first structure. Sitting higher up the hillside, it had a metal-railed patio that offered an excellent view of the mountains forming the east side of the valley across the Panjshir River, and a good view to the south out over our village and down toward the landing field, which was out of sight around a bend in the valley. Connected to this building was a smaller structure with what passed for a kitchen, and a small room with rudimentary toilet facilities. I recall glancing into the toilet area and noting it had a small washbasin. The "toilet" itself was a porcelain square fitted around a single hole in the floor, with a pair of raised footprints pointing away from the wall. I had seen similar setups throughout my years in South Asia and did not give it much thought. That little room would come to haunt all of us in the next forty days.

Jan Mohammad explained with pride that Ahmad Shah Masood had used this compound as his headquarters whenever he was in this part of the valley, and the higher building was the finest one in the village. The large double room overlooking the patio had been Masood's office area, and it would serve as our working area. The two other small rooms down the hall would serve as the sleeping quarters for most of the team. Chris, who loved to camp, immediately said he would sleep outside on the patio; Pappy ended up, as usual, sleeping in the office space next to his equipment. A small bare concrete room with a single drain hole in the floor and one water faucet would serve as our bathing facility.

About the time we finished the quick walk-through of the buildings, a large Soviet-era truck brought our equipment from the helicopter with Murray in tow, the horn blowing. Unloading was uneventful, except that the driver, while backing up to the front gate, smashed into a stone wall under construction and collapsed it completely. There was the usual confusion, the young Afghans now being directed by Jan Mohammad, with a lot of noise and scurrying about, but we were soon unloaded.

Pappy was busy setting up the communications equipment, with several of the team helping to unpack laptops, find electrical cords and cables, and set up the few desks and small tables provided by Jan Mohammad. We configured the room to maximize the work space.

A quick check with Jan Mohammad confirmed we had to run on generator power and had brought with us a five-kilowatt Honda generator as well as two one-kilowatt Honda generators. Pappy's vast field experience had forced him to develop great expertise in keeping these temperamental beasts running. We would need all of Pappy's skills, and those of the equally mechanically talented Buck, to keep the generators functioning through dust, long hours of use, and incredibly dirty gasoline.

I carried the black suitcase into one of the back bedrooms, cut off the metal banding straps, and checked the contents. All was fine. I would need regular access to the money, so I used just the suitcase locks (keeping the only key with me) and further secured the case with heavy-duty strapping tape. I wasn't worried about our guys, but the number of Afghan staff in the compound was bothersome, and I wanted the suitcase to blend in with the other gear in the bedroom.

The large wooden crate with our weapons was placed in the hallway just outside the door to the office space. It was a logical place to keep the weapons; they would be close at hand and under the watch of one of us all the time. Rick and I decided that, given our location deep in the secure heart of the Panjshir Valley, we would not carry our weapons in and around the compound or the village. Having the weapons together would make it easier for Stan, who was in charge of them, to keep track of them. However, we were still in dangerous country, and anytime we traveled away from our compound and the village, even down to the landing field, we would be armed.

Doc set up his medical kit and supplies in the hallway, under a stairway to the roof. He placed things so he would have easy access to the wide variety of medicines, drugs, and supplies he had brought along. One item that surprised me was a five-gallon plastic can of chlorine powder purchased from a pool supply store in northern Virginia. When I asked, Doc explained, "Chlorine is the best single thing to bring on any trip like this. We can use it to purify drinking water, keep the toilet and shower area sanitary, and put it on our feet after a shower to kill athlete's foot."

"Can we really use swimming pool chlorine in our water?" I asked.

"Oh, yes," said Doc, smiling. "Many towns in the United States chlorinate their public water supply. But you need only a tiny amount in the bottle to purify the water." I learned later that Doc's idea of a "tiny amount" resulted in a mixture that was strong enough to chlorinate all the swimming pools in northern Virginia for an entire summer. Luckily, it turned out that Jan Mohammad had more than thirty cases of bottled water from the last CIA team to visit the valley. With that, and the water we were later able to bring in, we never had to use the local stuff.

By about six that evening, things began to sort themselves out. The rush of adrenaline we felt on our arrival was wearing off, and the team had begun to congregate in the office area around the communications equipment. Pappy, with Buck's help, had the big generator up and running in one of the open, uncompleted areas of the building across the compound. It was not the most convenient location, but the noise would bother us less.

A few minutes after six, Pappy put the finishing touches on his equipment and turned things on. He checked the cable connection to the satellite antenna set up on the patio and declared the system ready to go. I sat down at one of the laptops and drafted a short cable announcing to CIA Headquarters our safe arrival in the Panjshir. I included our geocoordinates, to provide our exact location. A few minutes later, the message was on its way to Washington, and JAW-BREAKER was officially open for business.

PART FOUR

JAWBREAKER

26–28 September 2001

CHAPTER THIRTEEN

On the evening of our arrival, the local staff prepared what was to become the standard meal during our stay—rice and chicken, or what passed for chicken in the valley. We were awkwardly seated on a circle of cushions on the floor of the main workroom, and we spooned the food from platters onto our plates. There were fresh onions, some small tomatoes, and hot green peppers; with the various condiments and spices we had brought with us, the food was relatively tasty. At least we were not relegated to MREs or PowerBars, as we had anticipated.

Just as the meal ended that first night, Mumtaz arrived, announcing that Engineer Aref Sarwari, head of Masood's intelligence service, would visit the compound later that evening, sometime around eight o'clock. This would be our first meeting with a senior member of the Northern Alliance, and that was welcome news, because we needed to establish direct contact with the Northern Alliance leadership as quickly as possible.

I talked with Rick about the meeting and explained that I thought we should have a sizable amount of cash ready to pass to Aref, to impress upon him our seriousness of purpose and to emphasize to him and the other NA leaders that we were bringing them tangible support. We decided on $500,000, and Rick and I went to the rear bedroom to package the money. I knew from experience that no senior Afghan wanted to be passed money directly—cash from my hand to his. I would need to have it packaged, wrapped in paper or otherwise disguised, and have it placed in a bag for easy handling. The money would not be counted at the meeting, and I knew that Aref would work hard at showing no reaction to the payment of the funds.

Within the CIA, the handling of money is, as it should be, a serious matter, and proper accounting procedures are stressed. Yet in this crisis situation, I was authorized full personal discretion in how the funds I had with me were disbursed. I decided who to pay and how much they were to receive, and I did not require advance approval from Headquarters. This was out of the norm, but then again, this was not a normal situation. At the same time, I knew that at some point in the near future I would be called on to account for the expenditures I made. I kept careful records and made it standard practice to count, wrap, and pass money with another CIA officer present. In the forty days I was in the Panjshir Valley, I spent $5 million, the vast majority passed to our Afghan allies for their use, with only a small amount used as payment for essential supplies and equipment that the team required. That is a lot of money, but when measured against what the money helped achieve—the collapse of the Taliban as a military force, the disruption of the al-Qa'ida organization, and the denial of Afghanistan as a sanctuary for terrorism—it was money well spent.

Engineer Aref arrived at almost exactly 8:00 p.m., and after Mumtaz gave him a short briefing on the day's events, Rick and I joined him. Aref is actually an engineer, so in his case the title is appropriate. However, many people in Afghanistan and Iran who have graduated from college simply adopt the term as an honorific title. Aref was in his late thirties and is slim, with dark hair and a short beard. During my time with him in the valley, he was usually dressed in Western-style khaki pants, a matching khaki shirt, and a tan vest. I do not recall him ever wearing a hat or any other head covering, which is unusual for an Afghan. He is an animated speaker, full of energy, and finds it hard to remain still for long. He grew up speaking Dari; his Pashtu is equally fluent, and he speaks excellent Russian and fairly good English. In our meetings he preferred to speak Dari, and although my Dari was probably as good as Aref's English, we both preferred to use Mumtaz as our translator.

Aref recognized me immediately as having been one of the two CIA officers who met with Commander Masood in Paris in April 2001. I also recalled Aref from that meeting as one of the several Afghans who were part of Masood's inner circle. He and I had not really spoken then, but we had been introduced to each other. I recounted to Aref that I had met Masood in Kabul in September 1996 and again in Talaqan in late 1997. I noted that Mumtaz had been my driver when I visited Kabul in September 1996.

I asked after the health of my good friend Khalili, who was seriously wounded in the bomb blast that killed Masood on 9 September. I explained to Aref that my relationship with Khalili extended back to late 1988, and we were personal friends. Aref told me that Khalili was doing better than expected and would recover. However, his legs were badly wounded, and walking would be problematic. Also, it appeared that he had lost the sight in his right eye.

Aref noted that Commander Masood had saved Khalili's life. Just before the fatal meeting, Masood had placed Khalili's passport in his suit coat pocket, just over Khalili's heart. Nine pieces of small metal shards had hit the passport, but none had penetrated into Khalili's body. The doctors stated that any one of the metal pieces could have killed Khalili had they struck his heart.

I explained that Khalili had been the go-between who arranged for my meetings with Masood over the years. The April 2001 meeting in Paris was unusual, because Masood rarely left Afghanistan. On this trip, he visited Paris as a guest of the French government, with arrangements made by the French Internal Security Service (Direction de la Surveillance du Territoire—DST). Masood used this opportunity to explore possible support from the French and other European governments. After Paris, Masood visited the European Union Congress in Strasbourg, France, to plead for aid in his fight against the Taliban. The destruction of the two massive stone Buddha statues in Bamiyan Province earlier that month had shocked the European community, and Masood was hopeful that the European Congress would provide him much-needed support.

Khalili had arranged for me to have a room at the hotel in Paris where Masood's delegation was staying. When I checked in, I discovered that I was listed as part of the "Afghan delegation" by the hotel staff. I was well known to the French intelligence services, both the DST and the French External Intelligence Service (Direction Général de la Sécurité Extérieure—DGSE). I was using my true name on this trip. I often wondered what the DST thought when they reviewed the delegation list and saw my name as one of the official party. I'm sure it was something like, How did the CIA know of the visit, and How was one of their officers a member of the delegation? How can that be?

With my relationship with Masood established, and my personal connection to Khalili understood, I had immediate credibility with Aref. That credibility would extend to the other NA leaders I would be dealing with over the next weeks.

The meeting with Aref went well. He was anxious to know our mission during this visit. How long would we stay? What plan did the U.S. government have for Afghanistan? Would the Northern Alliance receive assistance? I went through his questions carefully. I explained that the U.S. government was deadly serious about eliminating bin Ladin and al-Qa'ida and ending the use of Afghanistan as a sanctuary for terrorists. This would mean breaking the Taliban, militarily and politically. I explained to Aref that I did not have the details of the plan, but it was certain that the president had directed the U.S. military to bring down its full might on the Taliban and their Arab "guests."

I said the United States recognized that the Northern Alliance was the single most effective fighting force in opposition to the Taliban, and most of the military strength of the Taliban and the Arab fighters was concentrated on the front lines facing the Northern Alliance, to the south, just above

Kabul, and in the west, on what was known as the Takhar front. My mission was to establish a solid relationship with the Northern Alliance leadership, to secure the cooperation of the Northern Alliance military forces in working in concert with the U.S. military in attacking the Taliban, and to arrange for the Panjshir Valley to serve as a base of operations for U.S. military Special Operations forces in the coming battle to crush the Taliban. Our team would stay until the mission was accomplished. Money would be provided to the Northern Alliance, and a first payment of funds would be made that evening. We would work with Aref and the NA military leadership to determine what materiel and supplies the Northern Alliance forces required to prepare them for the coming fight. Critical supplies that could not be procured locally would be airlifted into the valley, as well as to other locations in the north and west where Mujahedin were opposing the Taliban.

I explained that one critical early mission of our team was to work with the Northern Alliance to conduct GPS mapping of their frontline positions, so our aircraft would avoid attacks against NA troops and positions. We wanted to explore means to mark heavy equipment, such as tanks, so pilots could identify friendly forces and concentrate with confidence in attacking the enemy.

We also wanted to establish with Aref a joint intelligence cell, which would be located with my team at our compound. All the intelligence that NA forces collected over the coming days—whether from direct observation of enemy activities at the Northern Alliance front lines or intercepted enemy radio communications—could therefore be funneled into a single office, where it would be collated, analyzed, and shared with the CIA. In turn, we would share intelligence with Aref from our own sources. This was all good news to Aref, and I could see the relief sweep over his face as I spoke.

Since the late 1980s, as the role of the Soviets on the battlefields of Afghanistan began to significantly diminish, the single most important factor in deciding the outcome of any battle had been defections by individual commanders to the other side at critical moments in the fighting. Discouraged, disheartened commanders were prone to cut their losses and make a deal with the opposing forces. The Taliban, with funding from Pakistan and fundamentalist Arabs such as bin Ladin, had been able to buy the majority of their victories since sweeping out of the southern deserts of Qandahar Province in 1994.

There was no shame attached to these defections. Allegiances shifted easily, and defections were generally viewed as making the best of a bad situation. With Masood dead and the Taliban front lines growing stronger through the daily arrival of student volunteers from the religious schools in Pakistan, things looked bleak for the Northern Alliance.

The NA leadership was, however, connected to the outside world via satellite television, and they had followed the statements of America's leaders in the aftermath of 11 September. The notification of our team's plan to come to the valley had given them their first solid reason for hope since Masood was assassinated. Now we were in the valley, and I was saying exactly what they wanted to hear.

There was one point that bothered Aref. I had stressed that we would be dealing with commanders all around the north, commanders who were part of the Northern Alliance but operated semi-independently from the day-to-day command of the NA leadership. Aref pointedly said that this direct contact might create more problems than it solved, because it would confuse the lines of authority. He was sure that General Mohammad Fahim Khan, who had succeeded Masood as overall leader of the Northern Alliance, would prefer that all contact with NA commanders be handled through him.

I replied that I had anticipated Fahim's position, but success in the coming battles would require direct CIA coordination on the ground with any and all commanders willing and able to field troops to fight the Taliban. The CIA had already established direct contact with many of the key commanders—including General Dostum in the Mazar area, Ismail Khan in Herat, and the Shi'a leader, Khalili, in Bamiyan

Province—and we would continue to develop similar direct contact with Pashtun commanders in the southern areas of the country.

I touched on a key issue for Aref, stating that unlike 1992, when we walked away from the Mujahedin when victory was achieved, the U.S. government was in this fight for the long haul. We wanted to change conditions in Afghanistan, so that after the Taliban were crushed, and after bin Ladin and his Arab terrorists were eliminated, the country could rebuild, the economy could revive, and peace could finally come to Afghanistan. A peaceful, economically stable environment would ensure that the country would never again be used by foreign elements as a sanctuary for terrorists.

To guarantee that, the U.S. government would need to play the role of an honest broker in a post-Taliban Afghanistan. To accomplish that goal, we needed now to be in direct contact with as many of the leaders of the country as possible. I politely but firmly concluded by saying that we would do our best to ensure that Fahim and the NA leadership were kept in the loop on our dealings with their commanders around the north, but we would deal with those commanders directly. Aref reluctantly accepted that fact, but the issue would return to plague our relationship for weeks to come.

As promised, I produced the backpack in which I had placed the $500,000, and passed it to Aref. He hefted the bag but did not look into it, then handed it to Mumtaz. I told him the amount and said that this money was the first payment I would make to the Northern Alliance. I also stressed our hope that Aref's intelligence organization, the National Directorate of Security (NDS), should be permitted by the NA leadership to utilize the majority of this first payment. I told Aref that I wanted his intelligence organization to be able to operate effectively and the joint cell we were to establish to be up and running quickly. I said I was sure that General Fahim would utilize some of the money to secure supplies for his forces, but I asked Aref to stress to Fahim that much more money was available for purely military purposes.

Aref wrote the amount of the payment in his pocket diary

and repeated it to Mumtaz. I smiled to myself; it was clear that Aref was taking the same kind of double-check precautions with the money as I had. He wanted Mumtaz to be able to verify the amount of funds passed, just in case there was a question raised by Fahim or others of the Northern Alliance leadership.

With that, the meeting ended. We shook hands all around, then made plans for a meeting with Aref the following evening. Mumtaz was to begin efforts to organize the intelligence cell, and we would have Chris work closely with him in this effort. Aref was to coordinate with General Fahim to get team members to the Kabul front lines to begin the GPS survey of the NA positions. This would be a dangerous undertaking—the Taliban front lines were close enough to bring my officers under direct fire—and we all wanted this to be done in as safe and coordinated a manner as possible.

Rick and I returned to the other building, and I sat down to draft a cable about the meeting. Rick placed a secure telephone call back to Headquarters to speak with Hank C., who had just been assigned to manage the overall effort in Afghanistan for the CTC. At midnight we finished for the day. I felt good about the work we had accomplished, but physically I was not feeling well at all. The headache that had come on that afternoon was getting worse, and my lower intestinal tract was rumbling threateningly.

I went off to my room in the lower building. A sleeping bag on top of a locally made soft foam cushion, about five feet in length, served as my bed. I was too tired and sick to feel guilty about all the space I had to myself, because it was good to be alone. But I did note that I was a long, long way from the only bathroom facility, located behind the kitchen area, far across the compound.

Two hours later I awoke with a start. My bowels were churning, and I knew I had to make it to the bathroom immediately. Too many years in South Asia have given me a great familiarity with the onset of diarrhea. I struggled to get my pants on, but it was too late. Try as I might, I could not stop my bowels from giving way. I ripped a wad of paper towels from a roll to stop the mess but was only partially successful. I was in a panic. I knew I could not make it out of the building and across the courtyard to the bathroom, not in my condition. I grabbed the empty liter-size plastic water bottle I had finished just before turning off the lights and used my pocketknife to cut the top off the bottle. I jammed the ragged end of the bottle into place against my butt and relaxed. Somehow my aim was accurate. I squatted there in pain and shame, embarrassed and hurting. I was feverish and dehydrated, and my bowels were locked in spasms. I had soiled myself and the floor, and I knew it was not going to get any better that night. It was a great start to my time in Afghanistan.

CHAPTER FOURTEEN

For me the next day was a loss until just after noon. Early that morning I staggered over to the other building to find Doc. Buck, the two pilots, and Murray and Stan were getting ready to head out to the landing field at Astaneh to start repainting our helicopter. Its current paint job would make it stand out like a sore thumb in the valley, something we wanted to avoid. The new paint would match the green camouflage pattern used by the Northern Alliance.

I barely noticed their preparations and departure. Doc had no means of testing to determine what I had, but he felt that Cipro, a new, powerful antibiotic drug he had just started to use, would take care of whatever it was. I took one and dragged myself back to my room. With Imodium to slow the symptoms, I was able to rest and take some liquids. By late morning I was feeling a little better, although I stayed close to the bathroom or near one of the several altered water bottles I had in my room. Right after lunch, which I skipped, Rick and I discussed our plan of action and outlined our priorities for the next several days.

We needed to meet with General Mohammad Fahim Khan because as it was critical that we secure his agreement to fully cooperate with the CIA and the U.S. military, and to confirm Engineer Aref's statements that U.S. Special Operations forces could utilize the Panjshir Valley as a base of operations. I did not doubt Aref's word, but I needed to hear the same statement from Fahim directly. We would also need to secure General Fahim's agreement to begin the GPS mapping of the Northern Alliance front lines just north of Kabul.

We brought Chris into the conversation on the intelligence cell issue, and as I expected, he already had some solid ideas worked out. He and Mumtaz had scouted out an appropriate room in the lower building that would serve our needs, and arrangements were already under way to furnish the room with several large tables. Chris said there was ample wall space to put up maps of our area of operations, and Mumtaz was bringing over a number of the large-scale Russian maps that the NA utilized.

At 1:00 p.m., Mumtaz appeared and informed us that General Fahim, Engineer Aref, and the Northern Alliance foreign minister, Dr. Abdullah Abdullah, were to arrive in one hour for a meeting. Aref indicated the previous evening that our introductory meeting with Fahim would be held late at night, and I had been hoping the timing would hold. As anxious as I was to kick things off and meet with Fahim, I was tired and weak and badly needed a few hours of rest.

Although I had passed Aref $500,000 the night before, I wanted to pass a second, larger cash payment to General Fahim for his use in bringing his frontline forces nearer to combat readiness. Another payment of significant size would also impress on the NA leadership that the CIA was serious about providing assistance, and would reinforce the idea that cooperation with our team would yield direct, positive results. Rick and I went back to the black suitcase and got $1 million wrapped and ready.

The meeting took place right on time, with their three-car convoy arriving in a cloud of gray-brown dust. There was much scurrying about by the Afghan staff to greet Fahim and company. We met in the lower building, in the room that Mumtaz was occupying, which was furnished with a cheap felt floor covering, five or six chairs, and a number of locally made floor cushions. The windows were open to catch a breeze, which billowed the thin cotton curtains like sails into the room.

I had never before met General Fahim, and in fact had heard his name mentioned only once or twice in passing in all the years I had been dealing with Masood and the Northern Alliance. Fahim is of medium height, five foot nine or so, with a stocky but solid build that projects power. His face is round, and his nose has obviously been broken more than once and never set properly. He wears his Chitrali hat pulled low across his forehead, just above his thick eyebrows. He dresses in the tan khaki-style of camp clothing favored by Masood and Engineer Aref. He is clean-shaven, unusual among senior Panjshiris. When speaking to you, he has a habit of staring directly into your eyes, almost never blinking. He also watches you with equal intensity as you respond, leaning forward slightly, giving you his full attention. He does not speak English, nor does he have even a rudimentary understanding of the language, something that Aref and Dr. Abdullah used to their advantage during this and other meetings we held with Fahim. Mumtaz served as the formal translator for our discussions.

Over the next few weeks, I learned that when Masood returned to the Panjshir Valley in early 1980, Fahim joined him, serving as the commander of a small group of Mujahedin operating in the northern areas along the Tajik border. A tough, stubborn fighter, Fahim earned Masood's respect and was given ever larger command responsibilities by Masood. By the late 1980s, Fahim was Masood's senior field commander, with the rank of general. I was told that although Masood did not particularly like Fahim personally, he had full confidence in his battlefield abilities and found him indispensable.

Later I learned from Engineer Aref and Dr. Abdullah separately that on the day of Masood's assassination, it was Fahim who took charge and held the Northern Alliance leadership together. Both men said that they and the others around Masood were shocked, dazed, and shaken by the disaster. Fahim took charge, roughly exerting his will on the group, coming up with a plan that delayed the announcement of Masood's death until the other senior commanders in the north could be contacted and assured of the stability of the Alliance. He arranged for the helicopter flight that took Masood and Khalili to Dushanbe that afternoon, then personally reached out to all senior Northern Alliance commanders. Without Fahim's strength and decisive actions, the Northern Alliance might well have collapsed in those first few days after Masood's death.

I had met Dr. Abdullah on several occasions in the past, including an introduction in Talaqan in May 1997 when I visited Masood there, and again in Paris in April 2001 when I joined Masood at the beginning of his political tour in Europe to raise support within the European community. On both occasions, Dr. Abdullah was the only other member of Masood's entourage who actively participated in my conversations with Masood. Dr. Abdullah is of medium height, about five foot nine, and thin, with a slight, neatly trimmed beard. He is always stylishly dressed, preferring Western casual-dress clothing, usually a sport coat, dress shirt, and khaki pants. His English is excellent, and at all the meetings I attended with him he served as the expert on translations from Dari into English, politely correcting the translator (usually Mumtaz) to get to the exact English word needed. Dr. Abdullah is soft spoken, well mannered, and polite. He is not considered a true Panjshiri; only his mother was from the valley. This did not hinder Masood from developing real trust and affection for Abdullah. Over the years, Masood moved him from his role as medical adviser to one of his key political advisers.

I did not know how General Fahim would approach this meeting. I did know he certainly had been fully briefed by Aref on what I had said yesterday evening about our goals and intentions for our team. I expected Fahim to be positive and welcoming, but several of the issues we had placed on the table with Aref had troubling aspects for our Afghan hosts. The presence of large numbers of U.S. military personnel in uniform in the Panjshir Valley could raise the age-old Afghan objections to foreign troops on their soil. Our plan to establish independent contact with senior NA commanders in other areas in the north was another point of possible contention. Fahim might try to take a hard-line position on these and other issues.

I did not mind contention in our discussions. We were bound to disagree on any number of issues as we tried to secure larger U.S. interests and the NA leadership tried to protect their own fragile grip on the Alliance. But I wanted any disagreements to be handled in a collegial manner, with a frank give-and-take.

So I planned on being candid with Fahim on sticky issues, raising them even if our hosts were reluctant to bring up those topics themselves. There was no room for negotiation on the issue of our having independent, direct contact with NA commanders. The CIA would not only establish that contact, we would place CIA teams with those key commanders as soon as we could arrange to do so safely. This stance was sure to be the case on other issues. Sixteen days after 9/11, the U.S. government was in no mood to be thwarted in its efforts to engage the al-Qa'ida. Objections raised by Fahim on such issues as independent contact would be seen in Washington as petty squabbling to try to protect narrow political interests.

There were already rumblings from the Pakistanis, and from some quarters back in Washington, about the need to bring the Pashtun tribes in the south into the fight before fully engaging with the Northern Alliance. The Pashtuns were the traditional rulers of Afghanistan, and the Pakistanis were becoming increasingly vocal about what a disaster it would be if the Tajiks and other ethnic minorities of the north won control of the country. I did not want to add fuel to what could become a real fire.

The strategic situation seemed crystal clear to me. The Taliban and their Arab allies had the majority of their combat forces deployed in the north on two main fronts. One front ran west to east from above Kabul over to Jalalabad, near the Pakistani border. The other ran north to south, from the Tajik border down to connect with the lines above Kabul. On a map it was as if a large letter L had been drawn, isolating the northern corner of the country, with the Panjshir Valley forming the heart of that block of territory. The Northern Alliance forces, about eight thousand fighters, were deployed in static positions in lines opposite those of the Taliban forces. Neither side was strong enough to break the other, and the situation had been stalemated for well over a year.

In the southern areas of the country, the Taliban had succeeded in defeating all Pashtun tribal opposition to their rule and had effectively disarmed most of the fighters, at least of their heavy weapons. Whatever efforts the United States might make to rally Pashtun opposition to the Taliban in the south, it would take months before an effective military resistance could be organized among the fragmented tribal elements there.

Taliban frontline positions offered a clearly defined, target-rich environment made to order for U.S. airpower to strike. I was convinced that a concentrated bombing campaign on the Taliban lines would be devastating to the morale and effectiveness of the Taliban and Arab troops. Most of the successes by the Taliban had been won not in hard-fought battles but by siege and bribery, and most combat engagements had been small, short fights with few casualties. Taliban troops had not suffered the kind of bombardment and punishment they would face from American airpower in the coming fight. Heavy casualties, continuing for days on end, would break the Taliban troops. The Arab fighters might hold on longer and try to make a stand, but the Northern Alliance would be able to overcome their resistance.

If we could beef up the forces of such senior NA commanders as Ismail Khan in the Herat area and General Dostum and Ostad (Professor) Atta south of Mazar-e Sharif, they could tie down the Taliban forces in those areas. Once the breakout was achieved from the Panjshir area, the whole of northern Afghanistan would surely fall. With U.S. airpower working with those commanders to close roads leading south, most of the Taliban fighters would be cut off in the north and would surrender or die. With Kabul and the major cities of the north in NA hands, Pashtun tribal leaders in the south would be emboldened and begin to move against the Taliban. The fight in the south might drag on longer, because the Pashtuns were too fragmented and poorly armed to sweep to a quick victory, but once U.S. airpower focused on the south, the balance there would quickly shift against the Taliban.

The key to victory was in the north, and that victory rested on the shoulders of the Northern Alliance forces under Fahim's command. I wanted to avoid any shift in focus away from that strategic fact. I thought the situation was so clear that everyone involved in the war planning under way back in Washington would see things as I did. I did not realize what a fight lay ahead to convince Washington and American senior military planners to focus efforts in the north.

The meeting with General Fahim lasted almost two hours and covered much the same ground that Rick and I had reviewed with Engineer Aref the previous evening. Why were we here in the valley? What was our plan for cooperation? What would the United States do in the coming weeks? I made the same presentation as with Aref, touching on all the key issues. Fahim took the presentation well.

Rick discussed the possibility of General Fahim providing about thirty soldiers to be trained by our team to serve as a search and rescue (SAR) unit. Until the U.S. Special Operations units arrived, our Russian helicopter would be the only aircraft within range that could be used to extract a downed U.S. pilot from behind Taliban lines. Fahim agreed to supply thirty men, and initial plans were worked out to begin training them as soon as they could be assembled.

Rick stressed again the need for an accurate GPS map of the NA front lines. Because we did not know when the bombing would begin, this was a priority. Fahim agreed to arrange for members of our team to travel to the Kabul front to begin the work, stating he would assign General Bismullah Khan, who commanded the Kabul front, to personally work with the team. I then raised the subject of CIA contact with other commanders outside the valley, indicating that we were already in touch with Ismail Khan and Dostum, and said that I planned to meet directly with Professor Abdul Rasoul Sayyaf within the next several days.

As anticipated, Fahim voiced objections to this idea. However, he was polite in his argument, saying there was no need for the CIA to have direct contact with those commanders, that the NA leadership had well-established lines of command and control with all of their commanders.

Unilateral direct contact would blur those lines, confuse the situation, and create problems where none now existed. I went over our reasoning for wanting direct contact, and explained that Washington would proceed whether or not Fahim agreed. I pledged to keep Fahim informed of those contacts and of the assistance we provided to those commanders. He got the message; although he did not like it, he accepted the fact that the contacts would take place.

An interesting aspect of the meeting was the interplay between Aref and Dr. Abdullah, and their reactions to General Fahim. When dealing with military matters, Fahim spoke with authority and was clearly in charge. When the conversation moved to political issues, Abdullah and Aref would occasionally exchange pointed glances at certain comments made by Fahim. At those points, when Mumtaz finished translating Fahim's remarks for me, Dr. Abdullah would add a comment in English to amplify or modify what Fahim had said.

At one point, Dr. Abdullah said something to the effect that Fahim did not have the full picture on the issue, and we would work with him on that point. When he translated the comments he had made in English to Fahim in Dari, Abdullah obfuscated what he had said. My impression was that although Aref and Abdullah respected Fahim in the role of military leader of the Northern Alliance, at that time neither was comfortable with the general taking the lead in the political arena. From Aref and Abdullah's behavior together at that meeting and at later meetings, I suspected that they might be planning to use Fahim to win a battlefield victory, then work to marginalize him in the post-Taliban political struggle.

I produced the backpack with the $1 million and explained to Fahim that these funds were to assist in preparing his military forces for the coming battle. I said I had given Aref $500,000 the night before and hoped those funds would be used primarily to strengthen Aref's organization. I stressed that other money was available if and when specific needs were identified. I placed the money on a small table in the center of our semicircle of chairs, but no one made a move to pick it up. When the meeting ended, and we stood with hand-shakes all around, still no one made a move to pick up the backpack, even as we began to leave the room. For a second I had the foolish thought that they might not take the money. Then Aref motioned to Mumtaz, who casually picked up the backpack with one hand, then strained against its weight, almost dropping the bag. He looked at me and smiled, and I said, "Yes, a million dollars is heavier than you think."

I was exhausted. We waved good-bye at the front gate, and I went to the office area to draft a cable on the meeting. When I arrived, Chris briefed me on the progress that he and Stan had made in organizing the joint intelligence cell. The room was set up, maps were on the walls, and Northern Alliance communications gear was in place. Aref had assigned four young officers to work under Mumtaz as the rotating staff for the office. At least two of the officers would sleep in the room so it would be manned 24/7. Also assigned to the group was another Afghan, Hafiz, a seasoned combat veteran who was dedicated to the mission and incredibly hard-working. It had been Hafiz who had made things happen that afternoon. He and Chris hit it off immediately, and with Hafiz's help Chris already had enough information for three or four intelligence reports. Chris would get those back to Headquarters in Washington within the next few hours. I had not expected the Afghans to be ready for at least two or three more days. It was an impressive start, and an encouraging sign of Aref's commitment to the effort.

I sat down at the computer and worked on a cable report-ing the results of the meeting with Fahim. I told Rick I would do a first draft, then let him edit and put the cable into shape to send. I was feeling woozy and a little light-headed, and I knew I would not last much longer. As I worked on the cable, the rest of the team was discussing the events of the day.

The flight crew was happy with the results of the repaint-ing effort on the helicopter; they had completed the job by late afternoon. Buck was busy cutting out cardboard stencils of numbers so he could add the helicopter's "registration" number to the tail boom. I thought it was a little overkill—the number would be totally fictitious—but I felt too bad to even comment. I finished the cable, not overly happy with the results of my efforts but not really caring at that point. Rick took over to finish the cable.

I could feel another bout of diarrhea coming on, so I col-lected my next dose of Cipro from Doc and headed back to my room. I dozed on and off for the rest of the day and into the evening but was back in the office later that night to moni-tor contact with Headquarters. With a ten-and-a-half-hour time difference between us, they were just opening up in Washington as we were closing down for the day. I went to bed at midnight, leaving Chris and Stan at work on the intel-ligence reports and Pappy working hard getting the equip-ment in top shape. My modified water bottles continued to come in handy that night.

CHAPTER FIFTEEN

Although our living conditions in the Panjshir Valley could most charitably be described as spartan, there was a large guesthouse directly across from the helicopter landing field in Astaneh that turned out to be impressive even by Western standards. It was in use by a few Western journalists who had managed to work their way into the valley. Masood had learned years before of the power of good publicity, and the Northern Alliance had played host to numerous journalists since the mid-1980s. The guesthouse was one of several nicely appointed buildings that the NA maintained for journalists and visiting foreign dignitaries.

Security dictated that we be housed in a more protected, isolated location, which is why we were farther north up the valley. The small village of Barak hugs the narrow strip of land between the western hills and the river. The valley narrows just south of the village, so those moving north on the road can easily be funneled into a controlled checkpoint before they actually enter the village. At Barak, the Panjshir River widens to about three hundred yards and is fairly deep and icy cold, running in a swift current, forming a natural protective barrier for the village to the east. Additionally, the valley on the east side of the river, opposite the village, is bare and rocky, and movement there is easy to detect.

Just to the north, on the east side of the river, beyond sight of the village, was a Northern Alliance compound that was being used to house captured Taliban mullahs. Apparently these were senior clerics who were considered to be extremely valuable prisoners. Security around the compound was heavy, and the NA had placed a ZSU-23 antiaircraft cannon on a hilltop overlooking the compound, positioned so it could fire down onto the valley floor.

Our compound was built on a hillside, which rose to about six hundred feet above us, with a second and third line of hills rising behind that. We were at the northern end of the village, with many of the houses around us in various stages of construction. Jan Mohammad explained that the Soviets had invaded the Panjshir Valley eight times during their occupation of the country, trying to break Masood and his Northern Alliance. Barak was the high-water mark of those incursions into the valley. Although the Soviets had captured the village six times, they never succeeded in advancing any farther north in the valley. Each time, they were driven out and sustained heavy losses. Numerous rusting hulks of Soviet tanks and armored vehicles still littered the valley floor all around the village, blunt testimony to the ferocity of the fighting. Jan Mohammad said that every building in the village was destroyed, and for one three-month period the Soviets had bombed and shelled the village and the surrounding hills every day for four to five hours a day. Jan Mohammad assured us that there was no unexploded ordnance in the village area or on the lower hillsides; the number of children playing all around our compound seemed to prove that was true. He said there had been no accidents in more than three years, but that was true only for the lower hillsides. The upper hills had not been cleared, and we were not to try to move around up there without a guide.

As was Afghan tradition, our hosts insisted on preparing all our meals for us. The compound had a rudimentary kitchen, with crude, hand-constructed concrete wood-burning stoves and ovens. Round holes cut into the top of the stoves were sized to allow a pot or skillet to fit over the open flames. Meals were prepared in a cloud of wood smoke—the stoves/ovens had no chimneys, and the smoke vented into the room, where it formed a thick layer from the ceiling to a few feet off the floor. At times the smoke was so thick that all you could see of the cook and his helpers were their feet. The floor was usually wet from washing dishes and pots and pans in large buckets of water. Because of the smoke, much of the food preparation was done at ground level. After a few visits to the kitchen, we all decided it was best not to know exactly what was going on in there.

The food we were served was as good in quality as our hosts could find. It was late September when we arrived, so there were fresh tomatoes, onions, small hot peppers, carrots, and radishes available. Rice was a staple, but it had to be eaten with care, because it usually had a pebble or two in the pot missed by the cook in cleaning. Fresh bread was brought to the compound from the village each morning. It was typical of the bread in the region—rolled flat and baked in a stone oven to form a triangular loaf. It was stale by evening. My treat each morning was a piece of this still warm, delicious fresh bread with peanut butter and jelly. Small apples, sweet and crunchy, were available most of the time we were there. Eggs were inevitably cooked in ghee, a semi-liquid clarified butter favored throughout South Asia. It came packed in gallon cans and was used in great quantities in virtually every cooked dish we were served.

Meat was occasionally served at lunch and dinner but was always of the "mystery" variety. We never seemed to get a cut of meat that looked like a roast or a steak; rather we were served hunks of meat that had knuckles and joints and a lot of gristle and fat. The poultry came from scrawny chickens running free in and around the compound. Because they seemed to prefer eating the runoff from our toilet drain, we tended to avoid chicken—when we could recognize that it was what we were being served.

Soup was also prepared for lunch and dinner. It was mostly broth; only a few vegetables appeared in the pot. We assumed that the kitchen staff strained out most of the vegetables for themselves, probably to go with the better cuts of meat we never saw, but we couldn't prove that.

My typical lunch and dinner became cut-up tomatoes, onions, and hot green chilies in a bowl of soup broth with a spoonful or two of rice, and a piece of the local bread. Early on, Jan Mohammad produced a garlic and hot-pepper sauce made in Tajikistan that added a spicy jolt to the soup mix, and I made sure that the shopping list for the later food runs he organized to Dushanbe included mention of several jars of this mixture. With that, and the collection of condiments we had each brought with us—Tabasco sauce being the most popular single item on the table—the meals were tasty, if somewhat monotonous. Dessert was an apple or, if I was still hungry, a little peanut butter and jelly on the local bread. Between that diet and my chronic stomach and lower intestinal problems, I lost twenty pounds in forty days. I would not recommend this routine as a way to slim down.

Bathing was another adventure. The shower area was a bare ten-by-ten-foot room with a concrete floor. There was a single water tap on one wall about eighteen inches off the floor, and a small drain hole in the floor a few feet from the faucet. During our first several days there, the young Afghans working in the kitchen would heat water on the makeshift stoves and bring over a single bucket of warm water for each team member. The water was always murky, with a dirty sediment at the bottom. We dipped a plastic cup into the bucket to wet ourselves, then soaped up and used the rest of the water to rinse off. Within a few days we improved on the process by purchasing an electric heating coil at the local market. It could heat a bucket of water to a comfortable temperature in about ten minutes. Whenever someone used the heating coil, the lights in the hallway would dim dramatically. I was always afraid that someone would be electrocuted, but we all somehow survived our "showers." Within a few weeks of our arrival when the weather began to turn cold, the morning "shower" in that unheated concrete room took on an even less appealing aspect, but it did cut down on the time one had to wait to get a turn to bathe.

Jan Mohammad arranged for our clothing to be "washed" in the village. There was no way we could have managed the task ourselves, given the limited water sources and our cramped living spaces. The clothing would disappear midmorning and return late in the day, still damp but somewhat pressed and folded. The clothes had to have been washed in the river, because we noticed that our white undershorts and T-shirts got progressively grayer.

The first two days, we had our meals in the double-size room we used for our office. That quickly proved too disruptive and messy. At mealtime we would have to stop working and move the small worktables and chairs, laptops, and other gear out of the way. Our hosts would rush in, spread a plastic cloth in the cleared area, and set the bowls of food onto the cloth. We would then sit on the floor around the food, spooning it onto our plates and trying not to make a mess.

At the end of the second day, I asked Jan Mohammad to arrange for the large room in the lower building in which I was staying to be turned into a dining area and meeting room. The next morning my things were moved to the next room down, vacated that morning by Mumtaz. He had shifted to the intelligence cell office, where he would now sleep. The floor was covered with the ubiquitous heavy felt material that served as carpeting throughout the country. New white cotton sheets were cut into curtains, the window screens were repaired, and the shelves were cleaned. A large table that would seat twelve, with matching chairs, was somehow located to serve as our dining table and a meeting table. The other end of the room, furnished with two sofas and several overstuffed chairs, became our primary meeting area for contact with Aref. This change allowed us to expand the office area, adding tables and chairs for laptop workstations. Meals became more relaxed and enjoyable, and work was not interrupted three times a day.

We had expected that finding potable drinking water would be a problem, so we each brought along a small camping-type water purifier. Doc had brought his chlorine powder, which I suppose in a pinch we would have used. But we need not have worried. Jan Mohammad produced his stash of thirty or so cases of bottled water, brought in for the last CTC team that visited the valley, which nicely augmented the supply of

water we had brought with us. Doc advised that if the cap
was sealed and a visual check did not show any discoloration
of the water, we could drink it safely.

Although we adapted to the conditions and improvised to
make things run as smoothly as possible, one thing plagued
us throughout our time at the compound—the toilet facility.
There were ten of us on the team when we arrived in the valley, and over the next three weeks we were augmented by two
more officers. That meant there were twelve adult males utilizing one totally inadequate facility. The room itself was no
more than eight by ten feet. On the right as you entered was
a rusted, disconnected water heater. Next to it was a small
sink with a single cold-water faucet and a small, old mirror
with peeling silver backing. The toilet was next to the sink.
Mounted on the wall above the hole was a porcelain flush
box. A single small window, the glass broken, was set high in
the end wall of the room and provided the only ventilation.

To use the facility, you would step onto the footprints and
lower your trousers, keeping a tight grip on them so they did
not droop onto the wet and always dirty porcelain. You then
squatted and leaned back, bracing yourself with one hand
behind your back pressed against the wall. Once positioned,
you had to aim, looking down between your legs, trying to
hit the drain hole dead center, to avoid splashing. It was awkward and uncomfortable, especially with diarrhea twisting
your bowels.

But the real problem was the drain hole itself. It was about
four inches in diameter at floor level, but apparently about
two feet beneath the floor it necked down to a much smaller
diameter. If only two or three people had been using the facility, the small size of the drainpipe might not have caused
problems. But the toilet simply could not keep up with ten,
then twelve, adult males, especially as intestinal problems
developed among the team members. Using the facility became something to dread, especially in the morning. Stop-
pages were common, and one or two team members seemed
to have the constitution of a bear. I learned to time my morning visits to be ahead of them.

We kept a large bottle of Doc's famous chlorine water mix on the windowsill, to help keep the germs and the smell under control. We also had antibacterial soap on the sink, and I scrubbed my hands like a surgeon after each visit. Had there been some way to set up outdoor slit trenches, I would have done that, but the village children offered us no privacy once we were outside the walls of the compound.

The toilet situation became a source of black humor, under the assumption that it was better to laugh about it than cry. Particularly messy events, especially if the culprit could be identified, brought on rounds of raunchy kidding. We found ourselves talking about bowel movements more and more. Someone added a sentence to a resupply cable we were sending to Headquarters asking for small mirrors marked with crosshairs, so we could aim better. (We never did receive the mirrors.) In early October the toilet facility was hit with an infestation of small, pesky black flies, adding to the misery. Chris found old-fashioned sticky flypaper strips in the village, and those helped keep the fly population somewhat in check.

One other problem plagued us throughout our stay. It turned out that Pappy suffered from terrible flatulence. The man would start farting immediately upon waking up and would continue through the day until he fell asleep. We hollered at him, made jokes about him, and got mad at him, but it did no good. He would shrug and say, "I can't help it. It's this diet. What can I do?" Then a minute later he would pass another cloud of mind-numbing gas.

Despite this affliction, Pappy was the hardest-working member of the team, and he lived up to his reputation as being the best field communications officer in the business. The CIA's field communications system is much more cumbersome and difficult to use than the fantasy handheld cell phone and video/data transmission system seen in the movies. Pappy had a suitcase-size satellite transmitter/receiver system for secure data and voice transmission set up on the window ledge next to the two laptops he used. We would write cables on our individual laptops and put them on a floppy disk.

Periodically, Pappy would collect the floppy disks, then go through an elaborate process to transmit them back to Headquarters. After he sent our cables, he switched the system over to receive incoming traffic from Washington. All cable traffic to our team, regardless of where it originated, was held by Headquarters until we opened a channel with them. Given the fact that we were receiving perhaps a hundred cables a day and sending out thirty to forty cables and intelligence reports a day, it was a tremendous amount of tedious work for Pappy. Add to that his responsibilities of servicing the generators (which included cleaning the fuel filter two or three times a day), troubleshooting computer problems, and fighting the dust that constantly settled into the equipment, and it was usually a twenty-hour day for Pappy.

I, for one, decided early on that his flatulence was a small price to pay for his expertise and dedication.

CHAPTER SIXTEEN

Just before lunch on our third day in the valley, Buck returned from the helicopter and announced he had added the registration number to the tail boom. He was excited and asked me if we could take the entire team down to the landing field after lunch for a photo at the helicopter. Rick said he thought it was a good idea.

We arrived at the landing field just after lunch, with our Afghan pilot, Nasir, along to actually take the photo. Everyone acted as excited as Buck about the photo, which seemed strange to me. Yes, it was a good idea, and we would value the photo later, but this all seemed a little too much. As we moved toward the helicopter, I was admiring the new paint job. Then I saw the registration number. There in bold black paint on a light green background was 9-11-01. I turned to look at the team. They were all in on it and smiling broadly.

We gathered under the tail boom in two short rows, smiling at the camera as Nasir took four or five photos. There we were, ten CIA officers, the first Americans back in Afghanistan, just seventeen days after the 9/11 attacks. The smiles on our faces showed that we were all happy to be there.

By the afternoon of that day, intelligence from our joint cell was flowing well, thanks to the efforts of Chris and Stan and excellent cooperation from Mumtaz and Hafiz. The latter had a particularly remarkable ability to extract critical pieces of intelligence from the mass of information being collected by the Northern Alliance forces. From sites maintained by the NA along their front lines, Taliban radio transmissions were collected, transcribed, and sent directly to the cell. These same sites also regularly forwarded their battlefield observations of Taliban troop movements.

We also received, on a daily basis, reports from "human assets" who crossed over from the Taliban positions. These sources were either Taliban soldiers co-opted by the Northern Alliance, or civilians living inside NA lines—who had family or friends on the Taliban side—who took the risk of passing through enemy lines to gather information. Chris worked closely with Hafiz and the younger NA officers to ensure the quality and completeness of the reports.

In a one-month period, from 27 September to 26 October, our team produced more than four hundred intelligence reports, most from the efforts of the joint cell. This intelligence allowed U.S. military aircraft to strike Taliban and al-Qa'ida positions with great accuracy and a minimum of collateral damage. All and all an incredible accomplishment, especially given the conditions under which we were working and the mental stress and real physical danger we faced on a daily basis. Chris, Stan, and their Afghan colleagues should have been tremendously proud of their accomplishment.

We had a brief meeting with Engineer Aref late that afternoon, and he confirmed arrangements for the GPS survey of the Kabul front to begin the following day. He told us that General Fahim insisted the group be small, to keep as low a profile as possible. The NA front lines were close enough to the Taliban positions that visual observation of movements by either side was a real problem. It also turned out that the Iranian Revolutionary Guard Corps (IRGC) had a two-man observer team assigned with the NA forces on the Kabul front, and Fahim was anxious that the Iranians not discover the presence of U.S. personnel, at least not this early in the deployment.

Stan was an obvious choice for the GPS team; he was an expert in the use of GPS and had trained the team on the equipment while we were stuck in Tashkent. Murray would work with Stan; he had a great deal of field experience from his years with the SEAL teams. Rick would lead the team; he too had a great deal of experience with GPS, both in Africa and Bosnia. Aref said that General Bismullah Khan would personally work with Rick's team in this important effort. Mumtaz would accompany the team to provide translation.

Chris had managed to establish direct radio contact with Professor Sayyaf, who was enthusiastic about meeting with us. We explained to Aref that Chris and I planned on meeting with Professor Sayyaf the next morning. Aref was not happy with this news, but he agreed with our plans and said he would assign a driver and Hafiz to accompany us. Sayyaf was staying in a village named Gul Bahar (spring flower), just outside the Panjshir Valley on the Shomali Plains. This was the same road the GPS team would take, except once out of the Panjshir Valley and on the plains they would make an immediate right turn and head for Jabal-os-Saraj, a village area where General Bismullah Khan had his headquarters.

The three-man GPS team pulled out of the compound at daybreak the next day. I felt uneasy about letting them go on this survey mission without me, but ours was a small team and each of us had individual strengths. Chris and I were the best two officers on the team to handle political dealings with our Afghan hosts; we left an hour later for our meeting with Sayyaf.

As we were preparing to depart for the drive down the valley, it occurred to me that we would pass Masood's grave site. I asked Hafiz if we could stop and visit the grave, because we very much wanted to pay our respects to the Commander. I think Hafiz was a little surprised at my request; he looked at me carefully for a second or two, as if to gauge my sincerity. Then he smiled and nodded yes. As the driver signaled that he was ready, Hafiz said he had a tape of the Commander speaking, one he listened to frequently. We pulled out onto the bumpy, dusty road with Masood's voice filling the vehicle. He spoke in a clear, resonant Dari, with a rolling cadence that carried the listener along. Hafiz sat stiffly—at least as stiffly as the bouncing, jerking vehicle would allow—and I knew he was back in time, back with Masood.

Our beat-up SUV had seen better days, and the going was tough. When we had first arrived in Afghanistan we thought our short drive from the helicopter landing area was rough. However, it seemed like nothing compared to that morning's brutal thirty-five-mile drive down the valley. The "road" is, at best, one and a half lanes wide. There are not even remnants of paving left, the original surface having been beaten by armored vehicles; blasted by bombs, artillery, and heavy land mines; crushed by landslides; and eaten away by twenty years of erosion. Large potholes, often more like craters, appeared with wearing regularity. Dry as it was, the road surface was covered in an inches-deep layer of dust, which swirled up around the vehicle, obscuring any view to the sides and blinding anyone silly enough to be following closely.

The roadway runs along the west side of the Panjshir River and is cut into the sides of the hills that form the western wall of the valley. The elevation at a few places is actually river level but can be as much as six hundred feet above the river. There is no maintenance on the road except possibly that done by a few old men and their young grandsons, who stood in the shade by a particularly bad spot in the roadway. As a vehicle approached, they shoveled a little dirt into the pothole, then stood, shovel in hand and head slightly bowed, hoping the vehicle would slow long enough to allow the passengers to reward their "work" by throwing out a few cents' worth of crumpled currency.

On our trip we banged our heads on the roof or the windows and slammed our knees into the dashboard or the back of the front seats. But some potholes were so big that no amount of bracing would help prevent a jammed knee or, on the worse jolts, a compressed spine.

It was most unnerving to meet an approaching vehicle, especially on a stretch of road high above the riverbed. Drivers cooperated, and there seemed to be an unwritten code as to who would yield and hug the wall, allowing the other vehicle to squeeze by. I did not mind the passage if our vehicle was the one hugging the wall, but most often it seemed that it was our driver who took the outer path, with our tires fractions of an inch from a fall of hundreds of feet.

Riding a mule into the Grand Canyon for the first time comes close to matching the adventure of driving that road. I ended our first two-hour trip actually bruised, and convinced that we would more likely be injured or killed in a road accident than in hostile fire from the Taliban.

About twenty miles down the valley, the hills on both sides pull back and the broad river plain seems to expand into a large V shape. Nestled there in the curve of the river is an attractive village, green with trees, filling the area before us. A line of hills cuts across the valley from right to left, defining the limits of the village, and our road twisted to the right, then back to the left along the front edge of the hill line. The tape of the Commander had ended some miles back, and Hafiz sat in silence until now. He turned around and said, "Ahead, on the top of the high hill, that is where the Commander's grave is located."

From the backseat we bent lower to peer toward the hill line, and we could just see that the top of the last hill was scarred with recent grading and construction, making a large, flat area of most of the top. A number of vehicles were parked on one side of the flat area, and against the blue sky was a flutter of small green flags—the sign of a martyr's grave. Hafiz said that there were plans for a small monument to be constructed above Masood's grave, but work on that project had just begun. Now it was a simple grave, and the area around it was dirty and disrupted from the ongoing work.

When we reached the top of the hill and the dust blew clear, the view out over the village and back up the valley was spectacular. It was one of the few places in the valley we had seen that was rich with trees and bushes, which extended from the valley floor far up the sides of the surrounding hills. For the most part, the Panjshir Valley has a rough, rocky, stark beauty, but here the view was soft, comforting, and green. It was a perfect choice for Masood's final resting place.

Hafiz led Chris and me toward a dirt-walled structure topped with a canvas roof stretched tight on thick wooden poles. A walkway led into a rectangular "room," sheltered from the sun by the canvas. In the center was a long, narrow, rectangular earth mound, which was obviously Masood's grave. We were followed into the grave site by at least twenty of the Afghans who had been in the area as we parked, and now they all stood in silence watching the three of us. It could have been an awkward moment, with everyone staring, but I was able to withdraw from the surroundings and focus on my memories of Masood, picturing him on those occasions when I was with him. I looked at the mound of earth, finding it difficult to believe that a man of such vitality and strength could be resting there, gone forever. I made the sign of the cross, and we stood silently for several minutes. As we turned to walk around the grave and back into the sunlight, I saw that Hafiz had been crying. I realized that my cheeks too were wet with tears.

Professor Abdul Rasoul Sayyaf was pretty much an anachronism. He had been one of the "Big Seven" Mujahedin political leaders during the Jihad against the Soviets. His religious credentials—a graduate of Al-Ansar University in Cairo, and an affinity for the beliefs of the fundamentalist Saudi Wahabi sect—earned him financial support from private Saudi sources. This combination of education, religious belief, and money allowed him to build a strong military and popular following. The Philippine Muslim terrorist group that kidnapped and held three American citizens in 2002 is named Abu Sayyaf in honor of the good professor, whom I was about to meet for the first time. During the disastrous civil war that wrecked much of Afghanistan during 1992–94, Sayyaf lost prestige and influence, and in the years that followed he found himself increasingly isolated and on the sidelines. With the rise of the Taliban after 1994, Sayyaf realigned himself with Masood's Northern Alliance. Although not a real player in the political equation, he still controlled upward of two thousand fighters, and his forces manned NA frontline positions eastward from Kabul toward Jalalabad.

I was interested in meeting Sayyaf because, in the 1990–92 time frame, Sayyaf, through his Saudi connections, befriended a relatively unknown Saudi would-be Mujahedin named Usama bin Ladin. Already rabidly anti-Western and beginning to build the organization we would come to know as the al-Qa'ida, bin Ladin was then known only as a wealthy Saudi who was willing to finance Mujahedin combat operations. Bin Ladin was a man who enjoyed fighting from the sidelines, and he could pay for the privilege of a ringside seat. We realized that Sayyaf himself was not a friend of the United States—he was vehement in his public opposition to the United States during the Gulf War—but we hoped that in the aftermath of 9/11 he would be willing to assist us.

Just before it gives way to the Shomali Plains, the Panjshir Valley narrows into a gorge barely a hundred feet wide. At that point, the sides of the valley become almost vertical, and the river current becomes white-water rapids. The road rounds a bend and suddenly seems to pop out of the valley, and the Shomali Plains spread for miles ahead. The road soon splits, the right fork heading toward Jabal-os-Saraj and

Charikar, and the left going on to Gul Bahar village, our destination that morning.

Sayyaf's small compound was unimpressive, but we were greeted warmly. The previous night, Chris had been in radio, then satellite telephone contact with Sayyaf and members of his staff to finalize arrangements for our meeting. We were rushed to the main building and into a meeting room, where we were seated. After a short but appropriate wait, Sayyaf joined us.

Sayyaf is in his fifties, and with his long white beard, he strongly resembles the late Ayatollah Khomeini of Iran. His English is excellent, and he seems to enjoy speaking to visitors in that language. Although Sayyaf made all the right noises about combating terrorism and working against bin Ladin and the al-Qa'ida, he became vague and noncommittal when we pressed for specifics on how he might assist us. He did agree to help us go after bin Ladin's Arab lieutenants, such as Ayman al-Zawahiri, but nothing specific was worked out. Mostly he wanted to lecture us on why the U.S. government should not support bringing back the former Afghan king, Zahir Shah, from exile in Rome. I told Sayyaf that few in the U.S. government felt that the former king had any long-term role to play in a post-Taliban Afghanistan, but the king might provide some positive influence toward stability in the immediate days following the defeat of the Taliban.

As the meeting ended, I stated that I wanted to provide some assistance to Sayyaf, to help him better prepare his troops for the coming fight and to assist in any efforts he might make to lure al-Qa'ida leaders into our reach. I produced a $100,000 bundle of cash from my backpack and handed it across the table to Sayyaf, who instinctively took the package. Unlike the money I had passed to the Northern Alliance, I had left this bundle in its original clear plastic wrapping so that Sayyaf could see what it was. Sayyaf held the bundle for a second or two, looking at it, seeming somewhat confused by what he was holding in his hands. Then his eyes widened and he turned toward his hulking aide. He literally threw the bundle of cash at the man, as if he had been handed a hot potato. Sayyaf looked at me and his eyes narrowed. "That is the first time I have ever accepted cash directly from anyone." He shook his head as if he had been tricked, eyeing me carefully, a slight smile on his lips.

We rose and thanked him for agreeing to assist the U.S. government, and we each shook his hand. Chris stayed behind with the aide for an extra minute to discuss follow-on contact arrangements, then we were off for the two-hour return trip to the compound. Despite the jarring ride, I smiled a lot on the way back.

PART FIVE

SIZING UP THE ENEMY

29 September–1 October 2001

CHAPTER SEVENTEEN

While Chris and I were meeting with Professor Sayyaf, Rick, Murray, Stan, and Mumtaz were being bumped, banged, and beaten in their SUV as they drove to meet with General Bismullah Khan. A few miles after turning toward Jabal-os-Saraj, the road actually proved to be paved, although the asphalt surface was broken with potholes and an occasional filled-in shell hole. The relatively smooth ride came as a surprise to Rick, who had by now assumed that there were no paved roads left in the country. The buildings they were passing were much more substantial than any they had seen in the valley. Although many had obvious war damage, and all needed repair of some sort, they had a look of permanence that was lacking in the valley.

Suddenly, on their right, they saw a high chain-link fence topped with barbed wire, which surrounded a series of larger, better-maintained structures. Old T-72 tanks, Russian artillery pieces, and large trucks were parked among the buildings, and groups of soldiers were moving about. Their SUV speeding by drew no attention from the soldiers or the civilians they passed, a totally different reaction from what we usually received in the valley. Ahead of them, Rick saw a large hill that dominated the compound and was topped with a small complex of several large buildings.

As they drew abreast of the hill, they slowed and turned into the front gate of the compound. Two soldiers in clean green khaki uniforms and military fatigue caps, and carrying AK-47s, signaled the SUV to halt. One soldier approached the vehicle and spoke with Hafiz, who leaned across the

Afghan driver. The guard glanced at the three passengers, nodding affirmatively. Rick noted a 12.7mm machine gun manned by four additional soldiers in a sandbagged gun position to their left, in the shade of a canvas tarp. After a brief exchange and another glance at the passengers, they waved the car through. The driver turned immediately onto a dirt road, which serpentined around and up the back side of the large hill. This was not a guerrilla band's campsite but a true military installation, run with order and discipline.

Khan was waiting for them at the top of the hill, standing in a group of six or seven soldiers. The three Americans stiffly exited the vehicle, trying to stretch out the kinks from the long ride, as Khan approached them smiling, his hand extended in welcome. He grasped their hands in turn, vigorously shaking each, and Mumtaz translated as the general introduced himself, "I am Bismullah Khan. Welcome, welcome to my compound." Khan was about five foot ten, thick chested, with a pleasant round face and neatly trimmed beard. Unlike the other officers in the group, who were not introduced, he was not dressed in uniform but rather wore Western-style clothing—tan khaki pants and shirt, a black vest, and brown hiking boots. Rick guessed that Khan was in his early forties. Although he appeared a little stocky, it was clear that he was in excellent physical condition.

General Khan led them into a building, moving quickly through a labyrinth of rooms and hallways, then up several flights of stairs to a room on the top floor. He invited them to sit on chairs in front of a wide window. Its hinged frame was pulled inward and secured to hooks from the ceiling, providing a panoramic view of the Shomali Plains below, with Kabul a dark brown blur on the horizon. There was a neatly made bed in one corner, and several lamps were on a table that Rick assumed served as a desk. This room undoubtedly doubled as Khan's personal office and bedroom.

After they were seated, there was a flurry of activity as three or four young soldiers scurried in with trays of fruit and tea. Amid the clatter and bustle, Khan again extended his welcome to the team. He explained that General Fahim Khan had briefed him at length about their GPS survey mission, and he assured the team of his full personal cooperation in their effort. Because of his experience, he understood the importance of accurate mapping of the front lines for the coming bombing effort. Rick stressed that the U.S. military felt strongly about the need to minimize collateral damage to Northern Alliance allies, including Bismullah Khan's troops.

The general smiled. "Frankly, I am more interested that you bomb the enemy hard. Perhaps a few of your bombs will fall on my positions. That always happens in battle. We will accept such casualties without complaint—if you are hitting the enemy strongly." He paused, then continued, "But, yes, we must take precautions." In mid-October there were several unfortunate bombing errors that killed several NA soldiers and a number of civilians. Khan accepted the casualties calmly.

Khan stood, indicating that the introductory tea ceremony had ended. "Please, gentlemen, if you are ready, we will begin." Khan moved out of the room with the team following. There was another round of scurrying by the numerous staff waiting outside the room, with doors opening ahead of the party and staff pressing themselves against the walls to let them move quickly down the stairs and back through the maze of hallways and rooms.

Once outside, Khan took the front seat of a dusty but well-maintained Toyota Land Cruiser, and the team and Mumtaz piled into the rear, their daypacks already in place in the back of the vehicle. Khan had a small handheld radio that was crackling static. The SUV pulled out in a cloud of gray-brown dust, and a Toyota Hilux pickup truck lurched after it. Rick could see four armed guards jammed into the cargo bed of the truck, one man standing just behind the cab, holding on to the chromed roll bar as they bounced into the swirling dust cloud and headed down the hill.

Khan worked the radio, apparently contacting positions ahead of them that the convoy was moving. Between short bursts of radio chatter, Khan provided the team with a concise commentary on the tactical situation of the battlefield they were to visit.

"You will see that our front lines are not what you might expect. Many Western reporters have visited me here, and they always come expecting to see a continuous trench line on either side. We occupy the heights in this area, and we have strong defensive positions at key points along the ridge-line—sturdy bunkers with one-meter-thick walls and heavy roofs, with good firing positions. But, as you will see, we also hold the ground at the foot of these hills on the plains below." From Gul Bahar toward the west and most of Baghram Air Base, the lines in some places extended six to eight miles from the base of the hills. Just west of Baghram was a salient that extended even farther toward Kabul. The heights allowed Khan's forces to observe the enemy deep in his territory, making it difficult for the enemy to organize a major offensive without Khan's knowing well in advance about the preparations. "Our scouts keep us well advised of the enemy's movements. Our artillery and tank guns can in-flict heavy losses on any attack they launch on my lines below, and I can reinforce the lines below fairly quickly.

"If they should somehow break through on the plains below, it is very difficult for the enemy to attack uphill be-cause of the steep, rough ground to cross below us. A few men at the top can cause many casualties to the enemy as they try to attack. The Taliban artillery is not accurate, and their air strikes are ineffective. We do not have many men posted in these positions at any one time. Rather, we have the majority of our forces in reserve, stationed in three camps in the rear of the lines. Even those are but a small number of our total strength. I do not have the logistical structure to keep the front lines fully manned. The reserves—those we would use to hold off a major attack or, Allah willing, to make an offensive—we keep in the Panjshir. With my troops here, with my artillery and tanks, I can easily hold out for a full day; the Panjshir reserves can be here by then."

Khan paused to respond to a radio call, then continued. "On the enemy side, you will see, they hold a line of villages in the plains below. They have cleared all the local people from those villages, and now they use the houses as forts.

Thick stone walls, small windows, excellent for defense—
they are very hard to destroy. Direct artillery on the roof is
good, but"—he paused and smiled—"hard to hit, even for
my men. Close-in fighting is required, with tank fire or heavy
recoilless rifle fire to penetrate the walls. You will see also
that the villages are close together, and there are fighting positions between the villages, but those are manned only if we
attack. These villages dot the plains back toward Kabul, and
the line of hills midway between here and Kabul provides a
very good secondary defensive line. Many Taliban and Arab
reserve units are positioned on the rear of that hill line, safe
from my artillery. Frankly, I do not have the strength to force
a breakthrough of the enemy positions. But I and my men are
willing to try, if there is no other choice."

Stan asked, "What about the Arab fighters, General?"

Khan smiled. "Ah, good question. The Arab units maintain themselves separately from the Taliban forces, taking up
key positions within the overall front lines. Their positions
are easy to see. They have reinforced the buildings they
occupy with concrete and sandbags. They have money to afford such improvements. They are well equipped and well
trained. They fight like devils, especially those Muslim fighters from Chechnya and those from Uzbekistan. Unlike
Afghans, these devils aim when they shoot. Not like this."
He raised his arms above his head, one hand before the other,
as if holding a weapon. Then he closed his eyes and made a
back-and-forth motion with his hands, imitating the standard
firing position of Afghan troops throughout the long years of
fighting since 1978. "And they do not like to surrender. They
fight hard and they fight bravely. They will be the . . . ah,
what do you call it?" He paused, thinking. "Ah, yes, they will
be the glue that will hold the Taliban together when we attack."

Rick leaned forward to be heard more clearly over the
noise of the truck. "General, soon the U.S. Air Force will be
striking the Taliban positions. The damage will be incredible. We are anxious to pinpoint your frontline positions, but
once we have done that, we will want to plot the Taliban and

Arab positions. We need to work with you to make a priority list of which of those positions must be hit first. Soon, General, you will have the entire U.S. Air Force assisting you."

The general smiled broadly at that idea. "*In'sha'lah* [God willing]," he said. "If that happens, if their front lines are heavily damaged, my forces can complete their destruction."

The SUV braked, and the general had the door open and was outside the vehicle almost before it fully stopped. As the team exited and pulled out their daypacks, the general engaged in an animated conversation with a burly soldier dressed in traditional Afghan clothing, standing with three others. The man was smiling, and he looked over at the team, nodding. The general patted the man on the shoulder and turned to the team. "This is Major Haji Agha. He commands here. His men are at the top, waiting for us. It is a steep climb, but there is much to accomplish today, so we will hurry."

With that the general turned and started toward a well-worn path that zigzagged up the hillside toward the crest, which appeared to be at least eight hundred feet above them. The major waited as the team fell in behind the general. Rick noticed that the major had a slight smile on his lips as he nodded politely at each of them. The major fell in behind them as they started up the path.

The general's pace had started fast and, to Rick, seemed to increase with each zigzag of the path. The Americans were working hard to keep up; the path was steep, and in places loose and gravelly.

By the time they had climbed about five hundred feet, Rick was in a full sweat and breathing hard. He was thankful for the jogging he had been doing over the past several months. Although he knew he was in excellent shape, he also knew that they were at about 6,500 feet and climbing. Rick could hear Stan just behind him breathing equally hard, and he knew that if the path had been any wider Stan would be trying to get around him. Rick could hear Stan muttering to himself, something about "damn mountain goat" expelled between breaths.

Rick shifted the heavy daypack to the other shoulder and looked upward. Murray was dogging the general's heels, but Rick could see that Murray was straining to maintain the pace. They all knew that Khan was putting on a show for the Americans, and none of the three wanted to let Khan show him up by falling too far behind or, God forbid, having to stop to catch his breath.

As Khan reached the crest of the hill, he stepped back and waited for the team to catch up. He watched them carefully as they topped the hill and stopped to gather around him. Each man was breathing hard, face wet with sweat, but all tried to look comfortable. Mumtaz looked somewhat the worse for wear, breathing hard and sweating heavily, but he was smiling at the general as he joined the group.

The general was not breathing hard at all. "This is the left end of my line, and, as you can see, this is the last hill before the terrain drops toward the Shomali Plains to our left and front. You will get a good view of the battlefield and the hill line going back to our right and you can see the enemy positions and those of my troops below."

He turned toward the far side of the hilltop, then turned back. "Although the enemy cannot see us in detail, if they note unusual activity or movement up here, they may call in artillery on us. While not accurate, they do occasionally get lucky." On that note he turned and walked toward the positions on the far side of the hilltop. Major Haji Agha moved up by Khan's side.

Rick looked the position over carefully. There were three mud structures built into the forward edge of the hilltop, with foxhole-type fighting positions stretching between them. About ten soldiers were standing about, most of them looking at the team, smiling and talking quietly among themselves. They were dressed in Mujahedin-style clothing, but their weapons and web gear were clean and in good repair, and the troops appeared well fed and fit. There was a ZSU-23 23mm twin-barreled antiaircraft cannon dug into a position toward the front of the hilltop. Rick noted that the forward berm of the gun position was cut low, to allow the weapon to be depressed to fire down the front of the hillside, adding a tremendous amount of firepower to the defenders' capabilities. There was also a 14.5mm heavy machine gun positioned between each building, and what looked like an 82mm mortar in a foxhole on the far end of the flat area of the hilltop.

As they approached the middle structure, they dropped their daypacks and followed Khan and Major Agha into the dark interior of a bunker. The walls were at least three feet thick, and there were a number of thick logs posed as columns to support the weight of the roof, giving the dark room a cluttered, mazelike appearance. Khan led them through the forest of logs toward the three broad openings cut into the wall that provided the only light. Khan stopped in front of the center opening, and Mumtaz stood behind them and translated.

Khan motioned them forward into the opening, and as they moved together he gestured toward the view. "You see that from here we have good fields of fire down the hillside and onto the plain below. Look toward that clump of houses," he said, pointing. "There is a Taliban vehicle moving along the dirt road. It is routine to see them move so each day." The men could see what looked like an SUV moving along at a fast pace, trailing a plume of dust, heading for a group of buildings several hundred yards to the right. Only about eight hundred yards separated the Northern Alliance lines from those of the Taliban.

"Do you fire on them when you see them like this?" asked Murray. "They seem a fairly easy target."

The general looked at the SUV. "No, not usually. Not unless there are several vehicles together, or unless they have recently fired at us. We conserve our ammunition. But let us go back outside and begin your work."

With the general watching closely, Stan and Murray opened their packs and began to sort out their GPS equipment, maps, and a compass. Stan and Murray had calibrated their gear the previous evening and had selected map sheets from our stocks that covered the frontline area. "General, can you show us the map you use for this area, so we can compare your markings with our readings?" asked Stan. The general spoke to Major Agha, who pulled an acetate-covered map sheet from a canvas bag slung across his chest.

Stan and the major knelt on the ground with the two map sheets side by side, and the major pointed out their location on his map. Stan took the coordinates off that map and located the same coordinates on his map. The major's map was a Soviet military map and was very detailed, but it was immediately clear to Stan that the two maps were configured in slightly different scales. The calculations to convert one scale to the other were simple arithmetic, but it would be tedious to do the conversions kneeling there in the dirt. In the meantime, Murray took several GPS readings, then he and Stan compared those readings to the two maps. They agreed on the location and set of geocoordinates, then carefully marked their maps. It was going to be a long day.

The survey continued until a little after 6:00 p.m., the team somehow managing to cover the entire length of the Northern Alliance's front lines. It had been a strenuous, challenging day, the men stopping only long enough to take accurate GPS readings and mark the map before hurrying off behind General Khan to the next position. Lunch had been greasy fried chicken—at least they thought the scrawny meat was chicken—as well as rice and fruit, washed down with sweet warm tea and warm bottled water. Throughout the long, hot day, the general never lost his enthusiasm and never slowed down. He was smiling broadly as they eased into their vehicle for the pounding two-hour ride back up the Panjshir to the compound. The general shook each man's hand as they climbed back into the vehicle. "A good day of work. A few more days like this and we will make Afghans of you." Standing off to the side, Mumtaz shook his head wryly.

Rick smiled as the team pulled away, knowing that they had succeeded in impressing the general. He also knew that they would all pay for that success with aches and pains for the next several days.

CHAPTER EIGHTEEN

The next few days were filled with a variety of administrative details—the nuts and bolts of getting settled into our new environment. It did not help that I was still suffering from the lower intestinal problems that had plagued me since my arrival. Those problems, and my body's efforts to adjust to the elevation, kept me dehydrated and feeling weak and tired, although I was improving, albeit slowly. Luckily, other than Pappy's growing flatulence issues, I was the only one on the team having health problems of any consequence. Given our diet and the conditions under which our food was prepared, this was remarkable.

It was also becoming clear that as much as our hosts welcomed the team for the hope we represented and the assistance we were providing, they were concerned that our presence in the valley would become common knowledge, and that somehow that knowledge would cause "problems" for the Northern Alliance leadership.

On the morning of our fifth day in the valley, Jan Mohammad appeared just after breakfast with a large pile of new clothing, which he explained he had purchased for the team. He was animated and happy, explaining that Engineer Aref thought it best that we dress in local clothing rather than the L.L. Bean–style clothing we were currently wearing. He eyed each of us in turn, then pulled trousers and a baggy shirt from the pile and pressed them into our hands.

He also had a selection of the local neck scarves favored by men in the Panjshiri. These were made of light cotton fabric, white with a variety of black patterns woven into them.

Each was about three feet square, and virtually every Afghan male we had so far encountered wore one. Although they were normally worn tied around the neck, sort of like a cowboy bandana, they apparently were used for a variety of purposes. We saw them pulled up and tied to cover the nose and mouth to keep out the ever-present dust, or worn like a woman's head scarf against the rain or cold. As the weather worsened, we also saw men routinely use them to blow their nose (then tie the scarf back around their neck). Jan Mohammad explained that this white-and-black pattern identified the wearer as a member or supporter of the Northern Alliance; the white-and-black pattern was the one favored by Ahmad Shah Masood.

Jan Mohammad also provided each of us with a wool hat like those worn by virtually all the Afghan men we encountered. Made of a heavy, rough wool, the hat had a flat mushroom-shaped top that perched on a thick roll of wool that could be pulled down to cover the ears. In my earlier tours in Pakistan, we called these Chitrali caps, because they were the traditional headgear of tribesmen from the Chitral Valley area of northwest Pakistan.

Like the Chitrali caps, all the clothing that Jan Mohammad provided came from Pakistan. The shirt and trousers are referred to as *shalwar kamiz,* which means shirt and trousers in Urdu. The trousers are incredibly baggy. The waist is big enough to fit around two large men at once, but fortunately a cotton drawstring is threaded into the waistband to cinch the pants tightly. The shirts are long sleeved with a normal Western collar, but the shirttail reaches to the knees in front and back and is worn outside the pants. This allows the wearer to squat to perform toilet functions outdoors while remaining covered, something we saw every day. Despite the functionality of the shirt, I don't think anyone on the team attempted to copy that style of managing their "business" outdoors.

Soon we were decked out in our new clothing, adjusting the caps to the most stylish angle and practicing tying the neck scarves to achieve the best effect. I looked at my reflection in the window and thought that, although this was fun,

any Afghan seeing us would immediately know we were foreigners dressing up in local garb. I looked around at the other
team members, and even Murray, with his short-cropped
black beard, was instantly recognizable as a foreigner.

After Jan Mohammad left, happy with our obvious enthusiasm, we talked about the issue of our new clothing. From a
distance, all Afghan males tended to look alike to us—all of
them bearded, with similar clothing styles, hats, scarves, and
footgear. But an Afghan can instantly spot subtle differences
in dress and style and can pick a stranger out of a crowd immediately. In this tribal society, with life centered in small
villages or isolated valleys, everyone knows one another, and
a stranger stands out like a bandaged thumb.

A few years earlier in Pakistan, I was discussing with an
Afghan tribal leader the possibility of his sending several of
his men into a village far outside his own tribal area to look
for Mir Amal Kasi. He told me it was impossible. "You think
we all look alike, but an Afghan can recognize a stranger in
his village instantly. My men would be stopped and questioned as soon as they were spotted in that area. If their story
was suspected in any way, they might be killed." This also
proved true for us; no matter how closely we tried to mimic
the dress style of the locals, even those of us with full beards,
we stood out as foreigners everywhere we traveled.

Once when Chris and I were on a return drive with Hafiz
from a visit to the Shomali Plains, unexpected repairs being
made on the narrow road stopped us near a small group of
farmers' mud huts. A number of small children were playing
in the field next to the road while paying a lot of attention to
the roadwork under way. Two little boys approached our
SUV and peered through the open window at us. Chris and I
were "disguised" in Jan Mohammad's local clothing and
hats. The boys began to giggle, jabbering back and forth to
one another and pointing at us.

Then their little sister joined them. She was about four,
cute but very dirty, with mud-streaked face and hands. She
stopped and stared at me. Her eyes got wider and wider, and
she began to cry, her hands flapping up around her face.

Then, sobbing in fear, she turned and threw herself against her brother and buried her face in his chest. Chris and I were laughing hard at that point, and Hafiz spoke to the boys. He turned to us. "She thinks you are a monster. She has never seen a foreigner before."

Just then several young men came by on the other side of the vehicle, one pushing a wheelbarrow and the other carrying a heavy burlap sack on his back. This one paused and looked in at Chris, then asked in Dari, "Are you an Arab?" Chris responded in Dari that, no, he was not an Arab, he was from Europe. The young man smiled. "Lucky for you, because we are going to kill all the Arabs where we find them." He drew a finger slowly across his neck to emphasize his point. We continued to encounter those kinds of reactions in our "disguised" appearance as we moved around the valley.

So after the first few days, we resumed wearing our L.L. Bean–style clothing at the compound and within the village area. Even on the front lines, although a few of the team might wear at least some portion of the local clothing, most of us dressed in our own Western garb. Our hosts did not raise the clothing issue with us again after that day, but how the U.S. Special Forces personnel would dress when they deployed to the valley would become a major issue, one that almost derailed our relationship with the Northern Alliance.

Another issue that plagued us during those first few days was lack of transportation. Earlier CIA teams that had visited Ahmad Shah Masood in the Panjshir had provided the Northern Alliance with funds to purchase a Toyota Hilux pickup truck and a Toyota Land Cruiser. The agreement was that the two vehicles could be used by Engineer Aref's men but were to be made available for use by the visiting CIA teams. The two vehicles indeed were there, but they both had suffered great wear and tear from daily use by the Northern Alliance. Also, even though they were supposedly on standby for our use, we frequently found ourselves waiting for them to return from other errands.

We queried Jan Mohammad about locating additional vehicles that we could purchase for the team to utilize. He said there were usually a few used Russian jeeps available for purchase in the valley, and he would be happy to assist us in locating what was currently on the market. We assumed the term "used" meant "very well used," but we could not afford to be choosy. Murray was put in charge of finding two or three of these vehicles for dedicated—if not always reliable—transportation for the team.

A day later, Jan Mohammad took Murray to look at some used Russian jeeps he had located. Murray returned several hours later, dusty, grease stained, and enthusiastic. He had found three "good" vehicles; although all needed some sort of repairs, they appeared to be exactly what we needed. He had agreed on a price of $21,000 for all three, on the condition that the repairs he had identified were completed by the next morning. I peeled off the money, asking that Murray be sure to get a receipt and record the vehicle numbers on the receipt. We were sure to be asked to account for the cars at some later date, and I wanted to have at least a little paperwork to document the purchase.

The next morning, Murray and Jan Mohammad, with several young Afghans in tow, headed down the valley to the "used jeep lot." They returned two hours later in a billowing cloud of the ubiquitous gray-brown dust and a cacophony of blowing horns. Murray was grinning from ear to ear, his clothing again dirty and grease stained. "It was a hell of a bargaining session!" he said as we gathered around to look over our "new"wheels. "They tried to give me a bald spare tire, and the oil pan on one of the jeeps hadn't been repaired. I guess they thought I wouldn't crawl under the jeep to check, but I showed them." Jan Mohammad commented to me that, indeed, Mr. Murray was a ferocious bargainer and had beaten the price down to $19,200. He said he and Murray should reopen Jan Mohammad's antiques store in Kabul when the war was won, and between them they would become rich men.

As we anticipated, despite Murray's valiant efforts, the jeeps were only in fair running condition. Russian craftmanship was crude, and the vehicles lacked things like windows that could be rolled down, a ventilation fan, and such amenities as springs and shock absorbers (or at least it felt that way). The gearshift had two sticks, and putting the jeep into four-wheel drive was accomplished with much confusion and grinding of gears.

Because of the condition of the roads, our lack of knowledge of the area, and the constant threat that the vehicles might break down at any moment, our hosts insisted that we not drive the vehicles ourselves. In return, we insisted that at least two of their drivers be on call within the compound during working hours, so there would be no delays in our being able to move about when required. Our pilots and the mechanic needed to visit the airfield to pull maintenance or just check on the helicopter several times a day, and other errands came up frequently enough to justify keeping drivers on standby.

The same day that we purchased the jeeps, we met with Engineer Aref to try to work out another serious transportation issue—a reliable fuel supply for our helicopter. Since our arrival we had used the helicopter several times—to scout potential drop zones for humanitarian food supplies, and to look for an area suitable to land C-130 cargo aircraft. Each time, the issue of obtaining enough helicopter fuel to complete even those relatively short flights was a problem.

When we first arrived, we were assured that fuel was available. In fact, several fuel trucks were parked at the helicopter landing field we were using. We quickly learned, however, that fuel had to be brought in by truck over the roads from Tajikistan, and the trucks used were relatively small. Equally troubling was the fact that the trucks were old and their cargo tanks rusty and dirty, fouling the fuel and necessitating the use of fuel filters. It was common for a fuel truck to arrive at the landing field and have to be parked and left standing for two to three days to allow the dirt and rust that had mixed with the fuel to settle before we could pump the fuel out for our use.

Engineer Aref and I had discussed this problem several

times as sidebars to our operational discussions. On this day, Aref suggested that I give him the money to have a large fuel tanker-truck purchased in Dushanbe and he'd bring it fully loaded with aviation fuel from Tajikistan into the valley. The truck would be relatively new and the fuel tank cleaner, and it could carry significantly more fuel. I would, of course, also pay for the aviation fuel to fill the tanker truck. He also suggested the purchase of a large transport truck to move goods and equipment around in bulk rather than trying to make do with pickup trucks or SUVs. I agreed to both purchases and passed Aref $17,000 for the two trucks and $5,000 to purchase seventeen tons of aviation fuel. Aref said he would radio his men in Dushanbe and authorize the purchases, and the trucks would be on the road in two days. The pilots were happy, and we were all looking forward to the arrival of the fuel truck.

Actually the fuel truck never did arrive in the valley, or at least we never saw it. The whereabouts of the truck and the fuel became a running joke between Mumtaz, Aref, and me. Every time we met, I would mention the truck, asking where it was and when it would arrive. Depending on when I asked, the truck was either just on the other side of the Anjuman Pass and delayed in a traffic backup, or it was stuck in the pass, under threat of being weathered in there. Sometimes it had just crossed over the pass and would arrive in a day or two. Several weeks after providing the money for the truck, Aref told me that the truck had arrived in the valley. Strangely, however, it never appeared at the helicopter landing field. Aref explained that some of the fuel had been offloaded before the truck crossed the Anjuman, then General Fahim had taken some of the fuel for his own military needs when it arrived in the valley, and on and on. The bottom line was that the U.S. government was out the $22,000 I paid for the missing truck and the seventeen tons of fuel. This meant that the fuel available for our helicopter remained in short supply and was filthy.

When I returned to Kabul in January 2002 and met with

Engineer Aref in his new offices there, I once again asked if the truck had ever arrived. All he did was laugh. The joke was on me, and I managed to laugh too.

CHAPTER NINETEEN

With the successful completion of the GPS mapping effort on the Kabul front, the next step was to do the same at the Takhar front. This was a much more difficult task. For openers, the survey team would have to be flown back over the Anjuman Pass, then west to the front lines, a dangerous, tiring flight even under the best conditions.

The Takhar front was actually three separate fronts stretching from the Tajik border southward. This was a critical area, for behind the NA lines was an area of plains and low hills that skirted the north side of the Hindu Kush Mountains. A Taliban breakthrough there would threaten the vital supply line from Tajikistan into the Panjshir Valley. The main concentration of opposing forces was in the area just south of the Tajik border, where the Northern Alliance occupied the high ground along a spine of hills that extended to the south for ten or more miles. South of that point the terrain became extremely rough, the hills replaced by rugged mountains. Combat operations there were almost impossible except in two locations farther south where river valleys extended westward out of the mountains. These two river valleys formed natural entryways into the mountains, and a Taliban breakthrough into those valleys would allow them to push east into the Panjshir Valley. The NA forces were positioned to block the mouths of both river valleys, and these formed the second and third of the Takhar front lines.

Murray and Stan, who would conduct this survey mission, were flown out of the valley at first light on 1 October. Nasir, our Northern Alliance pilot, went along on the mission. He had flown this route to Takhar hundreds of times and proved invaluable in guiding our pilots, Ed and Greg, through the twisting valleys and cloud-shrouded mountaintops. The team's host for this mission was General Bariullah Khan, commander of the NA forces in the Takhar area. Khan was a striking figure, in his mid-thirties, slim with rugged good looks, and he moved with confidence and a sure sense of command. He had risen through the ranks, eventually commanding NA artillery units, and his personal courage was well known. He was extremely popular with his troops, and it was clear that he returned their affection. He did not speak English, but his Russian was excellent; he had been trained in Russia at some point. With Stan's excellent Russian, they were able to do without a translator. Bariullah Khan proved to be as energetic and enthusiastic as his Kabul-front namesake, Bismullah Khan. Stan and Murray soon learned that this survey would be conducted with much the same speed and vigor as that on the Kabul front.

Leaving the aircrew with the helicopter at the landing field at Khoja Bahauddin, Khan escorted Stan and Murray to the obligatory tea and cookies welcoming ceremony. It was held in a small, beautiful garden next to Khan's modest single-story house, located on a tall hill a mile or so behind the front lines. The view of the frontline positions from the garden was spectacular, and Khan pointed out his own and the enemy's key positions. He was candid in his assessment of his own strength—not strong enough to break the Taliban lines—and the enemy's strength—not strong enough to break through Khan's defenses. Although Khan occupied the higher ground, a line of hills just to the rear of the Taliban's most forward positions provided the Taliban a protected rear staging area and gave cover for the movement of reinforcements to counter attacks by Khan's forces. Khan recognized the advantage that the U.S. military bombing of those positions would provide him, and that it was in his best interest to assist in getting this initial survey completed.

There was one other significant difference between this frontline area and the lines north of Kabul. Here, the two sides exchanged fire on a regular basis, each reacting to any sign of movement. As Khan led Stan and Murray to his SUV, he warned them, "We will undoubtedly be shot at several times today. It is no problem if it is only small-arms fire. There are only a few Arab units on the front line, and the Afghan fighters have great difficulty aiming their weapons at the best of times. Also, firing uphill with accuracy is a skill few on that side have mastered." He paused alongside the vehicle, smiling at them. "But if they use mortars, that is more of a problem for us. They have had much practice with mortars, and that skill is one they seem to have learned well. We must be very alert." On that note he ushered them into the vehicle, then jumped into the front passenger seat.

He slapped his young driver on the shoulder, laughing, and said something in Dari that caused the driver to stomp on the gas and pop the clutch, jerking everyone back into his seat. With rear wheels spitting a cloud of gravel and dust, the SUV pulled away. As it slid into a sharp curve to the right just outside the front gate of Khan's villa, Stan grabbed tightly to the plastic handle above the door, visualizing the car sliding off the road and spinning end over end down the hillside. He turned to look at Murray, who was grinning, leaning forward with his hands on the top of the driver's seat, eyes shining with excitement. The SUV skidded a little to the left as the driver continued to stand on the gas, and Murray broke into a loud, full laugh. The thought of another long day went through Stan's mind as he tightened his grip on the handle.

They were fired on twice that day. Despite the general's cautionary warning, he proved almost reckless as he led them around the frontline positions. He moved about fully erect, bringing Stan and Murray to points where they would have the best view of the enemy positions opposite them. His troops showed good sense, however, and kept low, but they all watched Khan with what could only be described as amused awe. He joked with each man, laughing, slapping shoulders, sometimes adjusting equipment or commenting on their clothing or appearance. He seemed to know each man personally. Perhaps it was just a show for his men, or perhaps he was showing off for the two Americans, but Khan seemed fearless in exposing himself to the enemy.

At one point, about an hour into the first phase of the survey, Khan led them into a sandbagged gun position for a 14.5mm heavy machine gun. It was manned by five or six soldiers. Khan jumped up to the top of the berm surrounding the position, then turned and motioned for Stan and Murray to join him as he stood fully exposed to the enemy, who were just six hundred yards away. Murray immediately scrambled up to stand next to Khan. Against his better judgment, Stan followed Murray to the top of the berm.

"See, there is a concentration of Arabs, just next to that large, sharp boulder." Khan was pointing toward the position and offered Murray his binoculars to get a better view. "Tough fighters, those Arabs. Not like the Pakistanis. The Pakistanis are worse fighters than even the Taliban. But the Arabs, and those Chechens, they are well equipped, well trained, and they fight hard. The bunkers there at that position are very strong."

At that moment there was a sharp crack above their heads, and Stan recognized the sound of a high-velocity bullet. Immediately there were several more such cracks above them. They were being shot at! They turned to Khan as another series of rounds popped over their heads. Khan said calmly, "Ah, we are being shot at. Please jump down now," motioning them off the sandbagged berm. Stan was already in the air, leaping for the cover of the gun pit below them. Murray was a split second behind him. They both hit the ground and rolled, anticipating Khan landing behind them. They looked up toward the top of the berm, and Khan was still standing there, peering carefully in the direction of the firing. To Khan's right, about four to five feet from him, there was an explosion of dirt as heavy-caliber machine-gun rounds pounded the sandbags. Khan jumped down, landing lightly near the two incredulous Americans.

"They are getting better," Khan said, smiling. "A 14.5. They should have the weapon presighted." Stan knew that the 14.5mm heavy machine gun was the Russian equivalent of the U.S. Browning .50-caliber machine gun. It was a deadly weapon. "Come, take your GPS readings and mark the map," said Khan. "I will call for a few rounds of artillery to silence those Arab dogs. Unlike them, we have that position well registered for our guns."

True to his word, after a brief radio exchange, with Khan reading off the coordinates of the enemy position, there was the rushing sound of artillery rounds passing overhead, and the ground shook as the rounds exploded around the enemy position. "Perhaps those dogs will learn not to be so bold," said Khan, peering over the top of the berm to monitor the impact of the rounds. "Ah, my boys are good shots," he said. "That will make them keep their heads down for a while. Come, let's move on. There is much more to do."

The next time Khan's troop took incoming fire was an hour later, as they were moving between two forward gun positions on the crest of a low hill. Khan was, as usual, leading the way, although he was now moving in a semicrouch. The Taliban positions were relatively close, and Stan kept glancing toward them as they hurried forward. Stan estimated that the closest positions were only about four hundred yards away and that both hilltops were about the same height. Suddenly there was an explosion of earth below and slightly behind them on the hillside facing the enemy, with the sound of the gunshots following over the noise of the impacting rounds. Khan broke into a run, shouting words that Stan could not quite understand, but he was sure it was something like "Run for your lives!"

Stan broke into a full run, with Murray close on his heels. Stan recognized that they were being fired at by AK-47s, a sharper, higher-pitched sound than that of the 14.5mm heavy machine gun. The explosive impact of rounds continued behind them. They all dove forward into the gun position, landing hard and rolling to the forward edge of the hole. The rounds cracked into the dirt berm above them, and there was the now familiar crack of high-velocity rounds passing over their heads. Stan looked around and saw that Khan was laughing, obviously excited and enjoying himself.

The firing stopped as suddenly as it had begun. Stan found that his ears were ringing slightly and Khan's voice sounded somewhat muffled. He was saying, "Those Talibs are getting better. That was closer than with the Arabs. Come, my friends, take your readings. We can slip down from here out of sight of the enemy on the rear of this hill. I will have some artillery called in on them once we are clear, to reward them for their good shooting."

The flights to the other two frontline areas were uneventful, the helicopter landing well behind the frontline positions, with Khan accompanying Stan and Murray forward for the actual survey work. Although Khan was as energetic and enthusiastic as he was earlier in the day, he was much more cautious than before, keeping well under cover at the forward positions. Stan told Murray he thought Khan had finally realized that there would be serious problems for him from General Fahim should something happen to the Americans while under Khan's care. Whatever the reason, the afternoon was calmer, and the survey proceeded quickly.

The helicopter returned to Khan's headquarters area, and Ed and Greg got permission to refuel for the flight back to the compound. They also filled the large auxiliary fuel tank, saying that because Engineer Aref owed us seventeen tons of aviation fuel, he certainly would not mind our taking an advance on that shipment.

Khan was effusive in his farewells, inviting Stan and Murray to return and spend more time with him. Stan had no interest in returning to walk the battlefields with Khan, but Murray promised him he would return.

PART SIX

THE REALITIES OF WAR
2–18 October 2001

CHAPTER TWENTY

Over the several days following the Takhar front GPS survey, we began to sense that the bombing strategy was not as clear-cut or sharply defined back in Washington as it was to us sitting in the Panjshir. On 2 October, the CTC told us that U.S. bombing would begin in the southern areas of the country that evening. We informed Aref of this news and waited anxiously, but then we were told that the bombing campaign would be delayed "a few days." Aref was obviously disappointed. The reason given was the lack of a SAR capability in the region, which was a serious issue for the U.S. military. Without being able to at least attempt to rescue a downed U.S. pilot, our military was not willing to risk attacking what they considered "low-value" targets.

In the meantime, Doc and the pilots surveyed a potential landing field for fixed-wing aircraft at Gul Bahar, not far from Sayyaf's residence. It had been recommended by Engineer Aref, who said his staff thought there had been an airfield there. It was easy to spot from the air; there was a long, flat stretch of ground that stood out clearly from the surrounding terrain. Doc spoke to a couple of locals, using Hafiz as the translator, and learned that there indeed had been an airfield in the area, used by a "German beer brewery" in the 1930s. I gave Aref $10,000 to have the field graded, packed, and leveled, the work to be completed within a week. The pilots were sure the airfield would easily accommodate an L-100, which would give us a tremendous resupply capability. The problem would be that until the Taliban front lines were pushed back, the airfield would be within range of artillery and rocket attacks. But we wanted to have the capability in place, even if no other short-term use could be made of it except to serve as a drop zone for supplies.

Ed found further reference to our little airfield while reading a book on the history of the British wars in Afghanistan. In 1919, during the Third Afghan War, the British Air Corps had constructed an airfield just to the east of Kabul at a village named Gul Bahar. Later, our construction efforts turned up physical evidence confirming that our airfield was indeed the old British one.

The following day we learned from Headquarters the extent of the debate swirling around the issue of how to bring the Pashtuns south into the fight. Our chief in Islamabad was loudly beating what I thought of as the Pakistani drum song—that focusing on the north and concentrating our military efforts against the Taliban forces there would allow the Tajik Northern Alliance to capture Kabul and sweep across the northern half of Afghanistan. The Pashtuns would be left behind, still fragmented and militarily weak, which would embolden the Tajiks to press into Pashtun areas to gain political advantage and settle old scores even before the Taliban were overthrown. This theme played well in some circles within Washington, especially at the Department of State and some offices of the National Security Council (NSC). But if the Northern Alliance were held in place, we could focus on building Pashtun capabilities in the south. At the same time, we could weaken the Taliban with strategic bombing against their fixed military infrastructure. Then, in some weeks, when the CIA had the opportunity to rally Pashtun resistance to the Taliban, we could begin a coordinated nationwide bombing campaign. This would allow the Pashtuns a better opportunity to compete for a post-Taliban political position.

There were many problems with that interpretation of the situation, not the least of which was that the Taliban military was not conventionally structured. They did not have an infrastructure to strike. Bombing fixed military targets such as supply depots, vehicle repair facilities, and rear-area military installations would have little or no impact on the Taliban forces massed in the north facing the Northern Alliance.

On 3 October, I drafted the first of what would be three field appraisal cables outlining my views on the need to focus military efforts against the Taliban frontline forces in the north. The field appraisal channel is a unique, long-established process within the CIA wherein the chief, as the senior CIA officer on the ground, is authorized to send in his personal appraisal of a specific situation or problem within his area of command. This appraisal is distributed in the same manner as an intelligence report and therefore receives wide circulation within the Washington policy-making community. This channel is used infrequently, so these field appraisals have significant impact. I was told by Hank C. that my analysis was well received by the director of Central Intelligence, but the debate was likely to continue for some time, as the risks versus gains of the various military options were being studied. I was told to stress to the Northern Alliance that they hold their positions until an advance could be coordinated with military actions by U.S. forces. However, no time frame could be given as to when such actions might take place.

We also expected to receive word that some elements of the U.S. military Special Operations community would be deploying to join us in the Panjshir. We knew there were discussions of sending in Delta Force operators, who would use the valley as a staging area for raids on al-Qa'ida leaders behind Taliban lines. Perhaps a U.S. Army Special Forces A-Team would deploy, although it was not clear what exactly their mission would be once they were on the ground—classic training of indigenous military forces, or perhaps laser target designation along the front lines. Other units and other missions were also being discussed, but the simple fact was that there was no agreement within the U.S. military community as to what role U.S. forces should play on the ground in Afghanistan. Days dragged by as our Afghan hosts repeatedly asked when the promised U.S. forces would arrive and, more important to them, when the U.S. bombing campaign would begin.

As the weeks went by, the weather in the north began to change. On 4 October, we awoke to a cold morning with high winds and reports of rain in the mountains to the north, with snow at higher elevations. Winter was moving in already, and it would come fast in those high mountains. Our plan to fly to the northern end of the valley that morning to scout out potential helicopter landing zones (LZs) was canceled. Once winter settled in fully, the mountain passes would close, roads in the north would become extremely difficult to negotiate, and air operations in the northern half of the country would be severely hampered by bad weather. Traditionally, winter in the north meant that combat operations were reduced to rocket and artillery duels, with ground forces unable to attack in sufficient force to be effective. If the Northern Alliance did not break out of their lines, capture Kabul, and begin the push westward within the next four to six weeks, that opportunity might well be delayed until spring.

A call from Hank late that night confirmed the confusion among senior U.S. military leadership. Hank said that he was asked by the Special Operations Command in Tampa to have me, as team leader, "formally invite Special Operations forces to join [my] team in the Panjshir." I was flabbergasted. My response was "Invite them to join us? We have begged and pleaded with each of the commands—Delta, Special Forces, SEALs, Gray Fox—to send a team to join us. Hank, this situation is broken! We really need to get this confusion before the policy makers. Man, this isn't something I can fix from the Panjshir." I was preaching to the choir; Hank was as frustrated as I was with the vacillation and indecision on putting Special Operations troops into the valley with us.

Hank did have two pieces of good news. The bombing campaign was to begin on the evening of 7 October. Hank said this was a "firm date"; frustration at the slow movement by the U.S. military was growing within senior policymaking levels, and apparently General Tommy Franks had agreed to the seventh as the start date. That was great news, if the date held. I did not want to disappoint the Northern Alliance leadership once more by having the bombing delayed again.

Also, several lead personnel from Team ALPHA, the CIA's second team to be deployed from Headquarters, arrived in Tashkent in the early-morning hours of 4 October. Over the next week the team would assemble and eventually join General Dostum's ethnic Uzbek forces operating south of Mazar-e Sharif. CIA officers in Tashkent had established contact with Dostum months earlier, long before the 9/11 attacks, and coordination was now under way with Dostum to receive Team ALPHA.

Team ALPHA was commanded by R.J., an officer with whom I had served in Islamabad from 1988 to 1990. R.J. had handled a number of Mujahedin commanders, knew the tribal situation well, and spoke excellent Dari; he would be a valuable addition in the field. And as a former U.S. Army Ranger officer, he had the military background to fit in perfectly with Dostum and his Soviet-trained commanders.

Rick and I discussed what impact the U.S. bombing might have, and we focused on the possible need to relocate our base of operations to a location near the Kabul front outside the Panshir Valley. If the bombing was hard and continuous, the Taliban lines might weaken quickly, and we would want to be close at hand to monitor and coordinate actions by the Northern Alliance forces.

At a meeting with Aref at nine that evening, we discussed the bombing—or the lack thereof. I was happy to be able to tell Aref that things would finally get under way on the evening of 7 October. He smiled somewhat cynically and said he would contact General Fahim as soon as he returned to his office to pass on the good news. It was clear that after our false alarm on 2 October, Aref was taking a wait-and-see attitude. I told him our thoughts about relocating to the south, out of the valley, once the bombing campaign got into full swing. He agreed, and said he would scout out suitable locations in and around Jabal-os-Saraj.

We also discussed several other topics that had surfaced over the last several meetings. Aref's officers had extensive contacts with commanders serving under the Taliban in the lines above Kabul. Their loyalty to the Taliban was superficial, based on local circumstances and the benefits they could gain from serving what had looked like the winning side. Once the U.S. bombing of Taliban positions began, they would find themselves targets. Their loyalties would weaken, and an attractive cash offer to switch sides might cause many of those fence-sitting commanders to defect to the Northern Alliance. I agreed that it was a worthwhile investment.

We also discussed the Shelter Now hostages being held by the Taliban in a prison in Kabul. On 3 August 2001, the Taliban had arrested the entire staff of the humanitarian aid organization on charges that the staff was distributing Christian literature and attempting to convert Muslim Afghans to Christianity. The six non-Afghan staff members included four European men and two American women—Heather Mercer, twenty-five, and Dayna Curry, thirty. The group was placed in a Kabul prison, where they were still being held. There were regular threats by the Taliban leadership that the foreigners would be tried for the crime of being Christian missionaries—a crime that carried a sentence of death under the Taliban's enlightened law code.

International efforts to negotiate the release of the hostages prior to 9/11 had failed, and now, with the U.S. bombing of the Taliban soon to start, there was great fear for their safety. Aref stated that he had contacts at very senior levels within the Taliban Ministry of Intelligence and Security in Kabul and thought he could arrange to open secret negotiations to buy the release of the hostages. Although we needed more details, I told him to proceed as quickly as possible.

This issue became a subtheme for all of our discussions over the next weeks as we tried to come up with a plan to free the hostages. I passed Aref $250,000 to allow him to move forward with these two efforts.

CHAPTER TWENTY-ONE

On the morning of 7 October, Murray, the pilots, and Buck met with the thirty-man group of NA soldiers assigned by General Fahim to serve as our SAR team. We did not know what to expect, but Fahim had indicated that the men would be selected from among his best troops. What Murray found was somewhat different. Of the thirty, most appeared to be excited about the assignment, but four complained strongly to having been picked. Murray sent them away immediately. Most had brought along their personal AK-47s, although none had ammunition for the weapons. Six of them had no weapon at all, and three did not have boots but were wearing the locally made rubber-soled flip-flops.

The first several hours were spent with Murray passing out funds and sending off the men to obtain AK-47s, ammunition, and boots. Although we eventually prevailed on Fahim to provide additional new weapons, uniforms, and boots for the twenty-six-man team (of course, at our expense), the first day saw a pretty ragtag group of SAR trainees.

Buck supervised the removal of the two large clamshell doors at the rear of the helicopter to be used for the SAR operation, and Murray had divided the group into two thirteen-man teams. Officers were selected to head each team, and Murray set about putting the teams through the rudiments of exiting the aircraft, establishing a perimeter, and developing hand signals and fire discipline. The students proved to be enthusiastic, and they worked hard to please Murray. By late afternoon they had the basics fairly much in hand, and Murray returned to the compound pleased with a good day's work.

Murray spent the next two days running simulated rescue
missions. The helicopter would lift off, fly around the landing field in a long, low circle at top speed, then slow and descend, with a final flare movement that tilted the team toward
the open rear of the aircraft for a gut-wrenching second or
two before landing in a swirl of dust. Overseen closely by
Murray, the team leader would jump out and direct his team
into their positions. Only two or three of the Afghans had actually flown in a helicopter before, and these exercises left
the team members wide-eyed and grinning from ear to ear.
There were no mishaps, and by early afternoon on 9 October,
Murray pronounced the two teams trained well enough to
successfully conduct an emergency SAR extraction, albeit
with close U.S. supervision.

The biggest problem with using our helicopter in the SAR
role in conjunction with the possible rescue of a U.S. aircrew
was the lack of communications compatability between our
aircraft and the U.S. aircraft that would be flying with us
in the Afghan sky. We needed to be able to communicate
with the AWACS (airborne warning and control system) aircraft that would be in charge of the rescue effort and with the
CAS (close air support) fighters on station to protect the
downed pilot or crew. Without that capability, it seemed unlikely that the U.S. military would ever agree to our aircraft's
use in a rescue effort.

We were lucky that there was never a need for our team to
fly a SAR mission. By mid-October, the U.S. military had its
own SAR capabilities in place, with one helicopter element
stationed in the north in Uzbekistan and another positioned
in the south at an airfield in Pakistan in the general area of
Quetta, called Jacobabad. Once those assets were in place,
we turned one of our SAR teams back to General Fahim, and
we used the other thirteen-man team as guards at the airfield,
keeping them around for an unexpected contingency.

October 7 passed slowly in excited anticipation of the start
of the bombing campaign. In the meantime, Chris and Stan
headed for Gul Bahar to meet again with Sayyaf and to check
the progress on our airfield. They returned at 1:30 p.m. with

news that the airfield was almost completed and that their surprise visit had caught the full crew on the job and hard at work. They seemed to be on "American time" for a change.

We each spent some time in the afternoon going through our personal gear, packing so we would be able to move quickly toward the front should there be significant progress with the bombing campaign. At that point, we believed that the focus of the bombing would be on the front lines north of Kabul and on the Takhar front. A few days of heavy pounding, and the NA would be able to launch a breakout effort against the Taliban.

Late that afternoon, Jan Mohammad came to Rick and me with word that, if we wanted, he could arrange to have a TV satellite dish installed in the compound that would allow us to receive CNN and BBC news broadcasts. We were incredulous. Satellite TV, here in the Panjshir? Oh, yes, it was possible, Jan Mohammad explained. The dish was made locally, from what turned out to be sheets of misprinted aluminum beer can stock imported from the Far East, and thin iron construction rebar bent to form the dish frame. The electronics were imported from Tajikistan. These electronic components were not easy to come by and were expensive, but Jan Mohammad had located two complete sets. The satellite dish could be up and running within a few hours. We were as enthusiastic as we were news-starved. Our conversations with Headquarters were work focused, and we lacked the big picture of what was happening in the war on terrorism and how things were going back in post-9/11 America.

True to his word, Jan Mohammad reappeared within an hour with four or five Afghan "technicians," who brought with them a collection of odds and ends that looked more like junk than a satellite TV system. But with several hours of work, the dish took shape. Pappy helped with the electrical wiring for the system, allowing it to operate off generator power. Buck jumped in later, when he was back from Murray's SAR training program. Despite the language gap, he was able to communicate with the head technician on how best to mount the electronic receiver components.

As 9:00 p.m. approached, the time mentioned by Hank when the first bomb strikes on Kabul were scheduled, several of us moved to the roof, where we would have a more unobstructed view to the south down the valley toward Kabul. We thought we might be able to see the light flashes from the exploding bombs reflecting off the clouds above Kabul. Not much, but it would be a welcome sight. Rick was hoping that the satellite TV system would come on line before the bombing started, and we could "just watch it on CNN." That was exactly what we did during the 1991 SCUD missile attacks on Riyadh. When the air-raid sirens sounded, we would immediately tune in CNN and could watch the incoming SCUD being intercepted by the Patriot missile batteries. For Betsy and me, the TV pictures and the explosions overhead were often far too simultaneous for comfort.

This evening, 9:00 p.m. came and went. Ten minutes later, still nothing. Then there was a bright yellow flash in the clouds in the direction of Kabul. I hoped to hear the eventual rumble of the explosions, but we were too far away. Nevertheless, we were shouting and clapping one another on the back. Several more flashes lit the distant sky. I turned to Rick, pulling a cigar out of my jacket pocket, and offered it to him. "This calls for a celebration. It's less than a month since nine eleven and we've started hitting them at Kabul. Bombs are falling on the Taliban and Arab bastards who are protecting bin Ladin and his lieutenants." I produced a second cigar for myself and we puffed them into life.

Just then there was a noisy blast from the courtyard followed immediately by loud cheering. The TV set that Jan Mohammad had produced from somewhere was blaring, and the Afghan technicians and our Afghan staff were scattered around the yard laughing and talking excitedly. We joined them, and I must admit to being somewhat disoriented as I stood there in the middle of nowhere, watching CNN. Within a few minutes there was a breaking report that the U.S. military had opened the bombing campaign against the Taliban and al-Qa'ida forces in Afghanistan a few minutes after

9:00 p.m. Unfortunately, there were no live pictures of bombs exploding.

Mumtaz appeared and we shook hands in celebration. He was smiling and happy, and we talked about the impact the start of bombing might have on the Taliban. He was going to visit Engineer Aref and would pass on the good news. We sat around for another hour or so, smoking, talking, and making plans for our move south to the front lines.

We were somewhat premature in our planning. It turned out that the scope of the bombing on 7 October could best be described as modest. The following morning, we learned that the U.S. military had struck thirty-one targets across the country, with only three bombs dropped in the Kabul area. The majority of targets hit were strategic but low value, such as tank repair facilities, troop staging locations, and food and equipment storage compounds, with no frontline combat positions hit at all.

Engineer Aref arrived a few minutes past 7:00 a.m., unusually early for a meeting with him. If Aref's reaction was any gauge, the disappointment within the Northern Alliance senior ranks to the first night's bombing was palpable. Aref said he was happy that the bombing had begun, but the news from the NA commanders on the Kabul front reported no bombs falling on the Taliban or Arab positions. A warehouse facility had been hit, and a military transport vehicle repair station destroyed. Aref's men on the front lines, long adept at radio intercept techniques, had intercepted tactical HF radio communications from Taliban positions, and these indicated a sense of relief among the Taliban forces at the low level and limited impact of the bombing.

With Aref's blessing, I dispatched Stan and Doc to the Kabul front to join General Bismullah Khan's headquarters staff for a few days' stay. I wanted firsthand intelligence on the bombing, its impact or lack thereof, and the targets selected to be struck. Stan and Doc left for the long, rough ride south at about eleven that morning. As their vehicle pulled out across the open field next to the ammo dump and headed into Barak village, I thought, Well, at least part of the team is moving south. Unless the tempo of the bombing increases, they may be the only ones from the team heading that way for some time.

Hank called from the CTC later that afternoon. He reported that at the morning briefing for the president, which he had attended with the DCI, the discussion was of the start of the bombing and the need to hold the Northern Alliance forces in place for four to five more days, until the impact of the bombing weakened the Taliban. I told Hank not to expect much impact on the Taliban fighters if last night's effort was the best we could throw at them. I repeated my earlier assessment that the NA forces simply were not strong enough to break out of their positions and move on Kabul without significant help from U.S. bombs. Hank noted that the debate over the fate of Kabul continued to be an issue within the policy-making community. The Pakistanis, Russians, and Iranians were all publicly concerned about a Tajik takeover of Kabul and the "bloodbath" that was sure to follow. A lot of time in Washington was being spent coming up with a plan to allow the UN to take over the governing of a liberated Kabul while all the opposition forces, Tajik and Pashtun, stayed outside city limits. I could only shake my head in wonder. Hank and I said good-bye with a "well, let's see what tonight brings."

Engineer Aref returned at 9:00 p.m. for a second meeting that day, but this time he and I avoided the topic of bombing. I listened to Aref's thoughts on how he might arrange for operations inside Taliban-held areas of the country to go after bin Ladin or his senior lieutenants. Aref claimed to have numerous contacts with former Jihad-era Mujahedin commanders who had been associated with Masood and the Northern Alliance in the past and who, he thought, would be willing to cooperate on special missions of the type we were discussing—naturally for a price. I asked Aref to make contact with the commanders whom he most trusted, and open a dialogue with them on what they might be willing and able to accomplish against bin Ladin's senior lieutenants. Aref promised to send messengers across Taliban lines later that evening to contact several commanders living to the east of Kabul, where Aref's intelligence placed Amin Zawahiri, one of bin Ladin's closest lieutenants.

We talked again of the Shelter Now hostages, and Aref stated that he expected to have a reply the next day from one of the senior Taliban officers within the intelligence and security structure in Kabul on his willingness to deal on the release of the hostages. I encouraged Aref to make this a priority issue. Now that the bombing campaign had started, no matter how desultory, the Taliban might be prompted to take harsh action against the American and European hostages.

After Engineer Aref departed, I went back into the office area to compose a cable summarizing the events of the day. I found Rick and Chris sitting like bandits, half their faces wrapped with their Panjshiri scarves. Chris had three incense sticks burning in an effort to ward off the noxious smells emanating from Pappy. Unfortunately, I had no choice but to join them at the table. Wrapping myself with my scarf, I asked Chris, "How much of that incense do you have?"

"Two more boxes. Maybe forty more sticks."

I looked over at Pappy, who was trying to ignore us. "Forty sticks. Well, that may last us an hour or so. Guess I'll have to write real fast tonight." Pappy's face broke into a grin, and so did mine under my mask.

CHAPTER TWENTY-TWO

In hindsight, the next day, 10 October, was very important. Two events started the slow process of resolving the bombing strategy and the entry of Special Operations personnel

into Afghanistan. The day started as so many had over the
past week, with cold temperatures and cloudy skies threatening rain.

Shortly before 7:00 a.m., I got a cup of coffee and stepped
out onto the patio to call Betsy on the improved geostationary satellite phone system. I had spoken to her several times
earlier on another system that used the old Iridium low-orbit
satellites. The calls had been frustrating; it took forever to
connect to a satellite, and then, almost as soon as she answered the phone, I would lose the signal and the connection
would be broken. This was my first call to her on this system,
and I was pleasantly surprised at the clarity and strength of
the connection. It was good to hear her voice, catch up on her
activities, and learn how the kids were doing and what our
three dogs—all pugs—were up to. I told her that although I
was losing weight, I was feeling better; the Cipro was working well.

I suggested that when I returned to the United States, after
the Northern Alliance had managed to break out of their defensive line and move on Kabul, we spend five or six days in
New Orleans. Neither of us had been there, although we had
often said we would like to visit the city, and Betsy thought
it was a good idea. A foreign-service couple with whom
Betsy was longtime friends had retired to Louisiana, with a
home in Baton Rouge and a two-bedroom apartment in New
Orleans's French Quarter that they used on occasional week-
ends. They had invited us to use the apartment anytime we
were able to visit. The idea gave us both something positive
to look forward to. I was feeling good when we said our
good-byes. That glow would not last long.

As I entered the office area that morning, nursing my large
cup of strong black instant coffee, I was surprised to see that
Rick was agitated and upset. Pappy was there, working on an
incoming traffic dump, and was telling Rick about a phone
call that had wakened him at about half past three that morning. Frank A., one of the newly arrived senior officers drafted
into the CTC, had been on the line, and he started off mad as
hell as soon as Pappy answered the phone. It had something

to do with target coordinates, and Frank was under pressure to provide CENTCOM verification that there were no civilians at those specific targets. The team needed to provide immediate confirmation that this was the case.

Pappy told Frank that his request was impossible to act on. We did not have the capability to put eyes on the target; it was probably fifty miles south of our location, and it was the middle of the night here. Frank had exploded in anger and been abusive and rude. As I listened to the story, I too got mad.

We had been having problems with the CTC over the past few days in that they did not seem to be reading the daily cables and intelligence reports that we were sending them. We would provide an answer to a question they posed, and the next day they would ask for the same information again. We provided them with Taliban and Arab target locations on the battlefields north of Kabul. These coordinates were worked out in conjunction with Engineer Aref's intelligence officers within our joint cell, and we were positive that the coordinates were accurate and the targets valid. But there was no way we could ensure that innocent civilians were not located at those targets. Our Northern Alliance hosts assured us that all civilians in the villages on the plains north of Kabul had been forcibly evicted by the Taliban, but no one could tell who was actually sitting in a target area. It was unrealistic and unreasonable for Headquarters to expect any more information or confirmation than what we were providing.

For Frank or anyone back there to be rude and upset with Pappy, or with any of us here, for the stated reasons was unacceptable. I assured Rick and Pappy that I would take up the issue with Hank later that afternoon, when the day shift started at Headquarters.

We planned on flying to Gul Bahar to check on the airfield and pick up Stan and Doc, but Ed reported that Nasir, our Afghan pilot, had checked with NA forces at Baghram Air Base and the weather was too bad to fly. I looked out the windows and, sure enough, it was raining.

Engineer Aref arrived in the rain with news that the father

of one of the Afghan Shelter Now hostages had been contacted and agreed to cooperate with us in putting together a possible rescue plan. This man visited the prison weekly to meet with his son, and Aref was positive he could provide us with details of the prison's layout and security and where in the prison the hostages were being held. The man was scheduled to arrive late that evening, and Aref agreed to make him available to us for debriefing as soon as he arrived. As usual, this proved to be an "Afghan time" estimate; he did not show up until seventy-two hours later.

Later that afternoon I tried to call Hank, but he was out at meetings and would not be back until much later. I was still angry about the problems with Headquarters not reading our mail and the rude exchange with Frank. I wanted to talk to Hank personally about these issues, so I sat and stewed, writing cables on a number of pressing issues.

The phone rang and it was Mike W., an old friend who had served as my deputy in Islamabad for six months in 1996. He was deputy chief/SAD, and we had spoken once or twice since my arrival in the Panjshir. I was surprised when he opened the conversation by saying that Headquarters was upset with *me* because I had not yet resolved the issue of how to arrange for the Special Operations units to enter Afghanistan. He asked what *I* was going to do about this problem?

I lost it. I told him I wasn't going to do a damn thing about the issue. I was sitting in the middle of Afghanistan with a team of six CIA officers and we had limited communications with the outside world, and only indirect contact with CENTCOM or the other military commands involved in the issue. This was a U.S. military problem. Prior to our departure from the United States on 19 September, we had repeatedly asked our military contacts for their participation, but there was so much infighting among the various Special Operations components over who should be first that no progress was made. What did Headquarters think *we* could do about the problem? The more I talked, the angrier I got.

Mike insisted that I needed to reach out to Colonel John

Mulholland, commander of Task Force Dagger, who was setting up a base of operations at Karshi Khanabad Air Base, about a hundred miles north of Tashkent in Uzbekistan. Mike added that I should work with Colonel Mulholland on how he could bring in a Special Forces A-Team to join JAWBREAKER in the Panjshir Valley. I told Mike that if anyone back at Headquarters had read our cable traffic, they would know that we were already in regular contact with Mulholland. The colonel had made it clear that authorizing the insertion of Special Forces personnel into Afghanistan rested with CENTCOM and SOCOM (Special Operations Command) leadership, and despite his repeated requests, no such authorization was forthcoming. Worse, I explained, he could not even define what the mission of his A-Teams would be. We certainly could not solve these issues here in the field.

I told Mike that, frankly, this was all bullshit. It was an issue that needed to be fixed back at Headquarters, within the policy-making community.

"Well," he said, "that attitude is going to get you in trouble, and you need to somehow fix this problem." I told him that if people there were unhappy with me or how the team was performing, they could (a) kiss my ass and (b) pull me out and bring me home. Perhaps he might like the job out here. I then said, "This is a problem that needs to be 'unfucked' back there, and don't call me with this crap again."

I hung up and turned around, to find Rick, Chris, Pappy, Ed, Greg, and Buck all sitting very still, staring at me in surprised wonder. I shrugged and could only say, "Well, that was a pleasant exchange. Do you think Mike understood how I feel about the issue?"

Five minutes later the phone rang again; this time it was Rod, chief/SAD, calling to speak to me. "What's up? Mike says you were upset, angry." I was calm by then, and recognized this as an opportunity to get some things fully out on the table. Yes, I was upset. I reviewed the troubling lack of focus that was visited upon our responses to critical questions and issues raised by Headquarters. I realized that the CTC was just getting set up, but no one seemed to be reading our traffic. The result was irritating calls in the middle of the night, demanding answers to questions we had responded to twenty-four hours earlier, or requests for us to confirm information to which we had no possible access, such as "who actually is sitting in a two-hut, fortified compound in the middle of the Shomali Plains, twenty-two miles north of Kabul?" And then I get Mike's call saying that Headquarters wants me to get off my dead ass and resolve the issue of inserting Special Forces teams into Afghanistan. Between the CTC and NE divisions, there were literally hundreds of officers available for work, and there were other components at Headquarters whose only job was to facilitate the CIA's interface and coordination with the U.S. military and all other elements of the U.S. government. It seemed to me that the solution to the problems I described rested within Headquarters.

Rod is a great guy and, to his credit, he let me have my say. He responded in a calm, collected manner, and we talked for another fifteen minutes or so, reviewing problems. I provided specific examples of some of the difficulties we were having in getting our responses to Headquarters' queries and demands for targeting information noted and recorded within the CTC. Rod agreed that the issue of getting the U.S. military into Afghanistan was clearly a problem to be resolved by Washington. Rod made a commitment to bring the issue to the DCI that day, and also to talk with Cofer and Hank about getting a tighter grip on the organization structure in the growing CTC operation. My team was just the first of what could be ten or more CIA teams to be deployed across Afghanistan, and any kinks in the system had to be ironed out now, before those additional teams were inserted.

The last issue I brought up was the lack of impact of our bombing campaign on the Taliban and the situation on the front lines facing the Northern Alliance. We were three days into the campaign and the Taliban front lines had yet to be hit. The Northern Alliance leadership was getting worried, and from what we were seeing in their intercepts of enemy traffic, the Taliban were encouraged and their morale was high. Rod suggested that I do another field appraisal outlining the situation, spelling out how I saw things unfolding in the north if we were to shift strategies and hammer the Taliban forces dug in facing the NA. I hung up feeling much better.

I talked to Rick and Chris, and we decided that Rod's suggestion of a second field appraisal was a good one. It was one cable that I knew would be read and discussed, and I wanted our views to be part of the policy discussions back in Washington. I sat down and drafted the appraisal.

The Northern Alliance views the U.S. intervention in Afghanistan as "a dream come true." Yes, they are the best military fighting force in the country, but they lack the personnel reserves and logistical depth to turn the tide of battle against the Taliban and their Arab allies on their own. If we smash the Taliban front lines, the NA will take the Shomali Plains and Kabul. The Taliban will not try to hold Kabul but will flee to the south and east, down into Paktia, Paktika, and Gardez. The NA leadership realizes there is resistance within the U.S. government to their taking Kabul, but the realities of the battlefield will make that action an inevitability.

If the U.S. bombs the Takhar front in the northwest, the NA will also be able to break out there. Talaqan will fall quickly and the NA will push on to Konduz. With U.S. assistance, NA commanders Dostum and Ostad Atta can take Mazar-e Sharif, and Ismail Khan can do the same in Herat. We will control the northern half of Afghanistan within a few weeks of the beginning of a strong bombing campaign.

The Northern Alliance will not push beyond Kabul. Right or wrong, they see Kabul as part of their natural homeland area, and as the Taliban pull out of the city, they see their movement back into Kabul as justified by the historic, ethnic, and battlefield realities on the ground. They recognize that moving south and east beyond Kabul would bring strong political risks, and the NA frankly state that they do not have the military wherewithal to strike beyond Kabul. The NA will, at least in the short term, follow Masood's political agenda, working to form a national *Loya Jirga* (national assembly) and to cooperate in the formation of an interim government—one in which the Tajiks and other ethnic minorities will play an appropriate role.

Pappy sent out the appraisal just before midnight.

I learned later that the appraisal impressed the DCI, who briefed it to the president the following morning, 11 October. At that meeting there was the now standard discussion of how upset the Pakistanis will be if Kabul falls to the Northern Alliance and what can be done to get the Pashtun south motivated and moving. The DCI took the position that we should turn the NA loose in the north, allowing them to break out toward Talaqan and Konduz. Quick success could trap Taliban and Arab forces in the north, forcing them to surrender or be eliminated. We would hold the Northern Alliance north of Kabul, mollifying the Pashtuns (and the Pakistanis), allowing our successes in the north to energize into action the Pashtun tribes in the south.

Well, it was only some of what I had outlined, but it was a start toward breaking the logjam and coming up with a workable battlefield strategy. The debate was far from over, however. I sent in a long cable (not a field appraisal) outlining the Northern Alliance leadership views on the need to bomb the front lines and their comments on and perceptions of the problems that their capturing Kabul would create.

The points made were that the NA is grateful for our assistance but will press ahead with efforts to capture Kabul before winter sets in, whether or not we cooperate with them on the battlefield. The NA believe that the population of Kabul will welcome them, because it is primarily and traditionally a Tajik city. I stated that it was a mistake to withhold full military support to the Northern Alliance just to mollify Pashtun (and Pakistani) objections. Full cooperation now would strengthen our ability to influence Northern Alliance political activities in the future.

I had barely released my cable when one came in to us from

Islamabad, reviewing the first four days of bombing as a "political disappointment." The CIA station chief in Islamabad stated that the Pashtun tribes now remained even more firmly on the fence, and support within the Taliban was coalescing strongly around Mullah Omar. The cable stressed the importance of the Pakistani role in resolving this impasse, saying that President Musharraf had just made sweeping changes in the leadership of ISID (Pakistan's intelligence agency) to remove the religiously conservative director general and his cronies, who had opposed close cooperation with the U.S. government even after the events of 9/11. The new, more moderate leadership at ISID was charged by the president to cooperate fully with the CIA in the war on terrorism. The cable noted that ISID had years of experience in dealing with the Afghan situation and were already working hard to build a broad ethnic "Afghan Government in Exile" in Peshawar. The chief wrote that we should work closely with the Pakistanis on that effort, concentrate on the south, and go slowly with our bombing over the next several weeks, leaving the Taliban frontline forces untouched. Accordingly, this should be primarily a political struggle rather than a military one. Let the resistance to the Taliban regime grow within the Pashtun south as the CIA and ISID work to build an armed resistance movement there; this would balance the playing field in the post-Taliban political process in Afghanistan.

I read that message with total dismay. It was a blueprint for failure and political confusion. This push to allow the Pakistanis back into the Afghan game was disturbing and a real mistake. They had their own specific agenda for the country, and it did not track with anything the U.S. government would want to see emerge there in the post-Taliban period. It was clearly going to be a difficult, uphill struggle to convince Washington to fight a winning war in Afghanistan.

CHAPTER TWENTY-THREE

In my very first conversation with Engineer Aref, I promised that the U.S. military would be able to air-drop needed military supplies to Northern Alliance troops as well as humanitarian food supplies for the civilian population inside NA lines. I discussed this in cable traffic with the CTC and was assured that CENTCOM was in full agreement and would conduct humanitarian air-drop missions, although a number of issues had to be resolved before they could begin this effort.

The U.S. Air Force was unwilling to conduct the initial drops from low altitude, even though that would allow for much greater accuracy in hitting the drop zones. With several hundred U.S.-manufactured Stinger shoulder-fired anti-aircraft missiles in the hands of Taliban forces, and perhaps hundreds more Russian and other types of ground-to-air missiles in Afghanistan, and without a SAR capability in theater, the threat to the cargo aircraft making the drops was considered too high to risk. The first few drops would be made from twenty-seven thousand feet. This would require a long, broad, flat drop zone area, which ruled out the Panjshir Valley—at least until the drop altitude was lowered.

On 10 October, we were notified that the NSC had decided to conduct the first food drops in the north, just south of the Tajik border on the plains stretching east and south of Khoja Bahauddin. There were to be four C-17 aircraft dropping thousands of pounds of food packets. We were told that these food packets, similar to our own MREs, were manufactured for use by civilian humanitarian organizations, and each packet contained enough food to feed one adult for one day.

General Fahim happily approved the mission, and Murray volunteered to return to the north to work with his friend General Bariullah Khan to lay out the drop zone and coordinate preparations to retrieve the packets. On the morning of 12 October, our helicopter would ferry Murray to Khoja Bahauddin. The airdrop was scheduled to take place in the early-morning hours of the thirteenth. After dropping off Murray, the helicopter would fly on to Dushanbe to overnight, refuel, and pick up two additional officers for our team who were waiting to join us in the Panjshir.

As Murray was being flown north, with Greg and Nasir at the controls, four members of our team drove south down the valley in a two-vehicle convoy. Chris and Ed were in one vehicle, and Stan and Doc were in the other. Chris was planning to meet with Sayyaf again, and Ed was to do an official certification survey of our now-completed airfield at Gul Bahar. Stan and Doc were heading back to Baghram Air Base for another stay with General Bismullah Khan's intelligence staff. They would do their best to obtain additional information on key targets, to provide the most accurate targeting data possible.

The Predator, a new generation of unmanned aircraft, had made its appearance in the skies over Afghanistan a few days earlier. Our team was not in the direct loop on the Predator missions, and we had only after-the-fact, secondhand bits of information on when and where the Predator flew. We knew that on about half its flights, the Predator was armed with one or two Hellfire missiles, modified to engage fortified troop positions and the unarmored commercial vehicles favored by bin Ladin and his lieutenants. The Predator flights had little impact on us—until that day.

At almost exactly noon, we got a call from Washington. Rick and I were in the office area reading traffic, and Pappy took the call. He listened for a while, then covered the mouthpiece of the phone and said, "This is the mission manager for Predator flights. He wants to know if we have any information about a newly constructed airfield on the Shomali Plains near a village named Gul Bahar. Sounds like our air-

field, but he wants to talk to someone here about the place."
I took over the phone.

The voice on the other end of the line sounded young, male, and militarylike. We identified each other, and he said, "Sir, we have a Predator loitering above what appears to be a newly constructed Taliban airfield at the following coordinates." He read out the latitude and longitude numbers, and I wrote them down. I handed the numbers to Rick and motioned to the map pile on the other table. The voice continued, "CIA confirms this is a new Taliban facility, under construction for the past ten days or so. The Predator is looking at an SUV parked on the dirt landing strip, and there are two men, dressed in Western-style clothing, walking around on the strip. They are definitely not Afghans, and we think they may be al-Qa'ida. One of the men is very tall and thin and may be bin Ladin himself. We wanted to check with your team before authorizing a Hellfire shot against the vehicle and the two men."

I told him to hold on while we checked our maps. I turned to Rick. "You're not going to believe this, but I think the Predator is looking at Chris and Ed, and this guy thinks Ed is bin Ladin. They want to hit them with a Hellfire."

Rick came over with a map sheet that covered the Gul Bahar area, and traced the geocoordinates with his finger. Sure enough, the spot under his index finger was our Gul Bahar airstrip. "My God," he said, "they're going to kill Chris and Ed!"

I got back on the line and told the young man that he was to stand down on the attack, that the two men were CIA officers, part of our team, and they were walking on a CIA-constructed airstrip located well within Northern Alliance–controlled territory. The Taliban lines were at least five to six miles west of that location. Was I sure? I was absolutely positive. We had sent the CIA and the CTC regular reporting on the construction of the new airfield and included geocoordinates on several occasions. I could understand that the U.S. military might not know, but how could the CIA not know about it? And, worse, how could they not know where the front lines were located? A much-disappointed young officer assured me that he would inform all personnel involved of the mistaken identity, and ensure that the Predator was redirected back over Taliban lines.

Had the officer not thought to call us, the Predator might have taken a Hellfire shot at Chris and Ed. Another case of lack of attention to the traffic that we were sending in. We wrote a polite but firm cable back to all offices involved in supporting our team, pointing out the incident.

What we thought was equally remarkable was that neither Chris nor Ed had any idea that the Predator was overhead or that they had been in the Hellfire's crosshairs. I think that news took the joy out of what had otherwise been a welcome break for them from the office routine.

Murray called us the next morning, 13 October, to report on the humanitarian food drop that had taken place earlier that morning at Khoja Bahauddin. He said General Khan had gone all out in preparations to receive the drop. Murray marked the center of the drop zone, as instructed by the air force, and he and Khan waited with more than a hundred men and five large trucks to move in and collect what everyone expected would be large bundles of food packets. Sure enough, at just about 2:30 a.m., the four C-17s could be heard overhead. There was a long pause, then the sound of small objects cutting through the air in free fall, followed by hundreds of pops and bangs in the drop zone, like firecrackers going off, the sound quickly rolling off and away to the south. These were not the sounds that Murray had assumed he would hear—large bundles, dropped under cargo parachutes, each landing with a loud plop.

The men moved into the drop zone, and in their headlight beams they saw the ground littered with hundreds of small yellow packets. Murray retrieved several, and looked them over carefully in the headlights of the truck. They were indeed the individual food packets we expected to receive. Unfortunately, the packets were ruptured—exploded was a better description—and the food items inside were mixed together and dirty. The men collected as many packets as they could find in the dark, but these were spread far and wide for many miles, and the majority of the ones that Murray saw were in the same exploded, ruined condition. As dawn broke hundreds of Afghans from the villages in the area appeared, moving through the drop area scavenging the food from the packets.

It was clear to us—and confirmed by a Department of Defense film taken from inside the C-17s—that parachutes had not been used. The food had been pushed out of the rear of the aircraft in large cardboard containers, which quickly broke apart, allowing the food packets to fall to earth individually. From twenty-seven thousand feet, the packets quickly reached terminal velocity as they scattered for miles in the drop pattern. They hit the ground like small missiles, exploding on impact. The drop was another disappointment to the Northern Alliance leadership. Once again we made big promises but were unable to deliver.

In the early afternoon we received a secure phone call from Colonel Mulholland from his headquarters at Karshi Khan-abad Air Base, about a hundred miles north of Tashkent. Mulholland stated that he had been given the green light from CENTCOM to insert one A-Team into the Panjshir on the evening of 15 October—two nights away. I asked about the other clearances that would be needed, such as overflight clearances from the Uzbek and Tajik governments. Mulholland said he had no word on that but was planning to come as ordered. I told him we would coordinate with the Northern Alliance here and identify a good landing zone. I promised him that our pilots would be on the phone with his flight personnel to work out the safest flight route. I was happy to hear that the U.S. military had finally reached the decision to launch an A-Team to join us, but I was troubled by the apparent lack of overall coordination to prepare for the mission. Both the Uzbek and Tajik borders were protected by antiair-craft missile sites, some manned by Russian troops. Without official coordination with the appropriate governments, an unannounced, unauthorized flight over those borders could result in the aircraft being fired upon.

Just at 6:00 p.m., our helicopter returned from Dushanbe with Murray and the two additional team members on board. The two newcomers were CIA officers. Fred, a communications officer, was from the same office as Pappy. Fred had built a solid reputation on an impressive list of CIA deployments around the world, and we were all happy to have him join the team. Pappy needed an additional pair of hands, and we hoped that Fred's arrival would now allow Pappy to cut back on the twenty-hour days he was working. The other man, Brad, was a young Special Activities Division officer who had recently joined the CIA after a number of years in Special Forces. It turned out that Brad was an expert in the military's laser targeting system, the SOFLAM, having performed those duties while in Special Forces. Even though the CIA was not authorized to conduct laser targeting operations—that was restricted to U.S. military personnel—Brad had brought along a complete SOFLAM kit. This is a compact, portable laser device that allows a soldier to mark a target on the battlefield with a powerful laser and guide "smart bombs" to that target. We were happy to have the SOFLAM system; it might prove useful to the A-Team that would deploy to the Panjshir on 15 October.

After the initial flurry of activity of meeting the new team members, Murray motioned me over to him. I could see he was excited, and he was grinning broadly. "Gary, guess what else came in on the helicopter?" Before I could answer, he continued, "I have ten million in cash!" He had me there, as I was not expecting any additional money from Headquarters.

Sure enough, the Afghan staff was bringing into the hallway four large cardboard boxes, sealed with heavy duct tape. Murray pointed at the boxes and said, "Yeah, CTC sent the money out with the new guys. Ron, the chief in Dushanbe, said he was happy to see us take it off his hands. He said that much cash just lying around made him nervous."

Rick joined us, and Murray repeated the news about the

money. Rick kicked one of the boxes lightly and said, "I guess they thought we could use it, given how fast we've gone through the first three million." He was right, as the black suitcase was nearly empty; the last big payment to General Fahim had almost broken the bank.

I looked at the tape on the boxes, and said, "It looks like the boxes have been opened."

"Oh, yeah," said Murray, "I forgot. Ron opened the boxes and counted the money, to verify the amount."

"Well," I said, "we'll have to count each box ourselves and verify the amount." I looked at my watch. "We could do it tonight, but it's a little late. I want to be sure we get the count done correctly, and repackage the money so we can seal three of the boxes and just work out of one. Let's put them in the corner of the office area and we'll get to them tomorrow morning."

There was a scurry of activity back at the compound as the new arrivals settled in. We converted half of the large dining room that we were using for sit-down meetings with Engineer Aref into sleeping quarters for the new arrivals. Jan Mohammad found more large, flat sleeping cushions and arranged for a heavy red felt curtain to be hung across the middle of the big room, giving the two new men a modicum of privacy.

I found Mumtaz and informed him that a twelve-man Special Forces A-Team was set to deploy into the Panjshir on the night of 15 October, and we would need to find them quarters in a building or compound near our own. The addition of the two new officers to our team stretched our living space to the limits. The A-Team would have to be housed elsewhere. I asked our pilots to work with Nasir and Hafiz to select an appropriate landing zone in the general area of Barak village, and to coordinate with Mumtaz to arrange for the necessary transportation and security to be in place for the team's arrival. I asked Mumtaz to set up a meeting with Engineer Aref the following morning to discuss the arrival of the A-Team.

Things were finally looking up, I thought as I got ready for bed that evening. How little I knew.

A CHANGE OF PLAN?

CHAPTER TWENTY-FOUR

At about two in the morning, I awoke with that old familiar feeling of my bowels in turmoil. I had been doing well and had finished the course of Cipro that Doc had prescribed. I thought I was over the problem. Luckily, there was an empty water bottle already altered, ready and waiting. Between bouts, I was able to doze fitfully for the rest of the night. First light found me raiding Doc's medical kit to locate more Cipro. I also found the Imodium and Tagamet and helped myself. It was going to be another long day.

Mumtaz came by the office to tell us that Engineer Aref would arrive at 9:30 a.m. for our requested meeting. Rick and I were looking forward to it. We finally had something positive to discuss with him about the long-expected deployment of U.S. Special Forces soldiers into the Panjshir. With the dismal airdrop of humanitarian food supplies the day before, I suggested to Rick that we offer to provide the Northern Alliance $500,000 for the local purchase of food and other humanitarian goods. He agreed, and we got out the black suitcase to count and wrap the money. I was especially grateful for the extra funds we had received the night before, because this payment to the Northern Alliance would have left us with only a little over $120,000 of the original $3 million we had brought with us.

At 9:30 a.m., Aref arrived. Because our previous meeting area now housed our two new team members, we would use the intelligence cell office for meetings with Aref. He looked a little nervous as we got settled, and as soon as the mandatory tea and coffee were served, I learned why.

According to Aref, a meeting of the senior Northern Alliance leadership had been held late the previous night to discuss the deployment of the Special Forces team. The decision reached by the group, and ratified by General Fahim Khan, was that twelve soldiers were too many. Only two soldiers should be sent, and they must be dressed in civilian clothing, not U.S. Army uniforms. Rick and I must have looked stunned, for Aref stopped talking, his head swiveling back and forth between us, waiting for a response.

I asked him why this change of mind on an issue we had discussed and agreed upon more than two weeks earlier.

Aref stated that in our discussions with him we had stressed that the Special Forces A-Team would provide training for Northern Alliance troops. Aref said that, frankly, the NA forces had been fighting in the field for twenty-one years, and General Fahim said that, as good as the American soldiers might be, he doubted they could provide any training to his troops that would be of help in the coming battle. Besides, the presence of uniformed U.S. Army troops would cause the NA problems with its regional neighbors, who would resent the presence of American soldiers working with the Northern Alliance.

In our opening discussions with Aref on the day of our arrival, Rick and I had avoided mentioning the possible role of the A-Team in conducting laser targeting of Taliban positions. There had been no firm decision by the U.S. military on that role for the A-Team, at least none that had been communicated to Rick or me in our conversations with Headquarters, or with Colonel Mulholland in Uzbekistan. I had not wanted to promise the Northern Alliance something else that we would be unable to deliver. But this decision by the NA leadership was potentially a major stumbling block to the deployment of the A-Team.

I launched into a description of what LTD on the battlefield would mean to the accuracy and impact of U.S. bombing. Rick was able to offer a much more detailed description of how the A-Team members would operate, what kind of equipment they would be using, the communication links they would have with U.S. aircraft, and why the full team was required. We tried to stress that without an A-Team with their LTD capability, the U.S. bombing here in the valley would not improve.

In light of this clearer explanation of the LTD mission and the need for a full team to properly carry out this function, Aref agreed to revisit the issue with General Fahim. He said he would get back to me that evening on this issue.

As the meeting continued, we discussed the upcoming interview with the father of the Afghan Shelter Now hostage. The interview, by Chris and Hafiz, was scheduled for later that morning. Aref hoped that the interview would be helpful and we could begin making firm plans on how a rescue might be conducted.

I had planned to bring up the subject of a cash payment for humanitarian assistance, but with the sudden change in direction on the issue of the deployment of U.S. forces into the Panjshir, I opted to hold on to the money.

I did raise one additional subject, however—a suggestion that a visit to the United States by Dr. Abdullah to meet with senior administration officials might prove helpful in changing the views held by many in Washington that the capture of Kabul by the Northern Alliance could cause serious problems. Dr. Abdullah had visited Washington on several occasions in the past, and he was an articulate, polished spokesman who handled himself well in public meetings. He had also appeared regularly on CNN and BBC news broadcasts from the Northern Alliance frontline positions near Kabul over the past several days, and I thought he had done an impressive job of presenting Northern Alliance views, plans, and intentions. Aref brightened with this suggestion and became animated and positive as we discussed a possible visit. He agreed it was a good idea and promised to raise the issue with Fahim and Dr. Abdullah that morning. With that, the meeting broke up and Aref hurried off. The $500,000 went back into the black suitcase as soon as Aref departed.

At that point, I thought that the stumbling block for the

Northern Alliance over the insertion of the A-Team was our failure to clearly define the team's mission, that it benefited the Northern Alliance forces. The NA forces did not need the kind of training an A-Team could provide; they were a small but well-organized army, not a guerrilla force.

I also failed to take into account how strong the opposition to a visit to Washington by Dr. Abdullah might be within some areas of the policy-making community. I was so sure that the idea was a good one that I had put it on the table with Aref before checking on the reaction back in Washington. Both of these oversights would come back to haunt us over the following days.

The interview with the father of the Shelter Now hostage began shortly after Engineer Aref departed. Chris and Hafiz were handling the interview, which turned out to include the father and one of the young man's uncles. I sat in on the opening of the session to take my own reading on the credibility of the two. They seemed sincere, and the father struck me as somewhat naive and more than a little overwhelmed by the circumstances in which he found himself, not the least of which was sitting in a room with two CIA officers discussing the rescue of his son from a Kabul prison. I left Chris to the job and went off to write cables on the issues raised in my meeting with Aref.

Chris and Hafiz came out of the meeting with several pages of details, including a sketch of the exterior of the prison, a layout of the interior, which included the cell area in which the son was being held, and the locations of interior and exterior guard positions. The sketch of the prison exterior was a close match to a satellite image of a prison where we believed the hostages were located. Chris had given the two men a number of tasks, which included questions for the hostage about the health, welfare, treatment, and cell location of the two American women hostages. A follow-up meeting was arranged for the next week, immediately after the father's next authorized visit to his son.

* * *

Rick called Colonel Mulholland at Task Force Dagger and told him of the developments with the Northern Alliance over the insertion of his team into the Panjshir Valley. Mulholland confirmed that this first A-Team, ODA (ODA-555, or "Triple Nickel") would indeed conduct laser targeting as their primary mission. Rick and Mulholland discussed the uniform issue, and Mulholland was insistent that his men come in uniform and not civilian clothing. Mulholland was still planning on inserting ODA-555 on the night of 15–16 October.

When things quieted down, Rick and I counted the $10 million. Because the boxes had been opened in Dushanbe, I wanted to verify the amount as quickly as possible. I expected there to be $2.5 million in each box, but for some reason the amount in each box was different. Still, the $10 million was all there, and after filling the black suitcase with $2 million, Rick and I carefully repacked each box. We labeled the amount inside each box across the duct tape we used to seal them.

The question was how to secure the money. The four boxes were large, and there was no place to hide them. After some false starts, I decided to hide them in plain sight. We cleaned out a corner of the workroom and stacked the boxes two high next to each other. They quickly became just a bench to sit on or a place to rest a coffee cup or water bottle. They also proved to be an ideal spot to stretch out for a nap or relax and read. The most expensive mattress any of us would ever sleep on.

About a week after the money arrived, we received a call from a finance officer in the CTC. When I got on the phone, he thanked me for the cable acknowledging the receipt of the $10 million. Then he asked if we were storing the money in a safe. I told him we didn't have a safe.

"Well," he asked, "where is the money being stored?"

"It's still in the shipping boxes, sitting in a corner of our office."

There was some blustering and sputtering at the other end

of the line. When he caught his breath, he said he'd have a safe on the next supply flight out to the region.

"No thanks," I replied. "We have no way to move a thousand-pound safe around here. Besides, we'd probably need three four-drawer safes to hold all this cash."

There was more sputtering and some mention of regulations. I broke in and said, "Look, the cash is in our office space that is always manned by at least one CIA staff officer, day and night. No Afghans come into the office space without an escort. The money is therefore never out of the immediate control of a team member. It's as secure as possible, given the circumstances." I paused, then said, "Besides, the boxes make a great place to take a nap."

I spoke with Hank later that afternoon, and he had already read my cable on the issue of the number of Special Forces troops to be deployed and how they were to be dressed. I told him I thought the emphasis on the LTD of Taliban positions by the ODA would convince Fahim to agree to the team's insertion. However, I wanted assurance from the policy level within CENTCOM and the Department of Defense that the ODA would indeed be authorized for that critical mission. Otherwise, if the A-Team arrived and could not do LTD, it would appear that I had lied to the NA leadership just to get the ODA into their country. That would seriously undermine the credibility of the CIA and the U.S. military and would put our mission here in jeopardy. Hank said he would get this issue on the table at the day's NSC Principals Meeting. He also said he thought the suggestion of a visit by Dr. Abdullah to Washington was a good one, and he would begin to work on the issue with the State Department and the NSC.

Just before eleven that evening, Mumtaz came by to say he was off to attend a meeting of the senior Northern Alliance leadership on the question of the Special Forces team coming into the valley. He said the meeting would run late and suggested that Engineer Aref come to the compound the following morning with the results.

About the same time, Rick showed me a cable from Head-quarters saying that SAD officers had located a number of heavy-duty cargo parachutes, which had already been moved to a U.S. Air Force base in Germany. Our officers would train the air force cargo personnel in how to rig the parachutes for another humanitarian airdrop of food, this time utilizing the parachutes to drop the food in large bundles. They thought the cargo could be rigged in time to make the drop during the early-morning hours of 16 October. The drop zone at Khoja Bahauddin would again be used. This time the food should arrive in good, usable condition. Rick suggested that we have Brad, one of our new arrivals, go along with Murray to help coordinate the arrangements. They would be ferried to Khoja Bahauddin the next day, 15 October, to once again join General Bariullah Khan.

We had moved the TV from the courtyard into the hallway just outside our office area. It was too cold and rainy now to have the TV outside, even under shelter. The Afghan staff was disappointed that they no longer had access to the TV. We were somewhat disappointed also. After having a choice between CNN and BBC for three or four days, we lost the CNN signal. Jan Mohammad said his technicians claimed that CNN was blocking the signal to avoid its being hijacked for free (as we were doing). I thought the real reason was that Jan Mohammad had been offended by the good looks of the women newsreaders on CNN; his young Afghan staff had al-ways gotten somewhat agitated when a female anchored the CNN news desk. Pappy commented that there was no danger of that happening on BBC; their female newsreaders were obviously not selected for their looks.

After Mumtaz left, I sat down on the sofa facing the TV and tried to watch the BBC news. I felt dizzy, dehydrated, and a little feverish. I was able to keep down Gatorade, and the Imodium was helping with the symptoms, but I knew it would take a couple of more days of Cipro to get me back to feeling good. I watched part of a story showing an Afghan family whose home in the Qandahar area in the south of

Afghanistan had been bombed. These were the same photos I had seen off and on all day—a wounded man lying on a stretcher in a hallway in what passed for a hospital, and a little girl lying on a bed, her head bandaged, her eyes looking woefully into the camera. Ed said, "God, you'd think we only bombed civilian targets. How many times can they show this same family?"

I shook my head in disgust and stood up, feeling a little light-headed, and started off for my room. I stopped by the trash box next to the front door to collect two empty water bottles. I was sure I was going to need both of them before morning came.

CHAPTER TWENTY-FIVE

On the morning of 15 October, we learned from cable traffic that R.J. and the rest of Team ALPHA had arrived in Tashkent and were making final preparations for insertion. The only real holdup was getting clearances from the Uzbeks and Tajiks for the flight. ALPHA was to join General Abdul Rashid Dostum, one of the senior Northern Alliance commanders operating semi-independently in the west, with his forces centered south of Mazar-e Sharif. For some months prior to 9/11, the CIA had been in touch with General Dostum via his representatives in Tashkent.

Dostum is a classic warlord, a true opportunist who is skilled at shifting alliances and making deals to better his own self-interests. He is the leader of the Uzbek minorities in northern Afghanistan, and during the Jihad years he was the commander of the Jowzjan militia, a powerful fighting force that served the Soviet military. He defected to the Mujahedin side in early 1992, when he recognized that the Najibullah communist regime was doomed. His fortunes had waxed and waned over the years, but in early 2001 he reconciled with Masood and the Northern Alliance and returned to his tribal homelands in the Mazar-e Sharif area to take up arms against the Taliban.

The decision to place our second CIA team with Dostum was based on two simple but critical factors. First, we had an established communications link with Dostum, which allowed for real-time coordination with him in arranging for ALPHA's insertion. He was also a known quantity—an effective battlefield commander with forces fairly well equipped and well trained.

I knew, however, that our choice of Dostum to be the first commander outside the Panjshir to receive a CIA team would not sit well with General Fahim and the NA leadership. Despite Dostum's reconciliation with Masood, he was an Uzbek, and he had fought brutally for the Soviets during the Jihad, going toe-to-toe with Masood's forces several times in hard-fought battles. The NA leadership simply did not like or trust Dostum. Also, there was a second powerful field commander in the Mazar-e Sharif area, Ostad Atta, a trusted Tajik and longtime senior member of Masood's Northern Alliance. Atta's forces were about equal in size to Dostum's and were centered to the east of Mazar. General Fahim had mentioned Atta several times to Rick and me during our first meeting with Fahim, stating that Atta was really the power in the Mazar area and we should deal with him.

With the issue of the insertion of ODA-555 still unresolved, I did not look forward to telling Engineer Aref that we would send in a CIA team to join Dostum within the next several days.

Murray and Brad were making last-minute preparations to move north to Khoja Bahauddin. This would be a good introductory assignment for Brad, because Murray had already run the first food drop mission and had a good relationship with General Bariullah Khan, and the rapport and trust of that relationship would transfer quickly to Brad.

Aref arrived at 10:00 a.m. and we held a brief meeting. He said the NA leadership had met for several hours late the night before to discuss the issue of the A-Team coming to the valley. General Fahim had agreed that the entire team could deploy for the express purpose of laser targeting of Taliban positions. However, the A-Team must wear civilian clothing while operating with NA forces. Aref stressed that it was the laser targeting mission that convinced the NA leadership to agree to the A-Team's deploying to the valley. I listened politely, then told Aref that although I was grateful that the A-Team would be allowed to come, I thought the demand that they not wear their uniforms was a serious mistake. I said I would, however, communicate this requirement back to my Headquarters and to Colonel Mulholland at Task Force Dagger.

I told Aref the news that our second CIA team was staging in Tashkent and planned to join up with General Dostum as soon as logistical arrangements and overflight clearances were taken care of. Aref listened in an equally polite manner, then replied that he thought this deployment plan was a serious mistake. Yes, Dostum was a senior member of the Northern Alliance, but Ostad Atta was the key NA commander in the Mazar area. General Fahim would be unhappy about this decision. I could reply only that my Headquarters had made the decision after careful thought, and we were in direct contact with Dostum; the insertion of Team ALPHA would take place, regardless of any objections that General Fahim might make.

One of the things I had come to like about Aref was his ability to give and take frankly on contentious issues and still remain personable and polite. We might both feel that the other was wrong on a critical issue, but we kept the conversation positive and professional. Aref concluded the meeting with a request that I meet with Dr. Abdullah in the late afternoon to discuss the proposal I had made the previous day about his visit to Washington. Aref said Abdullah was enthusiastic about it, and General Fahim had also supported the

Approaching the Hindu Kush Mountains, heading into Afghanistan

JAWBREAKER Team on the L-100, flying to Tashkent, Uzbekistan, 20 September 2001

Loading the team's Russian-built cargo helicopter in Tashkent, in preparation for deploying into Afghanistan, 26 September 2001

"Pappy" monitoring the radio on the team's entry into Afghanistan

The helicopter with its new paint job at the landing field in the Panjshir Valley

A curious father and son from Barak village, checking out the foreigners

The team became an attraction for the village children, who found the snack items in our MREs a special treat.

An isolated Taliban-held compound on the Takhar Front

A traffic jam in the Panjshir Valley. Sheep, donkeys, and even camels were a constant sight on the roads in the Panjshir.

Members of the team being greeted by our Northern Alliance hosts, at the landing field at Khoja Bhaudin

A Soviet-era tank on the Takhar Front, in preparation for the upcoming battle, late October 2001

"Stan" (in the middle) working on his maps during the initial GPS survey of the Kabul Front

View of the Shomali Plains toward Kabul from General Bismullah Khan's frontline positions

The single-barrel ZSU-23 on the hilltop just north of Barak village. The compound holding the captured senior Taliban mullahs was located directly below this gun position.

One of the hundreds of destroyed Soviet army tanks that litter the Panjshir Valley, standing as silent testimony to the ferocity of the fighting that ebbed and flowed there for so many years

idea when it was mentioned at the NA leadership meeting the night before. We fixed a meeting time, and Aref said Mumtaz would arrange for a vehicle to take Rick and me to Abdullah's small villa down the valley below Astaneh.

Rick called Colonel Mulholland at Karshi Khanabad to tell him that the Northern Alliance agreed to receive ODA-555 but insisted that the soldiers wear civilian clothing. The colonel exploded in anger. He wanted his troops in uniform. Rick assured the colonel that we would revisit the issue with Dr. Abdullah when we met with him later that afternoon. We felt that Abdullah would be much more attuned to the political implications of the situation, and Rick assured Mulholland that we thought we could convince the NA leadership to change their stance on the uniform issue. The colonel would pass this news to his chain of command at SOCOM, but he anticipated he would be told to proceed with the insertion of ODA-555 that evening, whether or not there was agreement on the uniforms, because of the growing pressure in Washington to get the Special Forces into Afghanistan. Rick asked about flight clearances, but Mulholland said there was no word on that issue.

We informed Mumtaz that the A-Team was planning to arrive that evening and asked him to arrange to have transportation standing by. The pilots had agreed that the landing field at Astaneh, where we had our helicopter parked, was the best site for this first insertion of U.S. Special Forces. Stan would coordinate the placement of marking lights on the LZ just prior to the scheduled arrival time for the A-Team. For reasons of security, concealment, and surprise, the U.S. military conducts its SpecOps missions during hours of darkness. Their helicopter crews are the best in the world at night-flying techniques. In an operation such as this one, with friendly personnel on the ground to receive the incoming ODA, the landing zone is marked by a specific pattern of lights easily seen by the pilots using their night vision goggles. An improperly marked landing zone would result in the pilots aborting the mission and returning to base. Stan was the logical choice to coordinate the proper marking of the landing zone.

Later that afternoon, as Washington was opening for the day, I called Cofer Black, chief/CTC, primarily to discuss the U.S. military's bombing strategy as well as to bring him fully up-to-date on the problems we were having with the Northern Alliance on the issue of uniforms.

Cofer reported that CENTCOM was working targets in the Mazar-e Sharif and Konduz areas, because they "can't find high-value targets in the Kabul area." I was dumbfounded. Over the past two weeks we had provided Headquarters and CENTCOM with literally hundreds of geocoordinates for Taliban military targets in the Kabul area. The plains area, stretching north from Kabul toward the Northern Alliance lines near Charikar and Baghram Air Base, was as target-rich an environment as could be found in all of Afghanistan. I told Cofer I thought this reluctance to bomb the Taliban around Kabul was a political decision rather than a military one. The risk of civilian collateral damage in the Mazar and Konduz areas was just as great as on the plains north of Kabul. We had done all we could to provide CENTCOM with accurate target coordinates short of laser-designating those targets ourselves. Cofer said that indeed the political debate over what to do about Kabul, and the potential political ramifications of allowing the Northern Alliance forces to capture the city, was still dragging on within the NSC.

As for the insertion of ODA-555, Cofer told me that Washington had learned early this morning that the Uzbeks and Tajiks had refused to grant overflight clearance for tonight's insertion, saying that they "require more time to evaluate the situation." I, for one, was relieved at their reluctance. It gave me time to negotiate with Dr. Abdullah and Engineer Aref about uniforms. I stressed to Cofer that whenever the ODA arrived, they must be authorized to conduct laser targeting as their primary mission. Cofer assured me that the issue was being worked out.

Surprisingly, although refusing overflight approval for

ODA-555, the Uzbek and Tajik governments had granted approval for overflight by the CIA's ALPHA Team. The plan now called for ALPHA to deploy during the night of 16–17 October. Apparently the Uzbeks and Tajiks had no problem supporting covert CIA operations in Afghanistan, but they still had not resolved the political issues of offering such support to overt U.S. military operations in the region. Cofer said this was an issue for high-level diplomacy; phone calls between the president and the heads of both governments were made to try to break the logjam. Cofer assured me I would get a cable from him by the next morning with the results of all this diplomatic maneuvering.

I informed Mumtaz of the delay in the deployment of ODA-555, saying we hoped to have flight clearances in hand within the next several days. I stressed that the A-Team was delayed, not canceled. Mumtaz said he would leave immediately to pass this news to Engineer Aref, and I detected more than a little relief in his voice.

Our meeting with Dr. Abdullah took place at 5:00 p.m. Abdullah had a personal "villa" a few miles south of Astaneh, on a small one-lane road that climbed toward the hills, affording him a good view of the river and the hills on the east side of the valley. As I expected, Dr. Abdullah was alone, and he greeted us warmly. He was dressed in his usual casual Western-style clothing, and after the mandatory tea was served, he relaxed on his comfortable sofa and welcomed us.

He was happy with our cooperation and said he appreciated the money that we had so far provided. It was true that the bombing around Kabul was not what the NA leadership hoped for, but he recognized that political pressures were affecting how the bombing was being conducted. His candor opened the door for a frank discussion on my part about the political situation we faced back in Washington. I said there were fears that a Tajik victory in Kabul would lead to a bloodbath of revenge killings against Pashtuns who had supported the Taliban. There was also concern that taking Kabul might embolden the Northern Alliance to push farther south and east, moving into traditional Pashtun areas, to gain a strategic advantage in post-Taliban political negotiations over how power would be shared.

Dr. Abdullah said he was well aware of those concerns but felt they had no merit. He reminded me that the Tajik forces of Ahmad Shah Masood were welcomed in Kabul in 1992, and mentioned how those forces had behaved when they occupied the city. There were no executions, arrests, or persecution of those who had served the Soviets or the Najibullah regime. Abdullah felt that this was all Pakistani and Pashtun propaganda aimed at creating a climate wherein the Tajik and other ethnic minorities of the north would be isolated and ignored, allowing a conservative Pashtun government—under strong Pakistani influence—to come to power.

Dr. Abdullah was also aware that Abdul Haq, a senior Pashtun commander from the Jihad days, was in direct contact with senior policy makers in Washington and was being supported by several wealthy Afghan-American businessmen with strong connections to senior members of the U.S. policy-making community. In addition to his strong political ambitions, Abdul Haq had always opposed Masood and the Tajiks. His popularity with key officials at the State Department and within the NSC was troubling, because he would certainly be pressing the same negative line about holding the Tajiks back from Kabul and focusing on the Pashtun south.

Abdullah was convinced that if he could visit Washington to meet with senior policy makers, he would be able to clearly articulate the political policies of the Northern Alliance and, he hoped, reduce the distrust and fears of those who did not understand Afghanistan and its tortured history of these last twenty-plus years. I agreed that his visit to Washington was important.

Dr. Abdullah did suggest, however, that Wali Masood, one of Ahmad Shah Masood's younger brothers, and a member of the NA inner leadership circle, accompany him on this visit. I tried unsuccessfully to hide my negative reaction to that suggestion. Neither Wali nor his brother, Ahmad Zia, had the skills or polish to effectively represent the Northern Alliance in a Western political forum. Abdullah smiled at my uncomfortable reaction and explained that the NA leadership was anxious to have Wali Masood involved; it added the legitimacy of the Masood family name to the visit and would demonstrate to Washington that the Northern Alliance was cohesive and united, even in the aftermath of Ahmad Shah Masood's assassination. Neither of us expressed our opinions about Wali's political abilities.

Abdullah stated that he would be free to travel to Washington anytime after 20 October. I told him I would send that message to CIA Headquarters as soon as I returned to our compound. I thought the sooner such a visit could be arranged, the better.

As our meeting continued, I explained that tonight's planned insertion of ODA-555 had been delayed. Then I brought up the issue of how the team was to dress once on the ground in the valley. I explained the importance of the uniforms not only to the individual soldiers but for the impact this issue had with Washington policy makers.

Dr. Abdullah gave a slight smile and said he fully understood the significance of the uniforms. He personally supported the A-Team wearing their uniforms but understood how others within the Northern Alliance leadership circle would take offense at the overt display of foreign troops. Memories of the Soviet invasion were still fresh. Also, the ineffective bombing campaign, and its lack of impact on the Taliban and the Arab forces, were creating questions in the minds of many in the Northern Alliance leadership about the level of commitment by the U.S. government to bring the fight to the Taliban. He said he would revisit the issue with his colleagues and press for a positive decision on this point.

I left the meeting with the feeling that we were making progress.

CHAPTER TWENTY-SIX

The morning of 16 October opened with a mixed bag of news. First, as promised, there was an optimistic cable from Cofer Black following up on our conversation of 15 October. The CIA's plans for the insertion of Team ALPHA into the Mazar-e Sharif area on the evening of 16–17 October had prompted another round of discussions within the policy-making community about what to do with the Northern Alliance and Kabul. The president, apparently impressed with JAWBREAKER's analysis of the situation in the north, advocated turning loose the Northern Alliance forces. The delays in getting army Special Forces teams into Afghanistan compounded the urgency to make progress against the Taliban forces around Kabul and in other areas of the north.

As a result, Cofer levied onto me the following tasks. I was to meet with General Fahim to reassure him that the U.S. government was committed to working with the Northern Alliance, and to energize Fahim to bring his forces to full combat readiness. I was to provide Fahim with cash for his own combat forces, for humanitarian aid for civilians in the Panjshir, and for payment by Fahim to his NA commanders operating across the northern part of the country, with special focus on Ostad Atta, who was sure to resent the arrival of Team ALPHA with his rival, General Dostum. This was welcome news, because I was sure that the disappointments and disagreements of the past few days had cooled the enthusiasm of the Northern Alliance leadership.

At 7:00 a.m., Murray, who was in Khoja Bahauddin, made contact with Pappy using a portable, secure voice radio that interfaced with Pappy's larger base station unit in our compound. The airdrop of humanitarian food supplies, although delayed until two that morning, had taken place successfully. The CIA-provided cargo parachutes had done the job, and the heavy bundles of food packets had landed intact, right on the designated drop zone. General Bariullah Khan was pleased and had been on the radio with General Fahim at first light this morning with news of the drop. Khan's men were out collecting the last of the bundles, and Khan planned to begin distributing the food later that afternoon. We agreed that Murray and Brad should stay in Khoja Bahauddin to monitor the process, and we would have our helicopter pick them up the next morning, on 17 October. Something good at last to share with Engineer Aref.

But then I read the cable reporting the extremely angry reaction from CENTCOM over the Uzbek/Tajik refusal to provide overflight clearance, and to the Northern Alliance's "civilian clothing only" decision. The morning cable from the CTC reported that this delay was adding to the pressure that the Department of Defense was under from the NSC on the lack of progress in getting U.S. military "boots on the ground" in Afghanistan. The cable noted the fact that although JAWBREAKER had been in the Panjshir Valley for twenty days, and Team ALPHA was being inserted into the Mazar-e Sharif area on the evening of 16–17 October, not one U.S. soldier had yet been inserted into Afghanistan. These facts had been painfully pointed out to the secretary of defense during NSC discussions the day before.

Finally, there was a brief cable from Hank reporting that the initial reaction within the policy-making community, especially from the State Department, about a visit by Dr. Abdullah had been negative. The State Department was opposed to the visit because Afghanistan's regional neighbors would view the U.S. government's hosting the foreign minister of the Northern Alliance in Washington as a political endorsement of the Tajik NA. The Pakistanis would be especially upset with such a move. Then there was the negative impact the visit would have on the Pashtun tribes in the south.

The cable said that CIA Headquarters supported the proposed visit as a sure way to bring to a head within the NSC community the issue of how to deal with the powerful Tajiks. Hank wrote that he would continue to work on the issue. This was discouraging news for me to deliver to Dr. Abdullah and the rest of the NA leadership. I decided to hold off for a day or so before mentioning it, to give the CTC time to try to resolve the issue in our favor.

Engineer Aref arrived at around nine that morning to discuss the latest developments in the Shelter Now rescue effort. The meeting was brief but upbeat. Aref reported that he had dispatched to Kabul one of his officers, who had managed to reestablish contact with a senior officer within the Taliban's Kabul intelligence office. The contact had proved fruitful; Aref's officer and the Taliban officer were blood relatives, and the Taliban officer was interested in negotiating for the release of the Shelter Now hostages. Given his senior position, and the number of relatives he had working in the Kabul police and security organizations, the Taliban officer was confident that he could arrange for the quick release and transport of the hostages to Northern Alliance lines. He wanted $4 million as his reward for arranging the hostages' release. He did not expect to receive the money in advance but made it clear that this was the amount he insisted on to accomplish the mission. I said that $4 million was a fair reward for such a dangerous but important task, but we would have to proceed carefully.

The Taliban officer would have to provide full details on how his plan would unfold and what precautions he would take to ensure the safety of the hostages during the entire process, and we would have to work out a mechanism to pass the money to him once the hostages were safely in our hands. There would be no payments made to the Taliban officer unless and until the hostages were delivered safely to Northern Alliance control. Aref agreed to follow up quickly with the officer.

I marveled at the connections within Afghan society that allowed individuals from two warring factions locked in a

fight for survival to agree to work out a deal of this significance. Aref recognized that we must be highly suspicious of
the Taliban officer and his claims, but he was not surprised at
the man's willingness to betray his side for personal gain. In
his world it was what any smart man would do when he
found himself boxed into a losing situation.

Finally, I told Aref that I would like to meet with him,
General Fahim, and Dr. Abdullah as soon as possible. I explained that I had positive news from Washington and
wanted to provide cash to the Northern Alliance for specific
preparations in getting ready to carry the fight to the Taliban.

As we walked together to the front gate to say good-bye,
Aref said he had just remembered that Dr. Abdullah wanted
to meet with me in two hours. As we shook hands, Aref said
he would have Mumtaz arrange for a vehicle at noon to take
me to Abdullah.

Dr. Abdullah was again waiting for Rick and me at his
"villa" down the valley. This time I took a more careful look
at the house; to call it a villa was a stretch. It was a small
single-story structure with a peaked Western-style roof. I
was told that there had been a grassy yard and flowers
planted around the covered porch at the front of the building.
Still, despite obvious neglect, the house was attractive and
offered a good view over the Panjshir River and across the
valley. Abdullah greeted us at the front door, then seated us
in what had obviously been the living room. There was a
sofa, covered with a white sheet, and four comfortable
chairs, but there was also a large desk next to the windows,
with a typewriter and a Thuraya satellite telephone carefully
arranged within reach from the swivel chair behind the desk.
A double bed in the corner of the room was also covered
with a white sheet. All was neat and orderly.

The relaxed conversation quickly turned into a forum for
Dr. Abdullah to practice what he must have felt would be the
main themes of his discussions in Washington. He spoke of
the history of the Jihad and the role of Masood's Tajik forces
in the war against the Soviets, then moved into a review of

Masood's political views about the future of Afghanistan. Abdullah again acknowledged Washington's negative views of the Northern Alliance, and stressed that he saw the upcoming trip as an opportunity to set the record straight.

I felt bad listening to this gentleman going on about the need to talk to senior officials in Washington. On an earlier visit, Abdullah had been met by the Afghanistan desk officer from the State Department, and on a second visit he had met with the deputy assistant secretary for Afghan affairs; both were fairly junior officers. Now he expected to meet with the secretary of state and the president's national security adviser so his message would have real impact. I said nothing about the negative reaction that the proposal for his visit had generated. But I knew that the trip was not going to take place. The CIA could push hard for the visit, but ultimately the decision would be seen as a political one, and the State Department's views would carry the day. It was, however, a pleasant conversation, with a stimulating exchange of views on how the fight against the Taliban might go. I always enjoyed talking to Dr. Abdullah.

Rick and I made the drive back to the compound under low rain clouds that had moved in while we were with Abdullah. The wind had picked up, and swirling billows of gray-brown dust beat against the vehicle as we bounced and bumped our way down the potholed road. The first gust of rain turned the dust on the windshield into mud. A cold front was dropping the temperature, and I had a slight chill as the damp air seeped into the vehicle.

After a long period of silence, Rick spoke. "Man, you seem down. What's wrong? I thought the meeting went well."

"It did, but that's the problem. He's going to be so disappointed when the trip doesn't materialize. Just another example of us getting their expectations up, then not delivering."

"You really think the trip's not going to be approved?"

I turned to look at Rick and smiled. "No way, buddy. That cable this morning laid it all out. I know the fellow who's the PDAS [principal deputy assistant secretary] for Afghanistan and Pakistan. He served as counsel general in Peshawar at some point in the Jihad years. Then he was the DCM [deputy chief of mission] at the embassy in Islamabad in the late 1990s. He and I visited Masood in Talaqan in the fall of 1997." I looked out the side window down into the valley. We were about two hundred feet up the side of the hill, and the falling rain had only partially cleared the windshield of mud. "He doesn't like the Tajiks. Remember earlier this year when there were discussions about providing assistance to Masood to keep him in the fight against the Taliban? Well, this guy opposed providing any aid to Masood. According to him, we would only be 'allowing Afghans to kill Afghans,' and we would not be moving any closer to achieving our goal of capturing bin Ladin."

A solid bump banged me hard against the door, and I grimaced at the pain in my shoulder. "The only problem with his analysis then was that time was on the Taliban's side. They had the ability to grow stronger, with support from their Arab friends and the Pakistanis. Masood was standing alone. If Masood had been defeated, the Taliban would have owned Afghanistan, and we would not be here in the valley getting our asses bounced around in this SUV; we'd be sitting in Tashkent trying to figure out how to get teams in to rally resistance against the Taliban."

CHAPTER TWENTY-SEVEN

On 17 October, we received the news from the CTC that all eight members of Team ALPHA had successfully inserted into the area south of Mazar-e Sharif and linked up with General Dostum's forces as scheduled. The cable was short and concise, but reading the few sentences sent a jolt of adrenaline through me. We had a second team on the ground in northern Afghanistan! The plan was coming together.

ALPHA had been flown in on a U.S. Special Operations helicopter, the first such operational activity by U.S. military forces here in theater—another significant step forward. ALPHA's communication system mirrored ours, so we would have secure two-way communications with them. Rick drafted a brief cable to ALPHA welcoming them and asking about possible negative reactions from Commander Atta. He asked them to call us on the secure radio as soon as time and circumstances allowed. If there was trouble brewing with Atta, we needed to know before we met with General Fahim later that morning.

Over the past few days, the weather had continued to deteriorate as winter began to settle in. Heavy snow was reported in the higher elevations of the Hindu Kush Mountains to the north, and Jan Mohammad said that within a week or so Anjuman Pass would be impassable to vehicle traffic until late spring next year. The temperature that morning drove us into our heavier clothing, despite blue skies overhead.

Ed and Greg were planning to fly the helicopter to Dushanbe to pick up a shipment of supplies we had requested from Headquarters about a week after our arrival in the valley. The same flight from the United States to Dushanbe also brought a three-man CIA team to establish a temporary CIA presence there. Their primary mission was to support our team and other CIA teams operating in northern Afghanistan.

Nasir, our Afghan pilot, used the Northern Alliance radio at the landing field at Astaneh to check with the weather observer, who lived higher up the valley within sight of the Anjuman Pass. The weather there was clear. However, because it could change at any moment, there was a sense of urgency as the flight crew prepared to depart. Just before they headed off for the helicopter, I passed Buck an aluminum foil–wrapped bundle of $85,000 to pass to Ron, the newly arrived chief in Dushanbe.

In discussions with our Afghan hosts, it was clear that better used vehicles were available in Dushanbe. Rick had coordinated with Ron by cable to have him purchase three used Toyota SUVs. Ron would pass them to a Northern Alliance representative there, Amrullah Saleh, to be driven down to us here in the valley. Jan Mohammad assured us that the $85,000 would cover the cost of the three vehicles as well as the expense of moving them over the mountains. We could only hope that the weather held off long enough for them to make it over the Anjuman Pass before winter. Maybe they would also locate our fuel tanker truck and convoy. Yeah, right.

I kept the black suitcase open and Rick and I counted and wrapped a total of $1.7 million to give to General Fahim and Dr. Abdullah at the meeting later that morning. With Cofer's positive message the day before about energizing the Northern Alliance forces, I wanted to make this meeting significant, one that would help erase the NA leadership's doubts about the sincerity and commitment of the U.S. government. Of the $1.7 million, $750,000 was for use by General Fahim in bringing his forces to full combat readiness, and $250,000 was for the purchase of humanitarian supplies for the civilian populations in the areas near the battlefields. This would pay for their relocation to the safer rear areas in the valley as well as for food and winter clothing.

I especially wanted to provide specific monetary support to Commander Atta, to help sooth his irritation over last night's insertion of Team ALPHA with Commander Dostum. Another $250,000 was wrapped in a separate bundle and I wrote Atta's name in Dari in large letters on the package. I had no idea whether the money would actually be passed to Atta, but I wanted to make clear the CIA's effort to calm the waters between Dostum and Atta. The last $450,000 of the 1.7 million was for Engineer Aref for the daily operation of his organization, and for possible bribes to entice Taliban commanders to defect to the Northern Alliance.

I looked around for a bag in which to carry the money, but we had to settle on a beat-up, dirty cardboard box. Because the money was so heavy, we used duct tape to secure the bottom of the box.

The meeting took place down the valley below Astaneh, in a building that was new to us. Set on a hillside with an unobstructed view of the Panjshir River and the hills to the east, the structure was impressive, and certainly worthy of being called a villa. It had two stories, with exterior walls of basketball-size gray rocks. The surrounding lawn was as green and well manicured as a golf course, and the trees and bushes were well tended. The furnishings were surprisingly modern, with new Western-style furniture, brightly polished tiled floors dotted with colorful Afghan carpets, and tasteful white drapes covering the floor-to-ceiling windows. The house had belonged to a wealthy Afghan businessman who fled to the United States in the early 1980s. During the years of fighting in the valley, the building had been badly damaged. In gratitude for the forced departure of the Soviets from Afghanistan in February 1989, the businessman gave the property to Ahmad Shah Masood. The house was completely refurbished and served as a VIP guesthouse for high-level visitors to the valley. Ironically, the two Arab "journalists" who assassinated Masood had been guests there while they waited for their "interview" with him.

I hefted the beat-up cardboard box and carried it into the house. As we were ushered into the meeting room, I casually placed it on a chair just inside the door. After the usual round of handshakes and greetings, we sat in a semicircle in comfortable, cushioned armchairs. General Fahim was seated next to me, with Engineer Aref and Dr. Abdullah sitting to his right. Rick was on my left, and Mumtaz, who served as note taker, was next to him. Having requested the meeting, I was invited to open the discussions. I moved quickly into a candid review of developments since my team's arrival in the Panjshir. I acknowledged the disappointing level of the bombing campaign, especially on the Kabul front. I also touched on some of the other missteps, such as the first, disastrous airdrop of humanitarian food at Khoja Bahauddin.

Then I noted the successes, which included the effective joint intelligence cell being run by Engineer Aref, and the newly completed airfield at Gul Bahar. I assured the three Afghans that the U.S. government was committed to defeating the Taliban and removing them from power, then carrying the fight to the al-Qa'ida and bin Ladin.

I spoke directly to General Fahim during most of this presentation, focusing on him, meeting his fixed stare as I spoke. I told him that Team ALPHA had been successfully inserted with General Dostum in the late hours of 16 October. The Special Forces A-Team was ready to deploy to the Panjshir as soon as bureaucratic issues with the Uzbek and Tajik governments were overcome. This was clear, positive evidence that the United States was committed to the defeat of our mutual enemies. I told him that I had brought to this meeting a large amount of money for the Northern Alliance. We wanted to ensure that General Fahim had the financial means to bring his forces to full combat readiness and to provide necessary assistance to the civilian population, and to the NA commanders in the northwestern areas outside the Panjshir.

I pointed to the cardboard box on the chair near the door and said it contained $1.7 million. All eyes in the room turned to the box, and I could tell that the amount of cash had impressed our Afghan hosts. I reviewed the breakdown of the cash, identifying the amounts I had earmarked for specific purposes: military preparations, humanitarian assistance, and intelligence operations. Then I focused on the money for Commander Atta. I said I understood that the linking of a CIA team with General Dostum was not a popular decision within the NA leadership, and certainly not with Atta. I mentioned Atta's military strength and importance in the Mazar area but acknowledged that it was the CIA's well-established links with Dostum that had allowed Team ALPHA to get quickly and safely on the ground. We would establish direct contact with Atta and his forces as circumstances allowed. In the meantime, the $250,000 I had set aside for Atta was a token of our sincerity in wanting to deal fairly with all important commanders in the western areas. I hoped that General Fahim would tell this to Commander Atta and see that he received the money as quickly as possible.

Fahim responded candidly after thanking me for the funds. He said that the issues I had raised, especially the bombing's lack of impact, were troubling. It was good news that the U.S. government was moving forward with plans to bring the battle to the Taliban. He stressed that the key to success in that battle would not be airpower and bombing but Northern Alliance troops fighting and defeating the Taliban and Arab forces on the ground. He said he would contact Commander Atta later in the day and pass on my assurances of support. He said he wanted to discuss the situation on the ground with Atta now that a CIA team was linked with Dostum.

Dr. Abdullah spoke next, also thanking me for the funds. He covered some of the same ground as the general. He said he understood that the move to link up with Dostum was one of expediency—he paused and smiled slightly—not a political decision on our part. The money for humanitarian assistance for the civilian population in the frontline areas was welcome, and this gesture would be well received by the NA leadership. He said that his planned visit to the United States would help smooth out any differences of opinion on how best to proceed with this fight. I did not comment.

I did bring up the issue of uniforms for ODA-555. I reminded all present how important this issue was to the United States. These were American soldiers coming to fight a common enemy, standing side by side with Northern Alliance troops. They must not be in civilian clothing.

Again Dr. Abdullah and Aref exchanged worried glances, and Dr. Abdullah broke in when I finished. Speaking in English, he said that this was a sensitive issue within the Northern Alliance leadership, and although General Fahim was firm in his position, the issue was not yet fully decided within the leadership circle. Dr. Abdullah would continue the discussion within the group, and perhaps opinions would shift. He then quickly translated his comments into Dari for

General Fahim's benefit. My Dari was good enough for me to understand what Dr. Abdullah was saying. He said nothing about continuing the discussion or seeking a shift in opinion. Mumtaz, who had been translating into Dari up to that point, sat silently while Dr. Abdullah spoke.

With that, the meeting adjourned, and Rick and I were ushered out with warm good-byes. As Mumtaz escorted us to our vehicle, I was sure that General Fahim, Dr. Abdullah, and Aref were busy counting the money. Despite my allocation, I had no illusions about who would make the final decision over the actual division of funds once it came time to spend the money. My only hope was that General Fahim would see to it that Commander Atta received his $250,000. I did not want Atta and Dostum shooting at each other, not with Team ALPHA possibly caught in the middle.

That afternoon we learned that our helicopter had flown from Dushanbe to Khoja Bahauddin and picked up Murray and Brad, but it had been forced to return to Dushanbe because of bad weather in the high mountain passes. The men would overnight in Dushanbe and try again the next morning. Other than that news, the rest of the afternoon and early evening were relaxed, and I felt upbeat about the developments of the day. I drafted a cable outlining our meeting and touched on the impact of the payment on our three Afghan colleagues. I made specific mention of Dr. Abdullah's assertion that the uniform issue was still under discussion. Things were looking up, and I was looking forward to sharing a cigar with Rick on the patio after dinner. I should have known better.

At almost 8:00 p.m., we received a secure phone call from the CTC. Could we try to contact Colonel Mulholland and confirm that he was launching ODA-555 that evening? CENTCOM had contacted the CTC earlier with the news that Colonel Mulholland was proceeding with the planned insertion, but they had not been able to contact Task Force Dagger to confirm that report. The CTC had no better luck.

I stood there dumbfounded listening to this news. There

had been no coordination with my team on this insertion effort, and at that moment we were unprepared to receive the inbound A-Team. The CTC confirmed that neither the Uzbek nor Tajik governments had given overflight approval for this mission. We knew from earlier planning discussions with Task Force Dagger that ODA-555 would be flown in on two MH-53 Pave Low helicopters. They would now be flying unannounced over the border defenses of those countries, both of which were equipped with excellent Soviet surface-to-air antiaircraft missile systems. They were facing terrible weather at the higher altitudes over the Hindu Kush Mountains, a fact we could have confirmed because our own aircraft had been forced to return to Dushanbe by those same weather conditions earlier today. Flying in without coordination would mean that the landing zone would not be marked, and there would be no Northern Alliance perimeter security around the LZ to keep out curious (and potentially dangerous) individuals. There would also be no CIA personnel on hand with whom to establish contact and to move the ODA to waiting transportation.

This was a disaster in the making. The decision to attempt a totally unilateral, uncoordinated night insertion of ODA-555 was so rash and reckless as to be unbelievable. A catastrophic accident that killed and injured members of this A-Team could have major negative consequences in how the U.S. military would be able to prosecute this war. But, be that as it may, currently there were two helicopters in the air carrying American Special Forces soldiers into harm's way, and their safety came first and foremost.

Rick got on the secure radio and called Task Force Dagger at Karshi Khanabad Air Base and somehow got through. No, Colonel Mulholland was not available, but, yes, they could confirm that ODA-555 was airborne on two MH-53 Pave Low helicopters, inbound for the Panjshir Valley. Estimated time of touchdown in the valley was 10:00 p.m. this evening. We had less than two hours to get our reception arrangements in place.

I knocked on Mumtaz's door and ruined his evening with

the news that the A-Team was in the air headed to the valley. I requested he get the necessary transportation together to meet the team, with room for twelve new arrivals and what I expected would be almost two thousand pounds of gear and equipment. Mumtaz said he would have Jan Mohammad work on that while he informed Engineer Aref of this development and asked him to arrange for physical security in and around the landing zone. There were many villages in the surrounding hills, and the nighttime landing of two helicopters was sure to create curiosity. All efforts must be made to ensure that there was neither a friendly fire incident by the A-Team as they disembarked from the helicopters nor an attack on the A-Team by Taliban sympathizers.

Rick had our reception team assembled, and it was agreed that he would be in charge of marking the landing zone. We assumed that the incoming helicopters would land at the "airfield" at Astaneh; in their earlier planning discussions, our pilots had provided the Special Forces pilots with those coordinates and also advice on the best approach to the landing zone. Doc, his emergency field medical kit ready, would be on standby with our reception team for the landings. Rick would lead the reception team, and I would man the radio with Pappy. Rick's team piled into two of the Russian jeeps and roared away into the night.

I sat in the relative silence of the large work area, watching Pappy take incoming cable traffic from Headquarters, listening for a callback from Task Force Dagger with an update on the status of the inbound flight. I could only think about how screwed up this situation was. I considered all the potential political consequences of this stupid, uncoordinated effort, and how this action could backfire and damage the U.S. government's efforts to strike at the al-Qa'ida. But those concerns paled to insignificance when I thought of the unnecessary danger in which this mission placed the men of ODA-555 and the aircrews of the two Pave Low helicopters.

Rick called me on his HF handheld radio to report that the landing zone was marked with lights and that Mumtaz had arrived with a number of SUVs and Toyota pickup trucks. Engineer Aref was arranging for the local military commander in that sector of the valley to put out security forces to protect the landing area. We were as ready as we could be at this end.

At a little before 10:00 p.m., Task Force Dagger called to report that the helicopters were experiencing bad weather, with high winds and icing. They were going to push on, but it did not look good unless the weather broke soon. I called Rick with that news and settled down to wait.

Finally, at 10:45 p.m., Task Force Dagger called to say that the flight had turned around because of the weather, and the two Pave Lows were on their way back to base. I was glad to hear it. I thanked the radio operator, asking him to request Colonel Mulholland to call me first thing in the morning to review the events of this mission. I was angry with Mulholland and thought his decision to launch ODA-555 without any coordination had been reckless and ill-advised. We had dodged a bullet this evening, especially the soldiers on those helicopters, but it was a bullet that should not have been fired in the first place.

I called Rick and told him to break down the marking lights and bring the guys home. I asked him to tell Mumtaz I would try tomorrow to explain to Engineer Aref what had happened tonight, and explain why there had been no coordination on the insertion effort. I was not looking forward to that meeting.

CHAPTER TWENTY-EIGHT

The next morning, I fully expected Engineer Aref to appear at first light to demand an explanation for the botched insertion effort of the previous evening, but there was no word from him, even as the morning stretched toward noon. That worried me more than an angry visit would have. Weather in the mountains was still bad, and our flight crew called in by radio to say they would monitor the weather conditions from Dushanbe airport. They would contact us if the weather broke. It seemed likely, however, that our helicopter would be grounded in Dushanbe for at least another day.

The previous evening, Rick suggested that he take Stan and Doc to Baghram Air Base and overnight there with General Bismullah Khan's intelligence section. They could get a feel for morale, assess firsthand the impact of the bombing on the Taliban front lines, and check to see if our cash infusion of the day before was being put to use yet.

After they departed, I wrote a series of cables back to Headquarters, with info copies to CENTCOM in Tampa, detailing the events surrounding the aborted insertion. I tried to be dispassionate and straightforward. I could not gauge the degree of impact the event had on the Northern Alliance leadership, but I could speculate that it was negative.

Just before noon, Mumtaz came by to say that Engineer Aref would meet with me around 7:30 p.m. that evening. I told Mumtaz that our helicopter was in Dushanbe, stranded by the weather, but that some of the special operations equipment we had requested for Aref's use against bin Ladin and other al-Qa'ida leaders, to include silenced machine guns and silenced pistols, had arrived in Dushanbe and would be on the helicopter when it finally did return. I wanted to give Aref a little good news before I saw him that evening.

After lunch I took a long walk with Jan Mohammad on the road leading north up the valley. Although the weather was cloudy and cool, the day was quiet and pleasant. The Panjshir River ran just next to the road. Small trees and brush lined the riverbank, and the current was slow and the water shallow. Around a bend in the road, with the Barak village out of sight behind us, was a natural pond about five yards wide formed in the river by a line of trees and brush growing on a thin spine of land running parallel to the riverbank. Wooden duck decoys were floating on the pond and anchored in place by string weighted with rocks. It was a beautiful scene, simple and still, and we stood together talking quietly in Dari about duck hunting and how life in the valley was slowly getting back to normal after so many years of war and destruction.

We walked on and rounded another bend in the road. There on the east bank of the river, ahead and opposite us, was a compound of two medium-size, one-story mud buildings, with a flat open area about ten yards square in front of the buildings. A tall barbed-wire fence completely surrounded the complex and was broken only by a single large gate, which provided access. A third mud building was situated just outside the gate. Jan Mohammad explained that this was the prison where the Northern Alliance kept captured senior Taliban mullahs. He said that about thirty mullahs were being held there now. As we drew nearer, I could see four or five robed figures standing around the front of one of the buildings in the fenced area.

"They are doing cleanup of the compound," Jan Mohammad explained. "They must work each day if they want food." I could see two armed soldiers standing watch from outside the fence, AK-47s on their shoulders.

Jan Mohammad told me that the Taliban leadership knew exactly who was being held here and exactly where this compound was located. The mullahs were not mistreated, but living conditions were "heavy" for them. They were like an insurance policy, he explained, because these were important mullahs, and the "good" treatment they received helped restrain the Taliban from committing some of their more brutal excesses on Northern Alliance prisoners that the Taliban had in their custody.

On our way back to our compound, we passed the mullah prison again and saw a group of ten or so mullahs digging at some project in the corner of the compound. This time I noted that there were no windows in either of the two buildings, just three or four small slits near the top of the front walls, which I assumed let in breezes and light. Life for them was "heavy" indeed.

* * *

ALPHA Team called in the early afternoon. R.J. and I talked, and he was upbeat about the team's reception by Dostum. Apparently, for the most part, Dostum moved his forces by horseback, and ALPHA was now officially in the cavalry. The problem was not in riding the horses, which were somewhat smaller than the average U.S. horse, but in the saddles and tack used by the Afghans. The saddles were small, made of thin leather, and did not have the high ridge in the rear that U.S. saddles had. More troubling was the fact that the stirrups were too small for the big-footed Americans' feet. They were making do, but R.J. said they were sending a message back to Headquarters that day asking for U.S. Western-style saddles and tack on a priority basis.

R.J. said that Commander Atta was more than a little upset that ALPHA had been located with Dostum. Dostum assured R.J. that things would settle down between him and Atta, and this was just part of their longtime rivalry. R.J. was also requesting an airdrop of weapons and ammunition for Dostum's forces, to be made within the next several days. The drop would be made to an area identified and marked by ALPHA, which meant that all the supplies would go to Dostum. I speculated to R.J. that this airdrop might be the event that would bring the problems between the two commanders to a head, with ALPHA caught in the middle. In the meantime, I assured R.J. that I would pressure General Fahim to calm Atta and stress the need to work cooperatively with Dostum.

Around four that afternoon, we had a series of calls with Colonel Mulholland to discuss the botched insertion of the night before and to make plans for a successful next effort. He agreed that he should have coordinated his plans with my team to ensure a safe reception, but he was adamant that CENTCOM had given him the green light to insert ODA-555 when and as he saw fit. Arguing with him was pointless.

Mulholland said he would like to deploy the A-Team that evening, but the weather forecasts for the area over the mountains were worse than those of the previous evening. Things looked better for the following night, 19 October, and he said he would inform CENTCOM that it was the firm target date for the next insertion mission. I asked him to keep my team in the loop and have his pilots talk to Ed and Greg tomorrow, when they would be back from Dushanbe.

Just as we were sitting down to dinner, Mumtaz arrived with word that Engineer Aref could not make the scheduled meeting that evening. He would not be available the next day either; that was the 40th Day anniversary of Masood's death, and ceremonies and prayers would be held for much of the day at Masood's grave site. I knew that Mumtaz was being truthful about the significance of the 40th Day celebrations; that was an important milestone in the mourning cycle in Islam. However, I could not help but think that Aref's cancellation of our scheduled meeting was his way of showing his anger at the events of the previous night with the A-Team.

It was a quiet evening, with just four of us rattling around in the workroom. It was windy and cold outside. I went to bed relatively early. I was awakened around midnight by the arrival of a large cargo truck at the ammunition dump next to our compound. For the next hour or so, there was the continual crash of heavy boxes being violently moved around. That was worrisome enough, but toward the end of that time the noise changed to the clang of heavy metal objects being dropped. I looked out the window and saw a number of soldiers moving what appeared to be 122mm rockets from their open storage pits to the rear of the truck, where they were unceremoniously wrestled and dropped into a pile. There was nothing to do but go back to bed. If the ammo dump exploded, I would never know it anyway. I actually slept soundly the rest of that night.

PART EIGHT

THE A-TEAMS ARE IN

19–23 October 2001

CHAPTER TWENTY-NINE

The morning of 19 October started off with good news. A cable from the CTC notified us that for some reason—pressure from the Russians, or the successful insertion of Team ALPHA by the U.S. military on the night of 16 October, or just the skill of senior U.S. administration officials in twisting the arms of senior officials—both Uzbek and Tajik governments had officially authorized overflight clearance for the insertion of ODA-555. The A-Team would be flying in tonight, weather permitting.

We then received a radio message from our flight crew in Dushanbe that the weather over the mountains was clear and they were preparing to depart at 8:00 a.m. That would put them back in the valley at about half past ten. Rick, Stan, and Doc were not yet back from their overnight visit to Baghram Air Base, so I walked over and informed Mumtaz about the arrival time for our helicopter, and about the approval for the A-Team to arrive this evening—time to be determined. I apologized for the disruption this would cause Mumtaz in his plans for the 40th Day ceremonies, but he took the news well. He said that before he departed for the ceremonies he would arrange for transportation to be at the landing zone that evening and make arrangements for the reception for the A-Team when he returned late that afternoon.

Not having met with Engineer Aref the previous day, I had to assume that the Northern Alliance was still standing firm on the decision that the A-Team be dressed in civilian clothing when they arrived. I knew from Colonel Mulholland's reaction on the radio yesterday that he planned to have his men in uniform. With the 40th Day ceremonies taking place, it was unlikely we would see any of the senior NA leadership today. I would not raise the issue. The ODA would arrive, in uniform or not, and we would see what happened then.

The noise of the arriving trucks carrying Murray, Brad, and most of the cargo from the helicopter brought us all down to the front gate of the compound. Murray was excited, grinning broadly. "Gary, guess what I have?" he asked as he approached me.

"Another ten million dollars?"

"No, no, something better," he said, laughing. "I have a hundred pounds of Starbucks coffee!"

I was elated with his announcement but could not fathom why Headquarters would have thought to send Starbucks coffee.

"Don't you remember? In the big resupply request we sent in, Chris asked for a hundred pounds of Starbucks and a Bible. We all laughed, but, hey, here it is. They sent the two metal coffee percolators he asked for, and—oh, yeah—the Bible is here too."

Brad pulled out two large Starbucks shopping bags, each packed with one-pound bags of ground coffee. There were two more similar shopping bags in the back of the pickup. We all stood with our mouths open. Within thirty minutes we had our first taste of fresh-brewed Starbucks coffee. We showed Jan Mohammad how the "old-fashioned" percolator coffeepots worked and how much coffee should be used. Later that day he had set up a two-burner kerosene cookstove on the wide window ledge outside the kitchen and had the young Afghan staff manning the pots. It became our "coffee shop," and Jan Mohammad took great pride in keeping the area clean. He made sure that every day there was at least one pot full and ready for use until well after dinner. The boost to morale was remarkable, and that first cup of morning coffee became something we all looked forward to.

I never knew whether Chris actually read the Bible he had

requested, but it was a thoughtful gesture for the CTC Logistics officers to make the extra effort to purchase and ship it to him.

CHAPTER THIRTY

Rick, Stan, and Doc returned from the Kabul front a little after noon and reported that, when they drove by an hour earlier, Commander Masood's hilltop grave site had been jammed with mourners. I wished we could have attended the ceremonies, but we were not invited, and I didn't want to intrude on what was sure to be an emotionally trying time for our Afghan hosts. Our presence at the ceremony would have distracted them, and I felt that this was a private time of mourning for those who had lived and fought with the Commander.

The Starbucks brewing on the window ledge was quickly noted, and Rick, Stan, and Doc enjoyed their first cups standing around the coffeepot as if they were worried it would disappear before they could get seconds.

Mumtaz returned to the compound at around four that afternoon. He was somber and subdued and said that the ceremonies for Commander Masood had been very moving. I could see that he had been crying, and I knew it had been a difficult day for him. I told him that the weather over the mountains had been good, and our helicopter had returned from Dushanbe safely. We expected the A-Team to arrive as scheduled that evening. Mumtaz said he would check with the weather watcher by the Anjuman Pass, and ensure that the drivers and vehicles for tonight's pickup were notified and standing by.

At 6:00 p.m. we contacted Task Force Dagger at Karshi Khanabad Air Base, and Rick spoke with Colonel Mulholland. The weather report for that evening was good, although there would be a risk of icing at high altitudes. The Triple Nickel was ready to go. Eleven members of the team would be deployed using two MH-53 Pave Low helicopters. Touchdown at Astaneh was scheduled for 10:00 p.m. Ed and Greg were standing by, and spent ten minutes or so on the phone with the Pave Low pilots reviewing the flight route, the light marking patterns to be used, and the geocoordinates of the landing zone.

Jan Mohammad came by and asked Rick and me to visit the second safe house he had been working on for the A-Team. The house was about five hundred feet from our compound, located at the edge of the Barak village. It was a true residential compound, with a high mud wall surrounding three small, one-story mud-walled buildings. The first two buildings had a number of rooms, each one clean and well lighted. The floors were dirt and covered with new rough, feltlike carpeting. A third building contained a toilet facility (a concrete floor with a hole in one corner, and a large water jug next to it for flushing) and a small area that served as a kitchen.

Jan Mohammad had three young men hard at work cleaning and sweeping, and he assured us that the place would be ready for our guests well before they arrived in the valley. He said he would have a hot meal with tea and coffee ready for the soldiers as soon as they were settled into the compound.

As Rick and I walked back to our compound, I noted that the new safe house was just about as close to the ammunition dump as our compound was. "I guess Jan Mohammad wanted to ensure that if the ammo dump blows, he gets us all," Rick commented. I could still hear the clanging of 122mm rockets being tossed around a few nights earlier.

There are actually two landing areas at the field at Astaneh. The upper field could easily accommodate two helicopters simultaneously. The smaller second field was slightly downhill from the other, on a level area closer to the river. The Northern Alliance had two of their MI-17 helicopters parked on the lower field, and we had moved our helicopter down to join them, freeing the upper field for that night's air operations. The helicopters bringing the A-Team were to approach straight south, down the river valley, actually passing in front of Barak, then turning left around a bend in the river, after which the valley broadened nicely. The LZ marking lights would be easily visible to the inbound pilots for several minutes as they made their final approach. Rick would be in charge of marking the LZ. Doc, once again, would stand by with his medical kit for an emergency. Chris would work closely with Mumtaz to ensure that all the vehicles and drivers were in place and the A-Team's gear would be loaded quickly and efficiently. Murray and Stan both wanted to be included, as did I, but we would be tight on space in the vehicles as it was, so they were to remain at the compound with me and the rest of the team.

By 9:00 p.m. our reception team was in place and the landing zone marked. Rick called in on the HF radio to report that Mumtaz was there with the transportation—four Toyota Hilux pickup trucks and four SUVs. At about half past nine, Murray, Stan, and I went up to the roof of our building, each with our night vision goggle set, to watch for the helicopters as they flew past on their way to the landing zone. It was a mild evening, not nearly as cold as the past two nights, and the skies were clear. The moon was just coming out of its dark phase, and there was ample ambient light to get the most out of the NVGs. The inbound pilots could not have had a better night for flying.

By 10:10 p.m., Rick and I had exchanged radio calls to check on the status of the incoming helicopters. Our last message from Task Force Dagger had been at 9:45 p.m., and they reported that the flight was running a little behind schedule because of stiff headwinds and some mild icing. All we could do was stand by and wait.

Then, at 10:20 p.m., we heard the sound of the beating rotor blades of the two helicopters off to the north. They were flying low and, from the sound, we knew they were coming straight down the middle of the valley, following the course of the river. I was on the handheld radio to Rick when the two blackened helicopters roared past us, flying at about one hundred fifty feet altitude. They were past our position quickly and moved around the big left-turn bend in the valley just past the village. They had about one more mile to fly before reaching the landing zone. But as soon as they rounded the bend in the valley, the sound of their engines changed. It was clear that they were slowing and beginning to hover. Murray was straining to see down the valley. "They're getting ready to land," he said. "They must think they're at the landing coordinates, but they're a mile or more short!" The sound shifted again. "Ah, hell, they're landing! This is all screwed up!"

Rick called in on the radio, saying that they could see up the valley and the two Pave Lows were landing. Then almost immediately one of the helicopters took off, flying away from the other aircraft. As Rick talked us through what was happening, the second helicopter flew over what appeared to be a low hill; then it seemed to land. There was a pause of about a minute; then we could all hear the two helicopters taking off, engine roar building in strength. From the compound roof we could see the two aircraft heading back toward us, climbing now to about three hundred feet as they swept past us heading north back up the valley. For some reason they had missed the landing zone and had apparently dropped Triple Nickel in two separate locations. Rick's voice crackled on the radio. "We will move out from here to try to locate the team. They are split, and that second bird dropped its team way off on the east side of the valley."

I replied to Rick that Murray, Stan, and I would head out on foot to search for them also. "We're probably closer to the first group than you are, from the way things sounded. See you out there." We ran downstairs, grabbed flashlights, and headed out into the village and down the road toward Astaneh. We were moving fast, just short of breaking into a run, and asking ourselves the same rhetorical questions. "How could those guys have missed the landing zone? It wasn't a unilateral landing—the landing lights were on. They should have been able to see it two miles out. Why did the two helicopters split the team? Even if they realized they weren't at the correct landing coordinates and decided to drop the team anyway, why not keep them together?"

About a half mile past the village, the road dropped and ran next to the river. A series of small, separate, shallow channels flowed between the road and the actual riverbed, and Murray headed out across this low, soggy area to cut closer to the spot where we thought the first helicopter had landed. We could see flashlights ahead and to the east, where the ground on the other side of the river rose into small hills. That area was wooded and had a lot of brush cover, and there seemed to be a number of flashlights moving around. "That must be the team," said Murray. "They know they've been dropped in the wrong spot and are trying to signal us." He broke into a run, splashing across the shallow channels, heading toward the flashlights.

Stan and I worked to keep up with him, but Murray was really running now. The flashlights were moving toward us, and Murray called out, "Americans. Hey, we're Americans. Hey!" We were about twenty yards behind Murray when he reached the riverbank. The current was fast here, and in the dark it was impossible to judge its depth. Murray never broke stride but did a hard, shallow dive into the icy current. He swam furiously, the water splashing into white foam in the darkness. Stan and I stopped and surveyed the scene. The river was wide here but narrowed to our right, and Stan could see some rocks that led across the river down that way. We headed toward the rocks.

Murray reached the other side of the river and found he was facing a four-foot-high muddy bank. He scrambled through the weeds at the edge of the river, then kicked and clawed his way up the slippery bank to the top. As Murray straightened up, the flashlights were no more than ten yards away, shining on him. "Hey, Americans. I'm an American here to meet you. Hey! Why don't you answer?"

The figures holding the flashlights moved closer, and Murray could finally see that they were not U.S. Special Forces soldiers but rather about ten ragged Afghan villagers, out in the night to see what all the commotion was about. Murray stood covered in mud, soaking wet, hair plastered to his head, shouting to them in a foreign language. They must have thought he was a visitor from outer space. Luckily they weren't armed.

Stan and I made it across the river on the rocks with dry feet. We could hear Murray off to our left. The headlights from a number of vehicles bounced into view to our right, and we knew it was our reception team sweeping to find the A-Team. The vehicles shifted direction, and we began to jog toward them. Somehow Murray ended up ahead of us all, and there in a cleared area was half of the Triple Nickel. They had stockaded their equipment and packs into a circle and were hunkered down waiting for us to appear.

One soldier, Warrant Officer D., stepped out of the circle and cautiously moved toward the approaching group. Murray walked up to him, his wet, muddy hand extended, and said, "Hey, guys, I'm Murray. Welcome to Afghanistan."

The trucks had stopped about twenty yards away with only their parking lights on. I could see Rick moving out from the vehicles, and he and I met just as we reached the Special Forces group. I stuck out my hand and said, "Welcome to Afghanistan. We're the CIA team you're here to work with." The soldier looked a little stunned, and I could see over his shoulder that the other A-Team members were moving toward us. "We have trucks and vehicles ready to take you to the safe house just as soon as we find the rest of your guys. There'll be hot coffee and a hot meal for you after you're settled in. Let's load the gear into the trucks and keep on looking for the other half of your team."

As that was taking place, I looked at my watch. It was 11:15 p.m. Chris came over to report that the gear from just this half of the ODA completely filled the four pickup trucks. He suggested we take this load back to the safe house, then bring the empty trucks back for the other group's equipment. Warrant Officer D. agreed, and two of his men and several of our team headed out for the safe house.

We located the second half of Triple Nickel at 12:15 a.m. They too had stacked their equipment into a defensive position and hunkered down to wait either to be located or for first light. The team commander, Captain R., was very happy to see us.

We had the entire ODA back at the safe house by 12:45 a.m. True to his word, Jan Mohammad was having his boys set out a hot dinner, complete with tea and coffee. Starbucks coffee, no less. We made sure to point that out to Captain R. and his men. In the lighted safe house, I could see that the entire team was in uniform.

We never found out why the two Pave Lows missed the landing zone. We speculated the pilots had the wrong geocoordinates or had become confused and thought they were on target but the reception team was not there. Because no one was injured and the mistake was soon corrected, the worst aspect of all this was that it took place in front of our Afghan hosts. We had bragged to Engineer Aref that the Special Forces could land in the dark exactly on target, and we would have the A-Team collected and off the landing zone within minutes of their arrival. Instead, as we who served in the Middle East said, it had been a "goat grope" of monumental proportions. Villagers from all over that part of the valley had seen the search, and many had even taken part in it. I was sure the details of the night's events would be fully reported to Engineer Aref at first light, including the fact that the team had arrived in full uniform. It was going to be another interesting day dealing with Aref.

CHAPTER THIRTY-ONE

The morning after the arrival of the Triple Nickel, we woke early; there was a full day's work ahead of us. We would have to brief the A-Team on the situation here on the ground with our Northern Alliance hosts, make appropriate introductions to Engineer Aref, and arrange with Aref to move the Triple Nickel down to Baghram Air Base to link up with General Bismullah Khan. Rick and I asked Stan to attach himself to the A-Team as our liaison with them. Stan was the logical choice for this role, because he had a good working relationship with the general and several of his key senior staff officers. Equally important, Stan's excellent Russian would allow easy communication between the A-Team and our Afghan hosts. Murray had already made friends with several members of the A-Team, and he volunteered to accompany Stan.

Rick, Chris, Stan, Murray, and I walked over to the Triple Nickel safe house and found the soldiers sorting through their gear and getting ready for what they hoped would be their deployment to the south later that day. The team members seemed relaxed, and it was clear that they were happy to finally be on the ground in Afghanistan. It was also clear that the accommodations we were providing, the hot meals, and the Starbucks coffee were almost too much for them to absorb. They arrived thinking they would be camping out in tough weather conditions. The comfort and convenience seemed almost a disappointment. Almost. I outlined to Captain R., Warrant Officer D., and several of the senior team members how we anticipated the day would go, and told them that the plan was to get them deployed to Baghram Air Base that day. Rick and I left Stan, Chris, and Murray there to begin the briefings for the entire A-Team.

When we got back to the compound, Mumtaz told us that Engineer Aref would arrive at 10:00 a.m. for a meeting. Rick walked back to the A-Team's safe house to arrange for the team leader to be available to meet Aref. There was little else to do to prepare for the meeting.

We had sent a brief cable back to Headquarters the previous evening to report the safe arrival of ODA-555, but I needed to provide a full account of the operation. I wanted to make sure that the details were on record of our preparations for the A-Team's reception, the careful marking of the landing zone, the advance coordination between the SpecOps pilots and our pilots on the route in, and the confirmation of geocoordinates for the landing zone. I doubted that Task Force Dagger would make an issue of the A-Team missing the landing zone and the resulting confusion in getting the team together, but if that happened I wanted the facts of the situation in official cable traffic.

I found a cable in the morning traffic that contained a half-expected disappointment. Despite continued pressure from the CIA at the NSC level, the State Department had finally and firmly refused to host Dr. Abdullah in Washington. I would have to tell Aref when he came.

Aref arrived right on time and appeared in good humor as Rick and I accompanied him to the meeting room. He was clearly happy that the A-Team had arrived. I apologized for the confusion of the previous night but blamed a faulty instrument on the lead helicopter for the problem. I could not tell whether Aref believed my story, but he dismissed the incident with a wave of his hand. He said that the key thing was the safe arrival of the team.

Aref wanted to know when the A-Team could move to Baghram. I told him that the team was getting ready to move even as we were meeting; as soon as logistical arrangements could be made, and coordination arranged with General Bismullah, they would be ready to move south. I explained to him that Stan and Murray would be assigned to the A-Team to handle coordination with General Bismullah.

When I said I would like to introduce Aref to the team's leader, he was all smiles. As Rick went to get Captain R., I thought, Well, here it comes. R. is in uniform.

Captain R. entered the room ahead of Rick and moved to stand across the table from Aref. Aref rose, looked at R. as he leaned forward, hand extended to take R.'s hand. The smile never left Aref's face, and there was the usual exchange of pleasantries and inquiries about the accommodations and food. Captain R. assured Aref that the Triple Nickel was ready to deploy to Baghram as soon as they were given the green light by our Afghan hosts. Aref asked the question I had been waiting for—would R.'s men conduct laser target designation on the enemy positions on the battlefield? R. answered promptly, "Sir, that is exactly why we have come to Afghanistan. We will begin marking enemy targets for our bombs as soon as we are settled in place at Baghram Air Base." Aref's face expanded into a broad smile, and he said that was excellent news. Preparations for the movement south would start immediately following this meeting.

The subject of uniforms was not mentioned then or later by Aref or any of our other Afghan hosts. I came to believe that R.'s upbeat, positive answer to the question on laser designation of enemy targets resolved the uniform issue. Having U.S. bombs falling on the enemy was simply more important to the NA leadership than how the A-Team was dressed.

Alone with Engineer Aref again, Rick and I asked about the reaction of Commander Atta to the presence of ALPHA Team. Aref became subdued and said the situation was serious. Atta was grateful to the CIA for the cash we had given him, but the presence of ALPHA with Dostum was unacceptable. Atta was the major commander in the Mazar-e Sharif area, a region of traditional Tajik control. Atta had been in communication with Dostum and learned that an airdrop of weapons was to be made to Dostum this evening. Atta threatened to attack Dostum's forces if that airdrop took place.

I told Aref that Washington would be incredibly upset by such an attack. The lives of ALPHA Team members would be needlessly placed in jeopardy. And the evidence of two Northern Alliance commanders fighting each other in the face of the enemy would confirm the view held by many in Washington that the focus of U.S. assistance should be with the Pashtun south. I requested that Aref contact General Fahim and press him to calm Atta, and to get Atta to stand down on any plans for an attack on Dostum. Aref agreed to arrange for Fahim to contact Atta later that day.

At this point I realized that the State Department's refusal to support a visit to Washington by Dr. Abdullah might be used in a positive way. It would serve to reinforce my comments on the potential impact that a battle between the two most powerful NA commanders in western Afghanistan could have back in Washington. I explained to Aref that I was sorry the State Department turned down Abdullah's visit but said it confirmed just how deep the suspicion was in the senior levels of Washington of the Northern Alliance's long-term motives. I was doing all I could to represent the NA as our strongest ally in Afghanistan, stressing the need to put the full weight of the U.S. bombing campaign against Taliban forces here in the north to open the way for a Northern Alliance attack. My arguments had so far convinced the CIA's leadership and others within the NSC community of the correctness of this strategy, and eventually I hoped that the rest of that leadership circle would come to realize the wisdom in focusing the fight in the north. However, a battle between senior NA commanders over such issues as who hosts a CIA team and who gets a few weapons and some ammunition will be seen as proof that the Northern Alliance should be restrained and cannot be trusted to lead the fight against the Taliban.

Aref got the point. He said he was sorry that Dr. Abdullah would not be able to visit the United States, and he would personally inform Abdullah of the decision later that day. Aref assured me that he would ask General Fahim to contact Dostum as well as Atta to talk sense to both men. The meeting concluded with Aref confirming that he would coordinate with Mumtaz to move the A-Team down south to Baghram. Aref thought everything would be in place by late afternoon.

I got on the radio and raised the ALPHA Team. R.J. had just returned from a meeting with General Dostum, and he confirmed that Commander Atta was indeed threatening to attack Dostum's forces should supplies and weapons be air-dropped to Dostum. R.J. said the situation looked serious, and he asked what had happened with the NA at my end in the valley. I explained that we had requested General Fahim to intervene, and that he contact both commanders to force them to back off this potential confrontation. I asked about R.J.'s plans should Atta attack. He said that Dostum had assured him he would provide enough men to protect ALPHA in the event of an attack. R.J. said he felt the best course was to accept that assurance of protection and simply get on with the business at hand. If Atta attacked, ALPHA would deal with the situation as it developed. I asked about canceling the scheduled airdrop set for the evening hours, but R.J. thought it should proceed. Dostum's forces needed resupply; the drop tonight was essential to establish the CIA's commitment to support the NA in the northern areas outside the Panjshir.

The early afternoon was spent writing cables on the results of the meeting with Aref and the situation between Dostum and Atta. I advised Washington that I thought it would be prudent to hold off on making the airdrop to Dostum until the situation could be defused. The weapons were important but not absolutely critical to Dostum; and, with the expectation that General Fahim would intervene, delay in making the airdrop for a day or two seemed a good way to avoid unnecessarily adding fuel to the fire.

Mumtaz came by at 3:00 p.m. to say that all coordination had been completed with General Bismullah, and arrangements were being made to have transportation available at the A-Team's safe house at 6:00 p.m. to begin loading their equipment. I voiced concern about the team's safety driving that twisty, bumpy, dangerous road in the dark. Mumtaz assured me that his drivers had driven the road at night many times. They knew the road so well that they could drive it with their eyes closed. That, I said, was exactly what I was worried about. Mumtaz did not get the joke.

We gave Stan and Murray one of the Russian jeeps for their use in driving down with the Triple Nickel, so they would have their own transportation once at Baghram. A little before 6:00 p.m. we helped them load their gear into the jeep, then Rick and I walked over to the A-Team safe house to see them off. As scheduled, Mumtaz was there with a number of Hi-Lux pickup trucks and three SUVs, and his men were struggling with the huge, heavy bags of gear that each soldier had brought with him.

That morning we had helped sort and stack their gear for tonight's move and I had tried to pick up one of the canvas kit bags. I think I got it about an inch off the ground and gave up. It must have weighed almost two hundred pounds. The young Afghans loading the trucks were straining to move these same bags, resorting to three men to a bag. At one point, one of the Special Forces soldiers walked over to two young Afghans trying to lift a bag. He casually grabbed the bag with one hand, lifted it up, and swung it around onto his back with one easy movement. He shrugged twice to shift the bag farther up, then walked toward the waiting trucks. The two young Afghans—and I—stood with our mouths open looking at the soldier, who betrayed no strain as he moved.

I got on the secure phone and called Hank back at the CTC. He too was concerned about the situation developing around ALPHA Team, but R.J. strongly recommended that the airdrop take place that evening as scheduled. R.J. told Hank that Dostum had several of his senior commanders meeting with Atta and Dostum felt confident that the crisis would be resolved. Hank said that because R.J. was the senior officer on the scene, he would give him the support he needed to get the job done. The airdrop would take place. I did not feel comfortable with that decision, but what would be would be. I just hoped that ALPHA did not get caught in the middle of a firefight. Little did I know that we would come closer than ALPHA Team to being involved in a firefight that night.

A little after ten that evening, just as I was finishing up in the office area and getting ready to head off to bed, there was a sudden burst of automatic weapons fire south of us, past the village. The firing continued, with sporadic short bursts of what was now clearly AK-47 fire. Doc came out of his room down the hall and said he would open the weapons crate and stand by. I headed for the roof with my night vision goggles and was quickly joined by several other team members.

The night was clear and cold, and once we were on the roof the sound of the weapons was loud and sharp. Even without the NVGs, we could see muzzle flashes on the hillside behind the village. Through the greenish hue of the

NVGs, we could make out several men moving along a hill-side trail, firing down at figures moving up toward them through the line of trees at the lower edge of the hills. There were muzzle flashes from the other figures who appeared to be returning fire up the hill.

Chris joined us to say that Mumtaz had stopped by, excited and out of breath, and told him not to be concerned; it was "just a wedding celebration taking place." We turned to look at the hillside some four hundred yards away, muzzle flashes and noise rolling toward us. "Wedding celebration, my ass," I said. "Everybody draw a weapon. Let's get ready for visitors."

We headed downstairs, and Rick and I stood in the hall-way as each member of the team took an AK-47 and one bandolier of four thirty-round magazines out of the crate. Rick said, "Let's have a couple of guys get on the roof of the lower building, so they can watch down toward the river and the lower end of the village. We can man the roof here, and we can put one man on the roof of the kitchen. He can cover the front gate and the approach from the trail down from the hills from that direction." It was a good plan, and we hustled everyone to get into position.

The firing had slowed for a bit, but by the time we got back to the roof, the firing increased. Muzzle flashes lit up the hill-side about two hundred fifty yards away, but no rounds seemed to be directed toward us. We hunkered down behind the raised parapet of the roof, watching and waiting.

Taliban sympathizers were here in the valley, as Mumtaz admitted days ago. Maybe the arrival of the Triple Nickel last night stirred them up. Then there was another short, sharp exchange of gunfire on the hillside. I knew one thing—that was no wedding celebration.

We sat there for another five minutes, and the firing began to slow and shift away from us. The figures on the hillside appeared to be moving farther up, drifting away from their contact with the figures lower down the hill. Eventually we lost sight of the figures as they moved back into an area of larger rocks. Then the firing stopped. Another five minutes passed without any further shooting, and I thought I could see some movement on the lower part of the hillside.

I heard Mumtaz's voice at the front gate, then Ed's voice from the kitchen roof. There was some noise before the metal gate swung open; then I could hear Mumtaz talking. I headed off the roof and met him in the doorway to our building. "Oh, General Gary, everything is fine now. You can relax." He was nervous but trying to hide it with a big grin.

"What was all the shooting about? What happened out there?" I asked.

Mumtaz was fidgeting nervously, trying—unsuccessfully—to appear relaxed. "Oh, it turned out to be that several prisoners escaped from the jail in town. Our men chased them down. It's all over. No problem."

"Escaped prisoners, huh? Taliban prisoners?"

"No, not Taliban. Criminals. Robbers."

I nodded yes and said nothing else about the incident. There was little sense in pushing him for the truth. I was about to say good night when he said, "Oh, I forgot. General Bismullah called from Baghram. The A-Team and Stan and Murray arrived safely about fifteen minutes ago." I thanked Mumtaz for the news, then helped the others put the weapons back in the crate.

CHAPTER THIRTY-TWO

Over coffee the next morning, I scanned the incoming cable traffic that had arrived overnight. There was a brief cable from ALPHA saying that the airdrop of weapons and ammunition had taken place the previous evening as scheduled.

The cable did not contain any word on what Atta's reaction to the supply drop had been. Rick got on the secure radio and called ALPHA. The communications officer confirmed that the drop had gone well and all the bundles were recovered. Things were quiet there, and R.J. and the rest of ALPHA were off meeting Dostum. Rick requested that R.J. call us as soon as he had time. That there had been no immediate reaction from Atta was encouraging; our worry was what might happen later in the day.

There was an interesting cable from the CTC discussing the situation between Dostum and Atta. The cable made the point that one answer to the problem was to deploy a separate CIA team to join Atta. His combat forces were about as large as Dostum's, and once combat operations got under way around Mazar-e Sharif, having a team with both of the major NA commanders made sense. The CTC suggested that ALPHA Team split, with half of the team relocating to join Atta. This would be a short-term fix, because both groups would be understaffed, but the CTC would work to augment them with replacement personnel on a priority basis. It made sense to us sitting around the table in the workroom; it would be interesting to see what ALPHA thought of the idea.

The final cable from Headquarters stated that CENTCOM wanted to deploy a second A-Team to the Panjshir Valley. CENTCOM and Task Force Dagger were already coordinating the logistical arrangements. In addition, there was discussion of deploying an ODA/CCE Team (Command and Control Element) to the Panjshir, to coordinate the activities of the soon-to-be-two ODAs on the ground here.

Rick explained that a Special Forces A-Team was traditionally commanded by a captain or a senior warrant officer. With a number of ODAs deployed, there would be competing requests by the various A-Teams to bring in air assets to strike their targets. Because the individual ODA commanders were relatively low on the military food chain, this would make prioritization of resources difficult. However, a Special Forces ODA/CCE was commanded by a lieutenant colonel, and his rank allowed him to coordinate competing requests for air support and prioritize allocation of air assets.

I was enthusiastic. We would suggest that the second ODA be sent to Khoja Bahauddin to work with General Bariullah Khan on the Takhar front, the ODA/CCE stay with us here in Barak in the safe house just vacated by ODA-555. Rick said he would call Task Force Dagger to see where the planning stood for this additional deployment.

At 7:10 a.m., Mumtaz arrived with a message from Engineer Aref that he needed to discuss something with us. We moved across to the meeting room in the other building, taking our coffee with us. Mumtaz was nervous, and it was obvious before he started to relay Aref's message that it was going to be bad news. He said that the Northern Alliance leadership group had met last night to discuss the situation between Dostum and Atta. Mumtaz sheepishly told me that their conclusion was that the CIA must withdraw the ALPHA Team from General Dostum. General Fahim and the NA leadership felt that the CIA's decision to have a team join Dostum was a serious mistake.

This was not quite the response I had been hoping for. I knew there was no way that the CIA would allow the Northern Alliance leadership to dictate where and with whom we deployed our field teams. ALPHA was on the ground to stay, and at least three additional teams were being organized for deployment within the next two weeks. I explained to Mumtaz that we realized that the NA leadership here in the valley was unhappy with the independent deployment of CIA teams to NA commanders in the west. However, our strategy was to place CIA and U.S. Special Forces teams with effective commanders around the country, to better carry the fight to the Taliban. There was no intention in this strategy to undermine the authority of the Northern Alliance leadership. We recognized Commander Atta's concerns that the CIA connection with Dostum would work to isolate Atta, but that would not necessarily be the case. We were already discussing plans to assign CIA personnel to join Atta, probably within the next day or two. I asked Mumtaz to relay that information to Engineer Aref. I could tell he was not happy with my response, but he agreed to meet with Aref as soon as possible to pass on what I had said.

Mumtaz was back at 8:00 a.m.—Aref was obviously working somewhere close by—and he looked even gloomier than he had during his earlier visit. Engineer Aref had listened carefully to what I had to say about the Dostum/Atta situation, but the NA decision would not be changed. ALPHA Team must be withdrawn from Dostum.

I sat back in my chair, shook my head slightly, and said politely, "Mumtaz, the highest levels of the U.S. government have decided that the CIA will deploy teams with effective commanders standing in opposition to the Taliban regardless of ethnic, tribal, or religious background. We chose to send our second team to Dostum for security and administrative reasons, and because he is an effective commander. We will send a team to Commander Atta as soon as we can make the arrangements. We will not withdraw ALPHA from Dostum. Please tell Engineer Aref that this is the decision of the U.S. government. I will be happy to discuss this issue with Engineer Aref, or any of the other Northern Alliance leaders, as they want." I smiled at Mumtaz, shook his hand, and patted him on the back as I walked him toward the front gate. He was only the messenger, and he looked so hangdog that I felt sorry for him.

I must admit that I felt down myself. This was not going well. We needed some good news about the situation with Dostum and Atta, something that would defuse the tension and make Atta more willing to cooperate. Chris was smiling as Rick and I returned to the office area, and he had a cable from ALPHA in his hand. It was the good news we needed.

R.J. had written that Dostum had met with Atta's representatives the previous night, with R.J. and several ALPHA Team members in the room. Dostum told the group he realized that it was unfair that he receive all the support from the CIA team, because the Americans were in Afghanistan to help the Northern Alliance defeat the Taliban. The Ameri-

cans wanted this to be a joint effort, so the supplies that
were to come that evening would be shared equally with
Commander Atta. Dostum continued, saying that Atta's representatives, all respected commanders, were welcome to
accompany his men to the drop zone and observe the operation. The materiel would be returned to Dostum's camp,
where it would be divided equally. Commander Atta could
arrange to collect his share of the supplies when he was
ready. Dostum said that all future CIA supply drops to his
forces would be shared equally with Commander Atta.

R.J. said that everyone at the meeting was surprised at
Dostum's magnanimous gesture. It was so out of character
and such an unexpected decision on Dostum's part that it left
Atta's commanders with nothing to say but thank you.
ALPHA had visited Dostum's headquarters that morning to
witness the transfer of half the weapons and ammunition to
Atta's commanders, who hauled off their share in a convoy
of Hi-Lux pickup trucks. R.J. said that he fully supported the
idea of splitting ALPHA. He had already raised the issue
with Dostum that morning, and Dostum was also supportive
of the move. A meeting was set for later that afternoon at
which R.J. would present the idea to Atta.

This was incredible news. I knew that General Dostum
was an intelligent field commander, but my impression had
always been that he was more a man of action than a wily political manipulator. His move to equally share the CIA supplies with Atta was brilliant. His agreement to let ALPHA
split and send a small CIA team to Atta was equally far-
sighted. Dostum now had the high ground, leaving Atta little
choice but to agree to cooperate with Dostum or risk being
seen as a petty spoilsport more interested in his own prestige
and pride than in defeating the Taliban. If Commander Atta
did agree to cooperate with Dostum, this would pull the rug
out from under General Fahim. With Dostum and Atta cooperating and sharing supplies equally, there was no reason for
ALPHA to be withdrawn. If this worked out as I thought, I
would owe a "tip of the turban" to General Dostum.

Engineer Aref arrived at the compound at about half past

three that afternoon, and we sat down for what would be a ninety-minute meeting to thrash out this issue. In the end, Dostum's brilliant move in sharing everything with Commander Atta defused all the arguments Aref put forward. The two senior NA commanders in the Mazar-e Sharif area had worked out an accommodation, and they were cooperating to accomplish the mission—the defeat of the Taliban forces they faced. The situation was out of the hands of the NA leadership in the Panjshir Valley. ALPHA Team would split, with the portion joining Atta becoming BRAVO Team. We would reinforce both teams as soon as possible, and we would be pressing for Special Forces ODA Teams to deploy with both commanders. I made it clear that the CIA's decision to insert a team with as many effective commanders as possible across northern Afghanistan was not negotiable. There was little that Engineer Aref and the rest of the NA leadership in the valley could do but accept the inevitable.

CHAPTER THIRTY-THREE

The morning of 22 October dawned clear and cold, and we busied ourselves with our morning routine of several large cups of Starbucks coffee, a warm "shower" out of a bucket of murky water, and for me, a light breakfast of fresh local bread and peanut butter. Ed and Greg had planned a supply run to Dushanbe, and the weather report from the mountains was good—blue skies and low winds. They made quick preparations for an early launch; their flight schedule included a stop at Faizabad, just across the Hindu Kush Mountains, then a stop at Khoja Bahauddin, before returning that afternoon. They would drop off Brad, then link up with General Bariullah Khan. The helicopter would return for Brad the following day.

The stop in Faizabad was to conduct a survey of a potential L-100 landing field that had been suggested by Engineer Aref. The CTC was exploring all options for moving materiel into northern Afghanistan, and the idea of being able to use the L-100 to move cargo to a halfway point in the north sounded intriguing. Aref said the Northern Alliance used the Faizabad field for fixed-wing aircraft, and he thought it would support an L-100. The pilots were not enthusiastic; Faizabad was on the far side of the Hindu Kush Mountains, and that would place the burden of moving the cargo over the treacherous mountains on our helicopter. The odds were high that any goods delivered to Faizabad would be stuck there until spring, when the weather cleared and it was safe enough for the helicopter to fly, but we would conduct the survey as asked.

Mumtaz dropped by the office area to tell us that Engineer Aref wanted to meet that afternoon. Reading Mumtaz's demeanor—relaxed and smiling—I hoped the upcoming meeting would be much more positive than the back-and-forth negative exchanges we had the previous day.

Rick took a call from Colonel Mulholland at Task Force Dagger, and they discussed plans for the possible insertion of a second A-Team and the ODA/CCE Team. At that point, the plan was to bring both teams to the Panjshir Valley, then, on the following day, move the new A-Team back north to link up with General Bariullah Khan and work the Takhar front. We did not have a landing zone identified in the Khoja Bahauddin area for use in a night insertion, so it made sense to take the extra step of having the A-Team come all the way into the valley, then move back to the north in daylight on our helicopter. Mulholland said he would like to make the insertion this evening, because the weather report looked good.

Engineer Aref arrived at 3:00 p.m. and was upbeat. General Dostum's decision to share the weapons and ammunition with Commander Atta had defused the situation in the Mazar-e Sharif area. Aref said that General Fahim was happy with Dostum's move and had spoken directly with Atta to encourage full cooperation. The CIA plan to put part of ALPHA Team with Atta was equally well received. I knew that the issue of our dealing directly with commanders outside the Panjshir Valley would haunt us in the future, but for now the waters were calm.

Rick reviewed his conversation with Colonel Mulholland earlier that morning. He explained our desire to bring in two additional ODA Teams—one to link up with General Bariullah on the Takhar front, and the other to join us here in Barak to coordinate the efforts of the ODA Teams on the front lines. Rick discussed in some detail the ODA/CCE's duties and how their presence would add weight to their requests for strike aircraft over the Kabul and Takhar fronts. Aref gave his approval for the insertion, saying it would be a welcome addition to the effort. He added with a slight smile that he hoped the ODA/CCE Team would be able to get more bombs dropped on the Taliban, especially along the Kabul front.

We talked about progress, and the lack thereof, in the efforts to pull together information on the Shelter Now hostages. The father of the Afghan prisoner had not yet returned to the valley with answers to the questions that Chris had assigned him. Aref did say that the NA officer who was in touch with the senior official in the Taliban intelligence and security organization had gone to Kabul to confirm our agreement with his reward demands and to gauge his sincerity in proceeding, but his return appeared to have been delayed.

I asked Aref if he could arrange for me to meet with General Bismullah. I had not yet met him, and I wanted to get to know him personally. Aref said that the general had asked just two days earlier when I would visit. Aref promised to call the general as soon as he returned to his office and request a meeting for the following day. He said he would call Mumtaz with confirmation, but I should plan on making the trip down the valley to the Kabul front the following day. Before departing, Aref asked to be informed immediately when the decision was finalized to insert the two Special Forces teams.

Just after Aref departed, our aircraft arrived bringing two

surprises. The pilots and Buck drove up from the landing zone with great fanfare, and cartons containing a small microwave oven and refrigerator were lugged out of the back of their SUV. A group of team members followed the two cardboard boxes into the building in a state of disbelief. Buck immediately began to unpack the refrigerator while George returned from the SUV carrying two cases of Russian Baltika beer in half-liter bottles. Ed, standing next to me, said, "Chief, we didn't check with you first on the beer. If you don't want it here, just say so."

I looked at the faces of the team members standing around and said loud enough for all to hear, "As long as it's indulged in moderation, and we respect our hosts' sensibilities—no drinking in front of them, and no empty bottles lying around—then fine." There were smiles from everyone.

When Rick and I talked later on the patio, I said I would object to the beer only if someone abused the privilege or made it an issue with our Afghan hosts. I had made a pact with myself not to drink while in Afghanistan. I took seriously the responsibility of leading this team, and I wanted to be alert and clearheaded at all times. I had not expected to be tempted, but now, faced with the temptation, I would stick by my pact. My continued health problems and use of Cipro made that pledge much easier to keep.

The last piece of real news of the day came at about six that evening, when Colonel Mulholland's staff called to say that the insertion of the two additional ODA Teams would be delayed; the weather was turning bad at the higher altitudes over the mountains. Mulholland said they would see what the morning brought.

CHAPTER THIRTY-FOUR

The following morning, 23 October, was even nicer than the previous day, with slightly warmer temperatures, blue skies, and high, puffy cumulus clouds drifting by slowly. Although the weather had been bad over the mountains the previous night, it had remained good over the valley. Colonel Mulholland might get lucky tonight.

Just before 10:00 a.m. I left for the Kabul front. Mumtaz was accompanying me and sat in the front passenger seat; I took my usual spot in the middle of the backseat. We were using one of our Russian jeeps, and I had the small wing windows in the rear open for ventilation. There was no air-conditioning, and only a faint waft of warm, dusty air managed to get through the small openings. The driver popped a cassette tape into the dash, and we were entertained by the scratchy sound of what I was sure was an Iranian female singer belting out in Farsi the latest hits from Tehran. There had been no music performed—let alone recorded—in Afghanistan since 1994, so she had to be Iranian. I made myself comfortable, extending my legs toward the sides of the vehicle, with both arms back on the top of the seat to brace myself, trying to ride with the bumps.

I was looking forward to this visit. I needed to meet General Bismullah, because he was the most important player in what would be the decisive battle of the war, and he was the host of the ODA and my men. I knew from Stan that the level of bombing had not significantly improved with the Triple Nickel's arrival, despite their ability to laser-designate prime targets. I wanted to hear from them why they couldn't increase the number of air strikes on the enemy. The problem certainly was not a lack of high-value targets. I also wanted to get General Bismullah's views on this situation. This would be excellent ammunition for me to use in pressing Washington and CENTCOM to readdress the bombing strategy.

Something had to give. I had told Engineer Aref that the bombing would increase once the ODA Team was in place. Now they were on the front lines, working day and night, and the pace of bombing had not changed significantly. The daily target deck for planned CENTCOM air strikes still focused on Taliban "targets" deep in the rear areas, with supply and warehouse facilities being high on the list.

Every drive down the valley was a bone-rattling experience. The Russian jeep is a basic piece of machinery, with strong parts built to take a lot of punishment. Soviet-era jeeps built in the early 1930s still give excellent service on Afghanistan roads. Creature comforts, however, were not within the design parameters. The suspension system is stiff, and there is no give when hitting bumps. From my position in the backseat, I could not see well enough to anticipate upcoming potholes or protruding rocks, so I usually got the full impact of these obstacles as we collided with them. The occasional spectacular vistas off to my left, out over the river, hardly compensated for the beating I took to see them. It was with great pleasure that I recognized the narrowing of the valley into the final gorge before exiting onto the Shomali Plains.

We enjoyed the novelty of a stretch of paved road before turning into the main gate of Bismullah's compound. The general was waiting for us at the front entry into his headquarters at the top of a hill. After tea was served and the room quieted, Bismullah slid forward to the edge of his chair, elbows on his knees, and began to review the military situation just outside his window.

"Mr. Gary, we are grateful for the assistance you have provided to the Northern Alliance forces. I have made good use of the funds you gave General Fahim, and I thank you for the ammunition and weapons you have dropped to our command-

ers at Mazar. We are especially grateful for your A-Team soldiers, and for Murray and Stan." He paused, smiled, and continued. "But, to be frank, there has been little impact from
your bombing around Kabul, even with the arrival of the A-
Team."

He rose from his chair and walked to the large open window. "Look out there, Mr. Gary. Hundreds of Taliban positions, dozens of Arab fighting positions, all easily seen,
easily identified. Yet your aircraft come in ones and twos,
some with only one bomb left from earlier strikes to the
south. The Taliban laugh each morning as they survey their
lines. Once again, no damage!"

I said nothing, waiting—wanting—to hear his comments.
"I have a well-trained force behind these lines, more back in
the Panjshir. We are fairly well equipped. The men are strong
and well trained, and they are anxious to attack. But, in all
honesty, I am not strong enough to push down off these
heights and break through to Kabul. Not without help from
your air force. Break the Taliban lines as you promised, and
I will be in Kabul in two or three days!" He leaned back in
his chair, and a wave of weariness seemed to roll over him.
"There are reasons for the delay, I know. Political debate in
Washington. Questions. Fears. But the delay is causing frustration among my soldiers. Winter is coming, and soon these
heights will have snow. We do not want to face another cold
winter hiding in these holes."

He gathered himself, strength seeming to come back into
him. "And so I tell you, Mr. Gary, that even if the bombing
does not improve, I will attack Kabul before the snows of
winter come. The attack will not succeed, I fear, but we will
try with all our resources and all our strength."

I thanked him for his candor and honesty. "I will speak
equally frankly," I said. "You are correct—the bombing here
is not what I told General Fahim it would be. The debate over
the future of Kabul, which really rests outside this window between you and your enemy, is being debated in Washington
as we speak. I think the situation is clear—defeat the
Taliban forces here and to the west around Konduz and Mazar,

and trap the Taliban fighters in the north and destroy them. That opens the door for an eventual victory in the Pashtun south. I believe that soon those in Washington who debate the issue will come to see the truth. I came here today to hear your views and see the situation for myself, firsthand. I will fight the issue with Washington with the ammunition I gather here today."

Bismullah stood, smiling. "Good. That is all I can ask. Come, let's get started then." He rose, and Mumtaz and I followed him toward the door.

We were riding in a Toyota SUV, its dark blue paint covered in a mantle of heavy gray-brown dust. The driver was a young soldier—dressed sharply in new green khakis—who was obviously enjoying his role driving the general and the American guest around the battlefield. Bismullah was in the front passenger seat working his handheld radio. He had it in his right hand, which he kept just outside the vehicle—for better reception, I guessed.

As we had left his compound and drove west along the main road out of Jabal-os-Saraj heading toward Charikar, the general had explained that we would travel without escort, just one vehicle. "The Taliban occupy that mountain ridge ahead of us," he said, pointing toward a jagged ridgeline running north to south rising perhaps two thousand feet above the plains. "They have heavy artillery up there, and since the bombing began they are quick to shoot at any attractive target. One vehicle, traveling alone and fast, it is not so attractive. Also, they sometimes take out their frustration at missing a target by shelling a village or some other civilian targets."

The general commented on what we were seeing. The small groups of houses set back from both sides of the road were heavy with dust, and the trees were drooped, wilted, and dry. "Three straight years of drought," Bismullah said, shaking his head. "The people suffer. The crops are stunted, the animals die of thirst, and the wells are long dry. Sometimes I think even God has forgotten Afghanistan."

I had driven over this stretch of road in September 1996, with my friend Masood Khalili as my host. Then the countryside had been lush and green, with the fall harvest in full swing. Cornfields had shimmered, and great piles of melons lined the roadside. Even with the war's stark destruction, the abundance of the harvest and the natural beauty of the fields had held hope and promise. This scene—now parched fields and stunted crops wilting in the sun—was depressing. But as bad as this was, it was about to get worse.

We were heading south now, on what was called the "old road" to Kabul. In the early 1980s, the lush fields, numerous villages, and rolling terrain along the road had made it an ideal ambush area from which the Mujahedin could strike Soviet military traffic moving to and from their major base at Baghram. Cutting the trees, denuding the fields, and destroying buildings along the road had failed to stop the attacks. The Soviets then built a new road some miles to the east. It paralleled the old road but cut through barren, rocky terrain—much easier to defend against Mujahedin attacks. But the damage done to this area remained stark and ugly.

The land sloped slightly downward as we drove south, and the city of Charikar soon spread below and before us. We heard a sudden faint sound over the noise of the engine, a rushing, whirling noise that I knew was an artillery round streaking through the sky. At that instant, a blossom of flame and earth erupted from within the city, debris arcing away from the dirty black cloud. General Bismullah was on the radio, trying to raise someone, and was slapping the driver on the shoulder gesturing for him to speed up. Two more explosions, almost simultaneous, erupted near where the first round had hit.

The general finished speaking into the radio and twisted around toward me. "The bastards are shelling the city. That is the market area they are targeting, and they know they will catch many women and children there." He called the enemy something in Dari I did not understand, then said, "We will continue into the city. I must organize assistance. You understand."

"Yes, yes," I said, nodding, "let's try to help." I glanced at Mumtaz, and he looked as tense as I felt.

The vehicle was moving very fast now, and the thought

jumped through my mind that the driver was likely to lose control. He was tight-jawed and gripping the wheel with white knuckles. There were at least three more explosions ahead of us, but we were close to the edge of the city and our view was now restricted. We slowed as we entered the city proper, and Bismullah directed the driver, guiding him toward the impact area.

Ahead of us we could see smoke billowing upward—probably a fire. We stopped about half a block away from where a crowd was gathering, and the general was out of the car and running toward the scene before I could get out of the backseat. Ahead was a small, open square with wood-sided stalls in ragged lines on either side. It was now a killing field, with a fire blazing from a building just behind the stalls opposite us. Debris of all kinds littered the street, and fallen bodies were strewn helter-skelter—twisted forms in dirty, dark-stained fabric. People were running to reach friends and family members, and we heard voices rising in pain and anger.

The general was on his radio and standing almost unnoticed in the chaos. I stood behind him, trying to take in the scene. I stepped on something and looked down to find that I was standing on a severed human hand, which was resting palm upward, fingers curled in a natural arc. My stomach rolled, and I took a breath and moved my foot carefully off the hand, as if I might be injuring it.

The general waved at a small group of soldiers and walked toward them, shouting orders, pointing to the injured. As they moved into action, he turned to me. "Come, Mr. Gary, the villagers know how to care for the wounded. We can do little here. But I must get you away from here. The Taliban may fire another round or two in hopes of killing those who have gathered to help." As if signaled by his words, there was a thunderous explosion about three hundred feet from us, hitting the buildings to the west of the square. The concussion was tremendous and actually knocked me off my feet. I found myself on my butt, sitting next to the severed hand. The general gripped my upper arm and helped me to my feet. "See," he said, "they are indeed devils. Let's go on."

* * *

We drove out of Charikar and raced a mile or so to the south of the city. The general motioned the driver to turn left off the highway onto a dirt road that twisted toward a line of trees ahead of us. At the tree line, we turned down into what I thought was a sunken roadway, shaded on both sides by trees. The temperature seemed to drop, and the roadway was fairly smooth. I wondered out loud to the general as to who had constructed such a clever road.

"It is not a road. It is an old irrigation canal. It has been dry for two years now, and we use it to conceal our dust and keep out of sight of those damned Talibs on the mountain." I was doubly grateful for the shade of the trees as we drove along.

The general explained that we were taking a back way into Baghram Air Base. He laughed and explained that after more than twenty years of fighting here on the Shomali Plains, he knew every inch of the terrain. We would stop at a frontline bunker to get a firsthand look at the Taliban positions in that area, then visit the A-Team, and Murray and Stan, who were working out of the control tower on the base.

We exited the old canal and headed south, moving slowly now, staying on the narrow dirt road that twisted around destroyed Soviet military buildings. "A Soviet tank repair facility," the general said as we reached a desolate group of large buildings with broad, open work bays facing the road. We moved through the ghost town slowly, finally stopping in the shade behind the last building. As we exited the vehicle, I could see a line of low bunkers stretching from our left, running parallel to the road. A few soldiers were grouped at the rear of a bunker about twenty yards from where we stood.

"These are my forces and those bunkers are our front line," the general said. "The Taliban are less than three hundred yards away, in a line of bunkers facing these. We will be careful here." With that we moved into the open and walked casually toward the bunkers. There was a round of handshaking with the soldiers who were waiting for the general, then the general pointed to a sunken stairway at the corner of the bunker. He motioned for me to follow one of the officers down the stairs. "Now you will see the enemy up close."

The only light inside was from the doorway behind me and the two long, narrow gun ports cut into the front of the bunker. Keeping one of the windows directly in front of me provided a silhouette of the logs used to prop up the heavy roof, so I could avoid running into them. The general stepped next to me, bending slightly to peer out the opening toward the enemy lines. I bent with him and could see what looked like a weed-covered dirt berm about three hundred yards away. "Those lumps you see are Taliban bunkers. The weeds hide the shape a little. But look closely to your left, by that small tree. There is a Talib watching us with binoculars." With the general's directions, I could see a figure crouching next to the small tree. Then there was a flashing to the right, and as my eyes swung that way I could hear a machine gun firing.

"Ah, I'm afraid they are nervous today. They are firing at us." Heavy rounds were impacting to our right. There was a pause, then a second machine gun joined the first. This time bullets were hitting our bunker. "Come, Mr. Gary, it is time for us to move on. Stay next to the wall as you head toward the door." We paused in the shadows until there was a lull in the firing, then hurried up the dirt stairs into the sunlight. The bunker walls were high enough to give us cover. The firing quickly died down, then stopped. As we stood chatting in the sun for a couple of minutes, the general explained the situation in this sector. The two sides usually avoided shooting at each other, because neither was anxious to take casualties needlessly. "They were probably nervous because of the shelling of Charikar. They might think we are up to something." When things seemed calm enough, we moved back to the vehicle, then headed out to visit the control tower.

We drove east, winding through the ruins of the huge Soviet air base. Destroyed aircraft were scattered here and there, left where they had crashed. Even a number of two-winged Soviet aircraft of some type, like something out of a World War I movie, stood smashed and mangled but aligned in a neat, straight formation. As we turned onto what was ob-

viously a main runway, the driver accelerated quickly, pushing the vehicle faster and faster. The general turned toward
us. "The Taliban hold that village off to our left. They can hit
the runway with machine-gun fire. They are dug in very well
there, and it would cost too many lives to root them out. So
we drive fast here."

The control tower was a surprise. I had expected a huge,
tall structure; in reality, it was a two-story building with an
observation room on top. We parked next to it and were
greeted by a gaggle of Afghan officers, all anxious to shake
the general's hand. The building's walls were pockmarked
with bullet and shrapnel scars. A narrow concrete stairway
led up to the control room. Stan and Murray were there, sitting at a small table working on a map. Scattered around in
front of the windows on the east and south side of the room
were about six of the Triple Nickel team. Several telescopes,
substantially larger that the normal spotting scope used by
hunters, as well as radio equipment, maps, two or three types
of binoculars, and other gear were spread around the room.
All the men were intent on the scene outside. I noted that the
roof above the stairwell we used to enter had been cratered
open by a mortar round, and mangled pieces of concrete
pieces hung from rusting iron rebar. There was no glass in
any of the windows, and the inside walls and ceiling of the
control room were bullet-scarred. It seemed a very exposed
location in which to work.

General Bismullah greeted Murray and Stan, then shook
hands with several members of the A-Team before excusing
himself and returning to join his officers below. Stan and
Murray were effusive in their praise for the work being done
by the A-Team, and they introduced me to the NCO (non-
commissioned officer) in charge. He was candid in his assessment of the situation: the frontline area they were facing
was incredibly target-rich. He took me to the window and
pointed out a Taliban position about a mile away that could
easily be seen without binoculars. He said that the team's
calls for aircraft often went unheeded, because the aircraft
sorties were scheduled for other areas of the country. It was

only when an aircraft had struck its assigned targets and had ordnance left that it would be released to respond to a call from the Triple Nickel. They were getting aircraft in ones and twos, and usually with smaller ordnance, not the 2,000-pound bunker busters they wanted. The team worked farther forward during the hours of darkness, actually on the front line near the most forward Taliban positions. They were putting themselves in harm's way on a regular basis; they had been fired on each night by the nervous Taliban troops facing them. He was obviously frustrated but tried to be upbeat. He agreed that the CCE Team—once it arrived—should be able to improve the responsiveness to the Triple Nickel's calls for bomb strikes.

I talked separately to Stan about the situation, and he confirmed everything that ODA's NCO had told me. The lack of results on the battlefield was beginning to wear on our Afghan hosts, and the colonel in charge of this sector had made disparaging remarks about the lack of American commitment to the Northern Alliance. Stan added that the team's living conditions had improved over the past two days; they had been moved out of their original quarters—a run-down two-room mud-walled house with no toilet facilities—to a more comfortable compound. But they needed more bottled water, because even the water purification tablets did little to make the local water palatable. I promised to have a supply run made the next morning, and asked Stan to coordinate with the ODA Team for a full list of supplies.

It was time to go, and I said good-bye somewhat reluctantly. Here was where the action was, where the fight was being brought to the enemy. American soldiers and CIA officers were risking their lives. It made me proud and a little envious. But above all, the lack of support they were receiving for all their efforts made me angry.

The policy makers in Washington dithered on and on about whether or not the Northern Alliance should take Kabul. That was not the question to ask. I thought the pertinent question was, Do we want to defeat the Taliban quickly? If the answer was yes, then the way to achieve that goal was to bomb the Taliban front lines in the north, then turn loose the Northern Alliance. Given the complete lack of any organized resistance to the Taliban within the Pashtun south, the reality was that, sooner or later, Kabul would fall to the Northern Alliance forces. In the meantime, Americans were at risk on the front lines, calling for bombing that did not come.

At 6:00 p.m. we arrived back at our compound dusty, tired, and stiff, and I thanked Mumtaz for arranging the trip. In some ways it had been frustrating, but overall it had been useful. Rick greeted me with news that the insertion of the two additional ODA Teams was set for that night. Colonel Mulholland had called that morning, just after my departure, to suggest that the two ODA Teams be inserted at Khoja Bahauddin rather than trying to make it over the mountains. The forecast was for bad weather at the higher altitudes across the Hindu Kush. The weather pattern for the past several days had been for good weather during the day, with conditions deteriorating after dark. We could insert the teams tonight in Khoja Bahauddin, then fly the CCE Team down to the valley the following day when the weather was better. Brad was in place with General Bariullah at Khoja Bahauddin to receive the ODA Teams. The team's helicopters would use the same landing area that Ed and Greg used when they flew into there.

Rick had called Brad to have him get approval from General Bismullah for this change in plan, and to arrange for Bismullah to be ready to receive the teams this evening. There were a lot of moving parts, but Rick said they had all come together. Bismullah immediately contacted General Fahim, who, it turned out, was visiting the Takhar front. Fahim had endorsed the new plan. Ed and Greg had coordinated by secure phone with Colonel Mulholland's pilots, providing them with the geocoordinates and other pertinent information about the landing area. They also provided the light markings that Bismullah would use to identify the landing zone. Rick had called Colonel Mulholland, and everyone was satisfied with the plans.

CHAPTER THIRTY-FIVE

At 8:20 p.m. we got the call from Task Force Dagger that the helicopters carrying the two ODA Teams were airborne, and the expected touchdown at Khoja Bahauddin was around half past ten. We had Mumtaz standing by to pass that information on to Engineer Aref, who would then contact General Bariullah. Rick contacted Brad by radio and passed the message. Brad said that General Bariullah and his men were standing by. We settled in to wait.

At 9:20 p.m., Mumtaz returned to our office area in an obvious panic. General Fahim, who had joined Bariullah at the landing zone, did not approve of the location of the site for the A-Teams' reception. It was too public, too exposed. Fahim demanded that the insertion be postponed and the helicopters return to Uzbekistan. I could not believe what I was hearing. The landing zone was too public? Too exposed? We had been using it for our helicopter for days, and no one raised the issue.

I tried not to get angry with Mumtaz; he was only the messenger. I told him it was impossible to change plans this late in the mission. More than thirty American soldiers were in the air, at risk, and it would be a terrible mistake to change plans and abort the mission over such a stupid reason. I asked Mumtaz to contact Engineer Aref and see if he could get General Fahim to change his mind. Rick got on the radio with Brad to see if he knew what was really going on.

Mumtaz and I called Task Force Dagger. I was told that the flight was proceeding, although there were unexpected strong headwinds. Touchdown was now anticipated for 10:35 p.m. I explained that some sort of problem was developing with the landing location, that we might have to abort the mission, and we would know for sure in the next ten to fifteen minutes. The response at the other end of the radio connection was not a happy one. The radio operator said he would contact Colonel Mulholland and have him stand by the radio for our callback.

When Mumtaz returned at about half past nine, I could tell by his face that he had bad news. General Fahim insisted that the insertion be canceled. There was no sense arguing with Mumtaz. I asked Rick to contact Task Force Dagger, tell Colonel Mulholland the situation, and recommend he abort the insertion.

As Rick left to make the radio call, I tried to politely engage Mumtaz on the situation. I said I found it difficult to understand why our helicopter could fly in and out of that landing zone in daylight for a number of days, yet a nighttime insertion—a quick in and out in the darkness—was not acceptable. Every helicopter flight was dangerous, and a long night flight over enemy territory was especially hazardous. To add to that risk with a decision to turn the flight around at the last minute must be based on real, serious security concerns. I said that this had better not be a reckless decision on Fahim's part, and certainly should not be a signal of a change in Northern Alliance policy about hosting U.S. Special Forces teams.

Rick returned as I was finishing and said that a blistering-mad Colonel Mulholland had agreed to order the flight to return to base, but he demanded an explanation from the Northern Alliance by the following morning.

I said good night to Mumtaz, asking him to pass my message and Colonel Mulholland's reaction to Engineer Aref.

Rick and I sat and talked for a while about the incident. I was convinced that some political reason was behind Fahim's last-minute decision. Something was going on in Khoja Bahauddin that had convinced Fahim not to have U.S. troops landing there this night. We would find out why the next morning. We said good night, and I dragged myself to bed.

PART NINE

ALPHA TEAM AND THE BATTLE SOUTH OF MAZAR-E SHARIF

23 October 2001

CHAPTER THIRTY-SIX

Bringing his binoculars into focus, R.J. peered carefully at the open plain spreading out before him. He was resting behind an outcropping of boulders situated near the top of a small hill line, perhaps fifty to sixty feet above the level field below him. The Russian-made binoculars—purchased for less than ten dollars in Tashkent—were of surprisingly good quality, and the details of the terrain and the troops deployed out across the plain were sharp and clear.

Dostum had moved about three hundred of his infantry forces, mostly local militia troops assembled over the past four to five days, about two hundred yards onto the plain, into positions along the shallow banks of a dry streambed that cut diagonally across the field. They would take part in the coming attack, but for now they served as a screening element to protect against an attack by the Taliban forces facing them some eight hundred yards across the plain. Dostum did not expect the Taliban to attack—they had a relatively good defensive position—but one could never tell what the Taliban might do. Dostum's forces had been steadily hammering them for the past three days, driving the much larger Taliban forces northward, toward Mazar-e Sharif.

R.J. shifted his gaze to sweep the Taliban lines. The Taliban had not had much time to dig in, but the terrain they had chosen was excellent, and the high ground behind them would provide good fields of fire for their ZSU-23 antiaircraft cannons—they had at least two of those—and their T-55 Soviet-era tanks. Major Akram, one of Dostum's staff officers now assigned as liaison officer to ALPHA Team, estimated that about a thousand Taliban fighters were waiting in those positions. They were a large blocking force there to allow the main body of Taliban forces to establish stronger defensive positions closer to Mazar-e Sharif.

ALPHA Team had been split several days earlier, with half the team being shifted to join Commander Atta, the Tajik leader in this area; R.J. and three members of the team stayed with General Dostum and his Uzbek fighters. The past three days had been exciting; Dostum pushed to Mazar-e Sharif from the south while Atta drove toward the city from the east. The successes had been impressive. R.J. had come to respect the diminutive Uzbek soldiers, who fought with courage and daring and little apparent concern for their own lives. Dostum's strategy was simple—attack the enemy where you found him, hit him head-on with all you have, and let the devil take the hindmost.

Bob, an SAD paramilitary officer who had assumed the role of R.J.'s deputy when the team split, leaned against the boulder next to R.J. "What do you think the plan is, R.J.?"

R.J. turned his head slightly to look at Bob and smiled. "I would venture a guess that Dostum will send his cavalry forces straight at the Taliban lines and slam them into the middle of the enemy position. The infantry on the plain will move out behind the horses, firing on the enemy flanks, and Dostum's artillery will try to hit the ZSU-23s."

Bob gazed out at the plain. "Yep, that's a good guess. Especially since that's exactly what he's done in every fight we've had over these last three days. I think the general subscribes to the theory that if something works, stick with it."

R.J. shook his head and looked back out across the plain toward the Taliban positions. "I wish we had an ODA Team with us to call in CAS. With laser designators, we could open huge holes in the Taliban lines. Well, let's hope Task Force Dagger sticks to the plan to insert an A-Team tonight."

There was movement behind them, and they both turned to look back at where Frank, another ALPHA Team officer, was standing with their horses. Frank gestured to his left.

"Here comes Major Akram. I guess it's just about time to start the dance."

Akram rode with the grace of one who had grown up on horseback. He reined in and swung off the horse in a smooth, easy motion. He was in his mid-thirties, about five foot ten, lean with light skin and green eyes, his looks the result of a Tajik father and an Uzbek mother. He was wearing the uniform of Dostum's regular forces—dark green khakis, field jacket, and black boots.

"*Salam,* gentlemen," he said. He quickly shook hands with R.J. and Bob, and nodded to Frank. Akram glanced at his wristwatch. "We will attack in ten minutes. The artillery and tanks will fire a few rounds to make the devils put their heads down, and we will open up with our heavy machine guns." He motioned to the low hills that extended northward toward the enemy positions. "The general had several 14.5mm machine guns placed there. They will pour heavy fire onto the enemy's right flank. The infantry below will fire on their left flank, and of course the cavalry will attack up the middle." R.J. and Bob glanced at each other and smiled.

"Come on," said Akram, turning back toward his horse. "The general invites you to be with him as the battle commences."

Akram mounted and waited while R.J. and his men got on their horses. R.J. was an excellent horseman, having spent his teenage years on a Montana ranch, but even he was bothered by the small Uzbek iron stirrups. He could fit only the toe of his boots into the stirrups. Once on their horses, they tried to settle into the wood-framed, thin, leather-covered saddles. It was a painful experience trying to get their backsides to fit into the small, stiff seats.

As they rode off following the major, R.J. said a silent prayer that the logistics people back in the CTC had already purchased the Western saddles he had requested, and that they would be on the next resupply drop.

General Dostum was standing in a small group of his senior officers. He was of medium height, stocky but powerfully built, and was dressed in brown khaki pants, boots, and a heavy black wool coat cut like a military field jacket. He was wearing a turbanlike dark blue head covering, with a long piece of the material hanging down to serve as a scarf. His eyebrows and thick mustache were jet black. He moved with a strength and confidence that commanded attention and respect.

Dostum stepped out of the circle of his officers as the group rode to a halt and dismounted. He smiled at the difficulty the Americans had in getting down. "Welcome, welcome, my friends," he said in Dari, extending his hand to R.J. and his men. Although R.J. spoke excellent Dari, Major Akram translated for the benefit of the other team members.

"In just a few minutes we will start the attack." Dostum motioned them toward the battlefield. "The Taliban have not had enough time to be strongly dug in. That is good for us. We have beaten them in battle on each of the last three days. That is also good for us. But the terrain favors them in that we have a long ride across the open plain to reach them." He paused and looked across the field.

"If we had more ammunition for our artillery and our tanks, we could bombard them heavily. That would weaken them, because they are not accustomed to being under heavy, sustained artillery fire. Even better would be to have those U.S. aircraft you have promised bombing their positions before we move." He raised his hand to forestall a response from R.J.

"No, my friend, I do not complain. All that will come as Allah wills. So we deal with what we have. Today, losses will be heavy, but we will sweep the enemy from the field."

Dostum turned to his officers. "Colonel Nazmudin, please give the signal for the artillery to fire." Then he turned to the team. "Now let us mount our horses and move forward to watch the attack begin."

R.J. swung up and settled himself into the saddle. He did a quick inventory of his equipment. His AK-47, with metal folding stock, was on his left side; hung by its strap around his neck. His Browning 9mm automatic was in a holster on his right thigh. The canvas web pouch with four AK magazines was strapped on his chest. He had no body armor, and he was wearing a wool Chitrali hat. Only his blue jeans and L.L. Bean boots set him apart from the Afghan fighters around him.

R.J. turned to Bob and Frank, both of whom were equipped and dressed similarly. "All set, guys?"

Frank shook his head. "Yeah, just another day in the cavalry."

Major Akram took the lead, and they followed him toward Dostum and his group of officers as they moved toward the battlefield. The shockingly loud sound of an M-30 heavy artillery piece being fired shook the ground, followed within seconds by the round exploding downrange. R.J. watched a gout of flame, smoke, dirt, and debris blossom in the exact middle of the Taliban line. The battle was on.

There was firing all along Dostum's line. The 14.5mm machine guns on the left began pouring fire onto the enemy positions. The M-30 artillery—Dostum had four cannons—placed their heavy shells on the Taliban lines with stunning accuracy. Heavy Soviet mortars chugged shells overhead from positions on the reverse slope of the hill line. R.J. was watching the shells strike downrange and was impressed. The fire, although not heavy in volume, was right on target. These crew-served weapons were manned by Dostum's veteran soldiers, all members of his notorious Soviet-trained militia force that had terrorized northern Afghanistan in the early years of the Jihad.

Two columns of cavalry moved out from behind the hill line, quickly forming into a line abreast, the classic formation for a charge. R.J. was fascinated at the discipline with which the men moved. The first hundred-man group came on line and, without much more than a pause of a few seconds, stepped out and slowly headed toward the Taliban lines. The second hundred moved into position and stepped off with the same precision.

R.J knew that a classic cavalry charge was designed to deliver a tremendous shock to a stationary enemy, slamming into them as a solid, compact mass. However, he also knew that it was impossible to actually achieve that shock effect.

Each man would react differently as he rode toward the
enemy. Some of the braver—or more foolhardy—would
drive their animals at full speed; others would hold back, trying to drift to the rear of the mass. The animals would also
react to the noise, confusion, smoke, and incoming fire, with
some charging ahead and others fighting to avoid the coming
impact. Over a long distance, the cavalry line would break
up, and the impact of the charge against the enemy position
would be lessened.

That is why Dostum planned the attack as he had. The six
hundred men would charge in lines of a hundred men each,
with the first wave striking toward the center of the objective.
The second line would ride slightly toward the left of the first
to overlap them at the time of impact and spread the shock
outward. The third line would ride toward the right of the
two, overlapping the first line, with the next three lines of
cavalry repeating the process as their turns came. That way
the enemy would experience repeated strikes on his position
over a longer period of time, to compensate for the lack of a
single massive blow.

Fire from the enemy lines had been light, because the artillery and heavy machine guns had kept the Taliban bur-
rowed in their shallow foxholes. Now the artillery fire was
lifting and the mortars were slowing. There was not enough
ammunition to sustain the kind of barrage necessary to cover
the attack. R.J. knew that Dostum had two old T-55 tanks in
reserve that would pull forward as the attack started in
earnest, to try to hit the ZSU-23s, but it was going to be a
long ride across open ground under fire.

As the first of the ZSU rounds exploded near the line of
Dostum's dug-in infantry, there was a swell of incoming fire.
Cannon shells and heavy-machine-gun bullets began impacting around the infantry positions, with a few stray
rounds hitting behind them, near the approaching line of
cavalry. There was a slow, deliberate manner about how the
horsemen moved, and R.J. could see some of the men shifting their weapons, moving their AK-47s into better positions
for use as they rode.

As the first line of cavalry reached the infantry line, an officer in the middle of the line stood in his stirrups and raised a sword into the air. A shouted command could be heard above the firing, and the line of horsemen surged forward almost as one. Within a few steps the horses were moving at a gallop. A shudder of excitement swept through R.J. as he watched the riders bend low over the necks of their mounts, urging them on. The second line of riders reached the jump-off point, formed, corrected the line, and then broke into a charge.

The Taliban had now opened up all along their line, although R.J. thought the fire was not as massive as it might have been without the earlier artillery barrage. The ZSU-23s were firing rapidly now, their powerful rounds tearing through the flesh of men and horses. The infantry positioned along the streambed were now up and jogging toward the enemy's left flank. They ran in that peculiar crouch that men under fire assume, like running into a driving rain, only this was a rain of steel and lead.

A tank fired from above and behind R.J., and he could feel the shudder of the air as the round passed over him. He looked for the explosion and saw it on the slope of high ground above the enemy's right flank. Dostum's tankers had spotted a ZSU. A second round was fired by the tank to ensure its destruction.

R.J. sat on a small rise just above the level of the plain with Dostum and his officers, all leaning into their binoculars to see how the battle was developing. The churned-up dust from the pounding hooves further obscured the sight already dimmed by the blasts of earth and smoke from the exploding shells. The sound of the battle was like a huge and powerful hand shaking him, making his very bones hum. His adrenaline had kicked in, and he was more focused, more alert now. The fifth line of riders had started across the field, and the last line was nearing the jump-off point.

Dostum turned his horse toward them, raising his arm and motioning in a broad sweep toward the battle. "Come, friends, let's follow the attack. We can see nothing from here." And with that he turned and kicked his horse's flanks, riding into the fight raging before them.

"Shit, I knew he was going to say that," Bob let out as he nudged his horse forward. R.J. and Frank moved with him, gaining speed to keep up with the general.

The smoke and dust seemed to clear a little as they moved forward, and R.J. could see that the cavalry was near the Taliban lines. The ground around them was littered with broken bodies of men and horses. As they rode forward, the scenes of carnage were ghastly; the ZSU-23's cannon shells had inflicted incredible damage on the flesh they struck. Bodies exploded, were ripped apart, limbs lying here and there, their owners lost in the twisted shapes of torn and bloody clothing.

Dostum shouted something and picked up the pace to a full gallop. R.J. nudged his horse's flanks, and the animal began to accelerate. R.J. was aware of Frank on his left and sensed Bob to his left rear. Without thinking, R.J. found that he had pulled his Browning from its holster and was riding with his hand held low near his right leg.

The firing continued but seemed concentrated in front of them, focusing on the charging cavalry. Rounds were flying past them, hitting around them, and R.J. felt the heat of a round close to his right ear. They could sense the impact of the cavalry against the Taliban positions, and shouts from hundreds of riders rose as a single sound, for a few seconds louder than even the noise of the weapons.

They were coming up on the Taliban line now, and there was a whirl of movement as hundreds of horses and men struggled in dust, smoke, noise, and confusion. Dostum had angled toward the enemy's right flank. R.J. could see that the positions ahead of him were mostly abandoned and the areas behind the lines were filled with men running in panic. The Taliban had broken.

They slowed as they moved forward, trying to save their horses' strength. Several figures rose suddenly from the earth to R.J.'s right front, and there was almost instant recognition that these were Taliban fighters—the wide-wrapped black turban and oddly cut beard were easy markers. Even as R.J. swung his pistol toward the men, he heard shots from ahead and around him, as others in the group began to engage the Taliban fighters. R.J. fired twice at one of the men, saw rounds kicking the man backward, twisting as he fell. R.J. swept past the crumpled body, not sure he had even hit the man.

Frank was next to R.J. now, riding four to five feet out on his right. One of the fleeing Taliban fighters stopped and spun around to face them, raising his AK-47. Frank fired at him. R.J. saw the rounds hit the man high in the chest and head, his forehead exploding in a spray of blood and bone, turban flipping off as his body fell toward the gray-brown earth.

R.J. could see that Dostum had pulled to a halt and was trying to rally some of his fighters. Ahead of them, on the slope that overlooked the battlefield, was a ZSU-23, and Dostum was trying to organize an attack on the position. He dismounted and grabbed an AK-47 from one of his men, accepting two spare magazines for the weapon and stuffing them inside his heavy coat. R.J. could not hear what Dostum was saying, but it was clear that he was going to lead the attack. Men rallied to him, and when Dostum turned to start the climb he was accompanied by more than twenty men, including a number of his senior officers. They spread out into a loose line and started up the hill.

Major Akram wheeled his horse around and shouted, "R.J., dismount your men and we will form a defensive position here to protect the general's rear as he leads the attack." With that he leaped off his horse and began shouting at soldiers nearby to rally them and put some order and organization into their ranks.

R.J. handed over the reins to a young Afghan fighter who was moving the animals away from the area, then he moved with Bob and Frank to a clump of waist-high rocks. They settled in, swinging their AK-47s loose and taking their weapons off safety. Afghan troops—dismounted cavalry and a few infantry—were placed in a semicircle defensive position. There was heavy fighting on the enemy's left flank, and cavalry forces were riding after fleeing Taliban troops trying to escape through the narrow pass some two hundred yards behind the Taliban lines.

R.J. focused to the front, trying to spot Dostum in the moving figures advancing toward the ZSU position. They were all firing AKs on full automatic, and the sound swelled and rolled down toward R.J. There was a pause in the firing as the magazines emptied, and R.J. could hear Dostum's voice calling in Dari to advance. There was a stutter of firing, then the full volume of fire again rose and swept down over R.J. Then a pause in firing and a sudden shout of excitement; they were over the lip of the gun position, in among the Taliban fighters.

Within a few seconds, the firing stopped and a young Afghan militiaman stood on the edge of the ZSU position facing down toward the battlefield. He raised both arms toward the sky—his AK-47 in his right hand and the severed head of a Taliban fighter held by its hair in his left—and he shouted in a clear, ringing voice, "Allahu Akbar!" God is great. The fight was over.

The firing slowed on the battlefield, became scattered shots here and there, then stopped. As silence moved across the field, men stopped and shook themselves as if to clear their heads. They looked around at their fellows who had also somehow survived that long ride across the open field. As if on signal, a great shout of victory went up from the throats of all standing on that bloody field. "Allahu Akbar!" It was shouted over and over again.

At that moment it became clear to R.J. that although the fight against the Taliban was far from over, the outcome of the war was certain. The Taliban would be crushed.

CHAPTER THIRTY-SEVEN

There was a mixed bag of news awaiting us the next morning, 24 October. Because we had not sent anything to Headquarters about the cancellation of the insertion of our two additional ODA Teams, there was of course no reaction on that issue. ALPHA reported a successful battle south of Mazar-e Sharif by Dostum's forces the previous afternoon. Since the arrival of ALPHA and the subsequent truce achieved with Commander Atta, Dostum's forces had been on the attack south of Mazar. They had slowly been pushing the Taliban out of their defenses, driving them northward toward Mazar-e Sharif.

Yesterday's battle was unique—the climactic engagement of the fight had been a six-hundred-man cavalry charge by Dostum's men across a broad open field straight into the Taliban defensive lines. It was classic, straight out of an old Western, except no one was blowing his bugle. Dostum was now only about thirty-five miles south of Mazar.

The CIA team with Commander Atta, now designated BRAVO Team, was reporting that Atta's men were having equal success. Task Force Dagger was to insert an ODA Team that evening, 24 October, to link up with ALPHA, and the hope was that their laser target designation capabilities would help increase the Northern Alliance successes on the battlefields south and east of Mazar.

According to a cable from Hank at the CTC, these victories had been discussed in detail at an NSC meeting the day before, resulting in a push by the State Department to focus the bulk of military air strikes on the Mazar front. Hank said that he argued for a focus on Kabul; ODA-555 had men five hundred yards from the Taliban front lines, and a breakthrough could be had if the bombing was concentrated there. Still, Hank also reported that there had been grumbling around the table that General Fahim was holding back, not moving, and waiting for U.S. bombs to do the work.

We had reported many times that the Northern Alliance simply was not strong enough to defeat the Taliban forces massed against them in front of Kabul or on the Takhar front without U.S. bombing to weaken the Taliban defenses. It seemed incredible to me that at this date, after all of our reports and all the analytical cables outlining the situation here in the north, there remained such confusion and misunderstanding within the Washington policy-making community.

Rick called Brad at Khoja Bahauddin to check on developments there. General Fahim had visited General Bariullah at first light that morning to discuss an alternative landing zone for the insertion of the ODA Teams. It was located seven to eight miles farther east than the one we had been using. Brad assured Rick that a survey of the new site would be made that same morning.

We called Task Force Dagger to pass on the information about the survey. The weather forecast for the evening was not good, but we would keep our fingers crossed. All we could do was wait to see what Brad found.

Engineer Aref arrived in the late morning. He was upbeat and played down the problems of the previous evening. He said the new landing zone would be "excellent," and we would be able to get the two new teams into the fight as early as tonight. I sipped on my tea, then leaned forward toward Aref. "Engineer, please let me speak candidly. We were told last night that the landing zone was too public, too open. That seemed strange, because we have been using that site to land in the daylight hours. What was the real reason why General Fahim canceled the mission?"

Aref paused before replying. "Mr. Gary, as you know, General Fahim has been concerned about the presence of

U.S. Special Forces becoming public knowledge. Last evening, Professor Rabbani, our longtime political leader, was visiting Khoja Bahauddin. It was an unexpected visit. Of course when Rabbani learned that General Fahim was there also, he insisted on joining the general. General Fahim was concerned that Rabbani would learn of the insertion of U.S. troops, so the general decided to postpone the mission."

I thought about that for a few seconds. "So why was General Fahim concerned that Professor Rabbani would learn of the two ODA Teams' arrival? Surely that information will soon be common knowledge."

When Aref made no reply, I added, "Or was the general concerned that Rabbani would learn of the insertion and take public credit for bringing the Americans into Afghanistan?"

Aref smiled slightly and shrugged. He did not want to comment on what was looking like an internal Tajik political issue between Fahim and Rabbani. "Whatever the reason, Engineer, it cannot happen again. Not for those reasons. Security problems at the landing zone—yes, we would want to cancel the insertion. But not over internal NA political issues."

Aref shifted gears and brought up the Shelter Now hostages. He had a new lead to report. His men had contacted a guard at the prison who said that he and a group of seven colleagues would be willing to release the hostages and move them at night to a prearranged landing site near Kabul. They wanted one million U.S. dollars each, and the promise that their families would be moved to a safe haven in the Panjshir Valley prior to the operation.

It sounded weak to me—too many men involved to be able to maintain the security of the operation. Moving eight families out of Kabul across Taliban lines prior to the operation surely would be noticed by the Taliban. I instructed Aref to continue the contact with the guard but said it did not sound promising. I thought the previously discussed offer by the senior Taliban intelligence officer in Kabul to transport the hostages to Northern Alliance lines was much more realistic.

After Aref departed, Rick and I discussed his comments about the canceled insertion. I thought it made perfect sense in the context of Northern Alliance politics. Professor Rabbani was one of the old guard—leader of the Tajik-dominated Jamiat-e Islami and the last president of the failed interim government that tried to rule Afghanistan between 1992 and 1996. Masood had moved to distance himself from Rabbani and the Jamiat Party in the years following the expulsion of Rabbani's interim government out of Kabul by the Taliban.

Masood had a broader alliance of commanders and political leaders who opposed the Taliban, and his new organization—the United Islamic Front for the Salvation of Afghanistan (UIFSA)—had begun to assume the trappings of a political party by the time of Masood's assassination. Had Masood lived and the Taliban been defeated, I am sure that Masood would have used the UIFSA as a political coalition to assert his own political ambitions in a post-Taliban Afghanistan, isolating Professor Rabbani.

At about one that afternoon, Brad called from Khoja Bahauddin with bad news. The proposed new site was indeed located eight miles east of our current landing zone. Unfortunately, General Bariullah had failed to mention that the road to the new location was heavily traveled by civilians in the area and passed near several fairly large villages. Unusual movement over the road at night would undoubtedly draw attention from curious villagers. More important, the proposed landing zone was on the opposite side of a river that could be crossed only by ferry. Vehicle traffic backed up on both sides of the river at the ferry crossing; even with General Bariullah leading their convoy, the survey team had to wait twenty minutes to cross. We asked Brad to tell General Bariullah that we would recommend the landing site that we had been using.

We called Colonel Mulholland to discuss the issue. Rick explained the situation and the facts behind the last-minute cancellation of the previous night's insertion. We told Mulholland that the new landing zone proposed by General

Fahim was untenable, and we would insist on using the current site. The colonel was in full agreement and said he would delay the insertion of the two additional ODA Teams until the following evening, 25 October. The flight crews could use the rest after the previous night's long hours in the air. Rick assured Mulholland that we would thrash out the landing zone issue with Engineer Aref, and General Fahim if necessary, and provide him the details in the morning.

The rest of the evening was spent in writing cables back to Headquarters detailing the events of the past twenty-four hours and outlining our plans for the upcoming day.

CHAPTER THIRTY-EIGHT

On the morning of 25 October, I headed to the office area feeling better than I had in weeks. My weight continued to drop and my pants were loose around the waist; at least there were some positive results from what I had been through. The toilet area remained an overused and undercleaned horror, but beating the "bears" to their morning visit helped a little. The heating coil allowed us to have warm water for our "showers," but our room was still an unheated concrete box. By getting up at first light, I could usually manage to shower and have five minutes in front of the washbasin and mirror to shave before anyone else was up and stirring.

Despite the dropping temperatures, Chris was still spending his nights on the patio in his sleeping bag. I had the impression that this was all just a big adventure for him and he was enjoying every minute here. He had the joint intelligence cell humming, disseminating an average of ten intelligence reports a day.

The kitchen staff now ended their daily duties by preparing the two coffeepots for the next morning. The first of us to get up would start the gas stove and have coffee perking to greet the rest of the team. I had not particularly cared for Starbucks coffee before this mission, but after weeks of instant coffee, I now looked forward to that first hot cup with real anticipation. I liked sitting on the patio chair with my mocha, watching the sun rise over the ridgeline and light up the valley. For me it was the best time of day, a time to reflect on yesterday's events and plan for the coming day's activities. I always wondered what new surprises awaited me.

One development that I reviewed in my mind was Hank's plan to have the officers, selected to replace Rick and me, arrive in the valley in ten days' time. Hank said that Cofer Black was convinced that we could have a real impact on the political and military strategy discussions dragging on in Washington. I had mixed feelings. I wanted to stay to see the Northern Alliance break out of their defensive positions and see Kabul captured. Yet with the debate still raging about whether to commit to full support for the NA at Kabul, my presence in DC as a CIA officer who knew the senior NA leadership and could articulate the situation clearly might be a factor in changing the bombing strategy and setting loose the NA forces.

As soon as Mumtaz was up and about, I cornered him for a brief but important conversation. I told him that the new landing zone suggested by General Fahim in the north was unacceptable and pointed out its numerous problems. I asked him to contact Engineer Aref as soon as possible and tell him that the insertion would take place at the original landing zone that evening, weather permitting.

Mumtaz returned from meeting with Engineer Aref and said the engineer would come for a meeting around ten that morning. Mumtaz looked relaxed, which I read as a sign that the upcoming meeting would not be contentious.

When I reviewed the problems with Engineer Aref about the new site proposed by General Fahim, he made no objection to using the original landing zone. He did want to offer a suggestion, though. He noted that one of the two Special Forces teams deploying that evening would join General Bariullah, and the other team would be based here in the valley in Barak—both areas under General Fahim's immediate command. Aref said that the general suggested that all the additional ODA Teams we wished to deploy to commanders in areas of the country outside Fahim's immediate control first travel to the Panjshir Valley. Then, as circumstance allowed, these teams would be deployed to join the various NA commanders elsewhere in the north. This, he said, would simplify the command and control structure for the Northern Alliance and would make it clear to the other commanders that this overall effort was closely coordinated with and fully agreed to by the senior Northern Alliance leadership.

I tried not to smile; all I could think was, Fahim never gives up. I said that I appreciated the general's desire to maintain maximum control over his commanders, and understood that he wanted to obtain the maximum benefit of having an A-Team assigned to a specific commander. However, to have each new team fly into the valley, then be flown out of the valley to their final destination was a terribly inefficient way to manage future deployments. The flight over the Hindu Kush Mountains was dangerous even in good weather. With winter rapidly settling in, it was even more risky. I told him we would deploy CIA and Special Forces teams directly from Uzbekistan to the various commanders in the north and west, but we would coordinate with General Fahim in advance, so he could contact the commander to ensure that he was aware that Fahim approved the deployment. This would ensure that Fahim received the credit from the commander in question. It was the reply that Aref had hoped for, and he said he would pass on my answer to General Fahim.

We discussed the Shelter Now hostage situation again. Aref's officer had returned from Kabul, having met with the senior Taliban intelligence officer several times. Their discussions resulted in what Aref called a "simple plan," which went as follows.

First, one or two of the Taliban officer's men would cross through the front lines and proceed to Charikar, where they would link up with Aref's men. After being shown the $4 million reward, they would contact the Taliban officer back in Kabul by radio to confirm that the money was there. The Taliban officer would then arrange for the hostages to be released and moved in two vehicles, driving northward from Kabul on the "new road," with the senior Taliban official riding in the first vehicle to talk their way through Taliban checkpoints. Near the front lines, they would leave the road and proceed by creek bed to a small village near the Northern Alliance front lines. Moving on foot, they would arrive at a designated point near NA lines, where the group would be met by NA troops. Aref's officer would be waiting there to coordinate the linkup with the hostages and the senior Taliban officer. Once the transfer of the hostages was made, Aref's men in Charikar would be contacted by radio, and the money would be passed to the Taliban officer's two men.

Yes, I thought, it was a "simple plan." Except for the long drive up the "new road" from Kabul to the frontline area, which was at least thirty miles through who knew how many checkpoints and past several thousand Taliban and Arab fighters. Then there was the linkup in the dark in no-man's-land with a group of probably fifteen people, eight of whom would be frightened civilians, trying to find their Northern Alliance reception team. Yes, it was a "simple plan."

I told Aref we would need many more details as to how the hostages would be moved north out of Kabul and what assurances the Taliban officer had that he could get through the checkpoints, especially if challenged. Washington was certainly not going to buy into the plan as we just heard it.

Rick had been on the radio with Colonel Mulholland to confirm the insertion that night. Arrival at the landing zone would be shortly after midnight, and Rick said he would personally be at the landing zone to welcome ODA-585, Lieutenant Colonel H., and the SOCCE Team. Mulholland told Rick that there would be three Delta Force soldiers with the

SOCCE Team, and their job was to plan for a possible rescue scenario for the Shelter Now hostages. Rick then passed the radio to our pilots, who spent ten minutes talking to the lead pilot of the insertion mission about the best flight route into the landing zone.

Rick took off at about three that afternoon for Khoja Bahauddin. We all settled down to wait, fingers crossed that the weather would hold.

CHAPTER THIRTY-NINE

The rest of the evening passed slowly. After dinner we all drifted back to the office area to read cable traffic, and I called Hank at the CTC. He said that the press had started to comment that the U.S. military's strategy in bringing the fight to the Taliban was not working. Reporters at the Kabul front were picking up the same disheartened comments from Northern Alliance military commanders. He said the NSC was pushing for an increased number of American troops on the ground, although the Principals Committee (PC) was divided on this issue. The real problem was the U.S. military's slow progress in deploying Special Forces A-Teams. Hank pointed out that if the insertion of the two ODA Teams scheduled for this evening was successful, the military would have just two A-Teams on the ground along with one smaller SOCCE Team. How to deal with the Northern Alliance on the issue of Kabul was still a sticking point in shaping the military strategy. Hank shared my frustration, but there was little either of us could do but keep on pushing to get the situation on the ground here fully understood by the decision makers.

As the team members drifted off to bed, I made a pallet on top of the money boxes in the corner and stretched out to wait for a call from Rick on the outcome of the Special Forces insertion. Pappy was still taking incoming cable traffic. Other than an occasional "rip" from Pappy passing gas, it was quiet. I dozed there, resting on top of almost $10 million in cash.

At about half past one in the morning, the radio crackled and Rick's voice came in loud and clear. Pappy roused himself from his sleeping bag and quickly established the link. The insertion had gone perfectly. The two teams were safely on the ground, now guests of General Bariullah. Colonel H.'s SOCCE Team, plus the three Delta Force operatives, would bunk with Rick and our pilots in a small compound near the landing zone. The A-Team, ODA-585, was on the move to the frontline area, where General Bariullah was anxious to put them to work later that morning. We needed a CIA interface with the A-Team, and Brad was the logical choice for that assignment.

I returned to the office area a little after 7:00 a.m. to read the morning traffic and draft cables. Pappy was going to travel down to Baghram Air Base to work on Stan and Murray's communications equipment. They had been having trouble sending data, and Pappy would swap out some components in their system. Chris was going along to consult with Stan on the intelligence-gathering process in place there with General Bismullah's staff, then visit Professor Sayyaf at his Gul Bahar residence on the ride back from Baghram that afternoon. Chris was still trying to win Sayyaf's agreement to work on luring one of bin Ladin's lieutenants to a location where he could be captured or killed. I was convinced it was a hopeless mission, but I admired Chris's dedication. He and Pappy planned to be back at Barak by 6:00 p.m. at the latest.

At 10:30 a.m. the helicopter returned from Khoja Bahauddin. We got Colonel H. and his men settled into the safe house used by ODA-555. ODA-585 planned to be set up by noon, and Colonel H. expected to be working with both 585 and 555 by early afternoon. This was outstanding news; we all anticipated that Colonel H. would be able to call in a larger number of air strikes than ODA-555 had done on its own.

Within the U.S. government, cables are labeled by their urgency—ROUTINE, PRIORITY, IMMEDIATE, or FLASH—allowing the receiving offices to quickly determine which cables must be dealt with first. The FLASH precedent is reserved for true emergency situations, and in my nearly thirty-two years of service with the CIA I have probably seen no more than ten FLASH cables. Just before noon we received a FLASH cable from Islamabad reporting that former Pashtun Mujahedin commander Abdul Haq and a small band of his supporters were being pursued by Taliban forces a few miles north of Jalalabad. Apparently Abdul Haq and his party had crossed into Afghanistan from the Peshawar area in the predawn hours that morning, traveling by mule and on foot past Jalalabad, heading for the mountains to the north and east of the city, where they hoped to establish a base of operations. Islamabad had known that Haq was in Peshawar but was not involved in the planning of this operation.

Haq's support came from two Afghan-American brothers, successful businessmen who had latched onto Haq as a former commander who they believed could have great influence in the struggle against the Taliban. Well meaning but terribly ignorant of the political and military realities on the ground in Afghanistan, these two brothers had supported and encouraged Abdul Haq in his ambitions. The brothers, ensconced in a hotel in Peshawar, were in radio contact with Haq. They had just telephoned Islamabad in a panic, asking for U.S. military assistance in rescuing Haq and his men, who were in danger of being cut off and surrounded.

I had been monitoring the efforts by the two brothers to secure U.S. support for several weeks with growing unease. I was well acquainted with Haq from the Jihad years. Early in the fighting he had been a dynamic, effective commander,

managing forces south and east of Kabul. After he lost a foot
to a land mine, the U.S. government paid his way to the
United States, where he was fitted with a high-quality pros-
thesis. However, after his return to Afghanistan, he lost the
drive and willingness to risk himself on the battlefield. He
spent more and more time in Peshawar playing up to the press.
He became an articulate speaker, and the press loved him.
Within the CIA he became known as "Hollywood Haq," and
from then on, he did all his fighting with his mouth. He
played no role in the Mujahedin interim government of 1992
to 1996, so I thought that the effort to try to build him into a
political figure who could challenge the Taliban was a waste
of time. Haq had no tribal base of support to which he could
attach himself (unlike Hamid Karzai, whose roots in the
Tarin Kowt area north of Qandahar were strong and deep). I
predicted that if Abdul Haq moved into the Jalalabad area
without such an established base, he would be killed by the
Taliban. Now that scenario was being played out in deadly
earnest.

A cable came from Headquarters within a few minutes.
There was a Predator aircraft armed with a Hellfire missile
being flown in the Peshawar area. It was being diverted to the
Jalalabad area to see if it could locate Abdul Haq's group and
ascertain the situation on the ground.

About an hour later, a cable from Headquarters said that
the Predator had indeed located Haq and his group, who
were almost completely surrounded by Taliban forces. The
CTC had been told that the Predator had fired its Hellfire at
several Taliban SUVs and succeeded in destroying them, but
that had not slowed the pursuit. It appeared that Abdul Haq's
capture by the Taliban was inevitable.

Later that day, Engineer Aref's radio intercept teams monitored Taliban communications and learned that Haq and
about twenty of his men had been captured. The Taliban officer in charge of the capture had asked senior Taliban leaders in Kabul how to deal with the prisoners. Haq and one of
his relatives were to be put on trial, then executed by firing
squad. The others in Haq's group were to be hanged that day.

They were all to be "tortured severely" before being executed. The "sentence" was carried out that same afternoon—a brutal reminder of the Taliban's ruthlessness.

There was negative fallout from the Northern Alliance over the death of Abdul Haq. Supported by false press reports following the incident that U.S. military helicopters flew strikes against the Taliban in an effort to assist Haq, our NA hosts concluded that Haq's insertion was another unilateral CIA operation. Engineer Aref told me later that had we coordinated with him, he could have had NA-affilated commanders in the Jalalabad area standing by to assist Haq and his party. My denials of CIA involvement with Haq fell on Aref's polite but deaf ears. It was just another example of the CIA "ignoring" the Northern Alliance leadership and creating problems as we "blundered" around on our own.

I spoke to Hank on the phone at 5:30 p.m. We discussed Abdul Haq's fate and agreed it was a prime example of what happens when amateurs involve themselves in intelligence activities. The two Afghan-American brothers with their high-level connections to the fringes of the administration had allowed Abdul Haq to receive undeserved attention, which, unfortunately, had fed his delusions that he was still a player in the Afghan scene. The results were tragic.

Hank also pointed out that the policy debate continued in the White House on how to deal with the Northern Alliance.

We had a group of officers ready to deploy to augment ALPHA and BRAVO teams, to bring them to full strength, and one team set to join Hamid Karzai in the south. Karzai was proving to be the only Pashtun tribal leader willing to step up to the formidable task of organizing resistance to the Taliban in the south. Although not a military commander, Karzai was an excellent political organizer, and he had inherited his father's tribal leadership role following the Taliban's assassination of his father in Quetta a few years earlier.

He suggested that I write another field appraisal of the situation in the north. He said the president seemed happy with the CIA and our progress, and a thoughtful presentation on how the situation in the north might play out, should U.S. military bombing strategy shift, could prove helpful within the White House in clarifying issues. I agreed to draft the appraisal that evening, so it would be available when Hank opened for business the following morning.

After speaking with Hank, I sat in front of the phone trying to come to grips with the inability of the senior leadership of the U.S. government and military to grasp the basics of the military situation on the ground here in Afghanistan. Perhaps I was not being as clear or as articulate as I should have been to explain what I thought was a relatively simple set of conditions. The Taliban had the majority of their military forces—and all the troops of their foreign allies, including the al-Qa'ida fighters—massed in the north, positioned to oppose the Northern Alliance forces of the late Ahmad Shah Masood. Bombing Taliban facilities in rear positions here in the north or in the south had little or no impact on the ability or willingness of the Taliban military to fight. Theirs was not a conventional army, and our current bombing strategy was simply not working. It must be clear that the only military force on the ground here that could and would fight effectively against the Taliban forces was Masood's Northern Alliance. However, without U.S. military assistance—massive bombing—they were not strong enough to break the Taliban lines. We had to shift our bombing strategy to focus on the Taliban lines above Kabul and on the Takhar front.

A victory by Dostum at Mazar-e Sharif would not break the Taliban hold on the north. The key rested with General Fahim's fighters. As long as Fahim's NA fighters remained stalemated and ineffective, the Taliban would have overall control of the country. A breakout toward Kabul, and a drive west by General Bariullah Khan's forces toward Talaqan and Konduz, combined with a push to Mazar-e Sharif by Dostum and Atta would have an incredible impact on the Taliban leadership in the south. Reluctant Pashtun tribal leaders in the south would be encouraged to take up arms against the Taliban. The fight in the south would be less decisive and would likely drag on for several months, but with the Taliban forces defeated in the north, victory over the Taliban in the south would be inevitable.

I wondered to myself if I might not be more effective in making these points if I was back in Washington, personally participating in the ongoing debate. Sitting in the Panjshir Valley, I seemed to be shouting down a deep, dark hole. I tackled the field appraisal later that evening around 10:00 p.m. I crafted my thoughts into what I thought was a tight, concise, and logical presentation. Just before midnight I sent the appraisal on its way.

At 7:00 p.m. Engineer Aref came by to take Rick and me to meet with Dr. Abdullah. We had been seeing a lot of Abdullah on the BBC, and he was proving to be a well-reasoned, articulate spokesman for the Northern Alliance. His excellent English and his natty Western style of dress made him a popular figure for the TV reporters flooding the frontline areas. Our meeting was again held at Abdullah's small villa below Astaneh.

It was a pleasant meeting and I had come to like and admire Dr. Abdullah in the short time I had dealt with him here in the valley. That night, he was relaxed and in an expansive mood. He discussed without rancor the failure of the Department of State to support his visit to Washington, saying only that time would demonstrate that the decision was a mistake. We also talked about the current struggle over defining the strategy on Kabul and he said he was aware of the mistrust that some circles in Washington held for the Northern Alliance.

I mentioned to Abdullah and Aref that plans were afoot to send in replacements so that Rick and I and a few other team members could return to Washington to take part in the strategy debate under way there. Aref was not happy with that idea, but Abdullah said he would welcome having me back in Washington and speaking out for the Northern Alliance. There was, of course, no firm plan yet on when that might happen, and in the end it might not take place at all. Who knew? The strategy might change on the strength of logic and the realities on the ground here, and we could all be in Kabul within a week or so. *In'sha'lah,* we all said.

Chris and Pappy were back when we arrived. Chris had a story for Rick and me, told to him by members of the A-Team. Two days earlier, in the late morning, the control tower came under direct fire by a Taliban 14.5mm machine gun. Their aim had been accurate for a change, and rounds impacted on the exterior walls and zipped through the glassless windows. Everyone hit the floor. Everyone except Murray, that is, who remained seated with his feet propped up on a table casually sharpening his knife. When someone hollered for him to take cover, he just smiled and said, "The Taliban are lousy shots. If they can hit me at this range, they deserve to get lucky." He continued to draw the knife blade over the sharpening steel as bullets kicked up dust and concrete shrapnel.

Rick and I listened to the story with dismay. I thought we should bring Murray back here. Bravery is one thing, but this was another. I asked Rick to make the call to Murray ordering him back while I started the field appraisal.

PART TEN

EFFORTS IN THE SOUTH—FIGHTING NORTH OF QANDAHAR

CHAPTER FORTY

A small convoy of SUVs and Toyota pickup trucks bounced along the rutted dirt trail heading toward a group of mud-walled buildings on top of a small hill. Craig, chief of ECHO Team, the CIA's first team operating in southern Afghanistan, was in the lead SUV, riding shotgun in the front passenger seat. Frank, an SAD paramilitary case officer who was serving as Craig's deputy, was driving, cursing quietly to himself as he fought to avoid the bigger potholes or the larger exposed rocks in the roadway.

Craig looked at Frank and smiled. "Frank, you're going to run out of expletives to call these bumps if you don't slow down."

Frank laughed, then twisted the wheel hard to the left and back to the right, failing to miss a large rock protruding from the dirt track. He bounced in his seat, banging his head against the roof. "Not likely, Chief, because I'll switch to Russian when I run out of curse words in English. Now that's a language you can really cuss in." Craig laughed and shook his head. "These roads—or what passes for roads here—are enough to drive even a preacher to cussing."

Craig looked toward the small group of buildings ahead, and his mind turned to the meeting he was to have in just a few minutes. Hamid Karzai was a strange man to figure out. He was of medium height, slim, always well dressed—even in the field—and a true gentleman. His slight frame, his thin face with its close-cropped grayish beard, and his balding head gave him the appearance of a college professor, not an Afghan tribal leader rallying his followers to oppose the Taliban. Yet he had an iron core, and he was stubbornly brave—at times to the point of recklessness.

Karzai had been the first Pashtun leader to volunteer to cooperate with the U.S. government in helping create an armed resistance to the Taliban among the Pashtun tribes in the south. He met with U.S. officials, including CIA officers, at the U.S. Embassy in Islamabad a few days following the 9/11 attacks. Karzai was a well-known figure, having been active in the Jihad years in the fight against the Soviets, and he had served as political adviser to his father, one of the most respected Pashtun tribal leaders from Qandahar Province. The Karzai family's opposition to the Taliban was intense and public, resulting in the Taliban's assassination of Hamid's father in the late 1990s. Hamid stepped forward to assume his father's political mantle, and his quiet, dignified demeanor, excellent English, and political skills made him a popular political figure within the Afghan exile community in Pakistan.

During those first meetings in Islamabad, Karzai insisted on moving back into Afghanistan immediately, to return to his tribal homelands in the Tarin Kowt area north of Qandahar city and begin organizing armed resistance groups. The CIA's advice was to hold off on his return until the U.S. government had assets in place that could provide Karzai and his followers with equipment, weapons, ammunition, and combat air support. But Karzai would not wait.

Accompanied by only three of his supporters, he started from Quetta, in southwestern Pakistan, at first in the back of a cargo truck, then by motorcycle, and made his way through Taliban-controlled territory to the rugged mountains around Tarin Kowt. Many of his tribal followers rallied to his side. But the lack of weapons and ammunition, as well as the lack of a mechanism to receive support from the outside, plagued Karzai's efforts from the start.

Taliban supporters in the area had quickly informed the Taliban leadership in Qandahar of Karzai's return, and their reaction was swift and decisive. A full-scale military operation was organized to find and eliminate Karzai and those close to him. Poorly armed, poorly organized, and vastly outnumbered, Karzai went on the run. Surrounded in the remote mountains east of Tarin Kowt, Karzai and his small group of followers slipped away and headed back toward Pakistan. Hounded day and night, they somehow made their way back across the border. Karzai barely escaped the fate of Abdul Haq.

Craig's first meeting with Karzai was held in Quetta in late October, shortly after he was assigned to lead ECHO Team into southern Afghanistan. ECHO was to work with Karzai, helping him prepare a base of support for his return, and arranging airdrops of weapons and ammunition to his supporters.

Craig and Karzai hit it off immediately. Craig, an experienced SAD officer with almost twenty years of successful involvement in CIA paramilitary operations around the world, is a no-nonsense guy. Just under six feet tall, lean and hard, Craig looks the part of the field operator that he is.

Frank pulled off the dirt trail and headed across a rocky, barren field toward the group of mud buildings, followed by the other vehicles in the convoy. Craig gazed to his right as they bounced toward the buildings, and saw a group of Karzai's fighters gathered around what looked like most of the A-Team, ODA-574. Several trucks were parked there, and boxes from the early-morning resupply flight were stacked in and around the rear of the trucks. Craig could see that their radio and equipment was set up, and some of the ODA (call sign TEXAS 12 on their radio net) were apparently getting ready to call in air strikes on Taliban positions located on a line of tall hills about a thousand yards across the valley. The group was set up just behind a low stone wall about two hundred and fifty yards from the building where Craig was to meet with Karzai.

As Craig exited the SUV, he waved at TEXAS 12 Team commander Captain A., who saw Craig and waved back. Craig turned to Frank. "Looks like our SF buddies have broken down the supplies that came in last night. Why don't you take our Mujahedin over and have them load up our share of things, then join me with Karzai."

Frank smiled. "Be happy to handle that, Chief. The Starbucks we asked for was supposed to be on this flight. JAW-BREAKER had the right idea when they thought of asking for Starbucks. I just hope our TEXAS 12 compadres don't say it didn't make the flight." Frank turned toward the other vehicles, the gray-brown dust they had raised drifting off toward the A-Team, and started toward them, muttering something that sounded to Craig like "another Alamo if they can't find the coffee."

Craig watched as Frank spoke to the young Afghan who served as the team's translator, then he turned and tuned out the noise behind him as he focused on the upcoming meeting. He heard the sound of another vehicle driving toward them, and looked to see Karzai's blue Toyota SUV speeding toward them, a cloud of dust billowing a heavy tail behind the vehicle. Craig continued up to the door of the main building and stood waiting for the SUV to reach him. He thought to himself as he watched the truck draw nearer that he was smiling, happy to be meeting with Karzai. He could not remember any earlier time in the field when he had more enjoyed and respected any other man with whom he had dealt.

The room was sparsely furnished with a beat-up sofa and an overstuffed armchair with a spring peeking through, a small wooden table and a couple of chairs, and a wood-framed bed with heavy rope strung to serve as the mattress. The windows were empty squares; even the wooden frames were gone—victims of the poverty of the area.

They sat on the sofa, plastic cups of hot tea resting on a small wooden board placed on the seat cushion between them, the thermos bottle that Karzai had used to bring the tea sitting on the floor at his feet.

Karzai leaned forward and spoke quietly. "Tell me, Craig, what is the news from around the country? How is the battle going?"

"Actually, things are going well, sir." Craig bent down and

reached for the envelope on the floor by his feet. "I have the map here, and we can go over developments."

Outside, TEXAS 12's newly arrived air force tactical control NCO was on the radio with a B-52 bomber overhead, calling for a strike on a Taliban troop position just confirmed in the hill line about a thousand yards across the valley. The NCO was working to finish the sequence of steps necessary to identify the geocoordinates to be hit. He made a small mistake, but a grave one, and did not realize that the geocoordinates he was reading to the circling B-52 were for his own team's position, not the Taliban target across the valley. The bombardier asked for confirmation of the coordinates, and the young sergeant assured him that they were the coordinates where he wanted the bomb to strike.

The B-52 released one GBU-31, a 2,000-pound high-explosive bomb, programmed to strike the geocoordinates provided by TEXAS 12. It would take nearly half a minute for the bomb to fall from its release altitude and land on the target.

Craig had moved the teacups off the middle cushion and had the map of Afghanistan open and spread out between them. He was pointing toward the eastern provinces, telling Karzai of the Taliban fleeing Kabul, when a tremendous wall of air and heat traveling at incredible speed smashed into and through the building, crumbling the walls and roof and slamming Craig into Karzai, tumbling the two like rag dolls across the room. The compression forced the air from their lungs as they were lifted and flung forward. Then the wave of pressure and noise passed, leaving a numbing silence. Craig was conscious, and although he hurt all over, it was not the localized pain of a serious wound but more like what he had felt once when he was caught in a huge wave while surfing and was pounded under and bounced and tossed on the bottom for nearly half a minute.

The air was full of smoke and dust. Craig looked around and saw that the wall at the rear of the building and part of the roof over that area were blown away. Karzai was lying a few feet from him, twisted onto his left side, his clothing torn and dirty. Craig crawled to Karzai and pulled him onto his back, then he shifted forward to cover Karzai's body from any falling debris. Craig pressed his cheek against Karzai's mouth and could feel that he was breathing. He raised himself off Karzai and did a hands-on pass over his body, feeling for broken bones, cuts, and other obvious injuries. There were several small cuts on Karzai's face, and bruises were already beginning to show faintly on his forehead, but Craig could not see any serious injuries.

He sat up next to Karzai and checked himself. He had several sore spots on his back, probably from debris from the collapsed wall striking him, and could feel small cuts on the back of his neck and head. He felt as though he had been hit by a truck; his entire body ached and tingled. His ears were ringing, and sounds seemed to be coming from a great distance. He did not know what happened except that something big had exploded close by. Looking around at the damage and destruction, he realized how lucky he and Karzai were to be alive.

The bomb had hit exactly on target, exploding about ten yards in front of the low stone wall behind which most of the team had been standing or working. Three of Karzai's Mujahedin fighters had been seated on the wall, relaxing, waiting to watch the fireworks as the Taliban positions across the valley were systematically destroyed. The three Mujahedin were blown apart, their bodies disintegrating in the blast. Three of the Special Forces team were killed outright, and the rest were wounded, some seriously. A number of the Mujahedin in the area working to move the supplies around were wounded as well. Frank, the ECHO Team officer, had been near the mud house where the meeting was taking place and was knocked unconscious, but other than minor cuts and bruises he was fine.

*   *   *

Much later that afternoon, Craig walked the site with Frank, looking at the chaos caused by one small mistake in misreading the geocoordinates for the target. Had the bomb landed ten yards closer to TEXAS 12 or hit on the same side of the stone wall where the team was working, those in the meeting house might have been killed and a potential national leader lost.

CHAPTER FORTY-ONE

Craig leaned on the hood of the SUV and steadied his binoculars, bringing the scene on the hilltop opposite him into focus. The sixty Mujahedin fighters he had sent forward last night to secure the hill line were in place, and he could see them moving around slowly in the cold of the early morning. A few small fires were burning, sending thin white lines of smoke into the clear sky, and around each fire three or four men were gathered waiting for the water to boil for morning tea. Craig scanned the line, noting the shallow defensive positions the men had put in place the night before, and he could see their equipment scattered around each position. Poor discipline, although these were not seasoned veterans but men from the local villages. Some of them had experience in fighting against the Soviets or the Afghan communist regime in the early 1990s, but even these were farmers or shopkeepers now, grown soft by village life.

Craig was parked just behind the crest of a taller hill line about three hundred yards to the rear of the hilltop he was observing. He knew that a force of several hundred Taliban fighters was on the line of hills about eight hundred yards farther on. Karzai's forces, with the help of massive U.S. air support, had been driving the Taliban southward at a steady pace for the past four days. Losses among the Taliban had been heavy, for every time they dug in to make a stand, bombs would rain from the skies, bringing down death and destruction around them. It was no wonder that Karzai's men on the next hill were relaxed and confident. The end of this long, slow battle seemed assured. The Taliban were beaten; they just did not know it yet.

Craig looked around him, smiling at the difference in the way his line looked. The defensive positions built by these Afghan troops were well constructed, with deep holes and protective dirt berms topped with heavy rocks. Equipment was stacked neatly, and there was one man at each position, even as breakfast tea and rice were being prepared in the rear.

The three members of ECHO Team with Craig were working around their two SUVs, coffee perking on a small camp stove, while Rocky, the communications officer, was bringing his equipment online to take the morning traffic from Headquarters. Frank, Craig's number two, was looking at a topographical map of the area with José, another SAD paramilitary officer. Their weapons and field gear were stacked near them. All were dressed in the odd mix of L.L. Bean field clothing and boots, with the U.S. military canvas web gear and military holsters and ammo pouches that all the CIA had adopted in Afghanistan. Just twenty yards away, about six members of the Special Forces ODA-574 were also engaged in morning duties, centered on brewing coffee, establishing communications, and getting things lined up for the day.

Craig motioned to Frank and they made their way over to greet the SF troopers and get the word on the day's close air support assaults. The air force tactical air operator told Craig that he had a B-52 inbound to their location, to be on station within thirty minutes. The rest of the morning's air package was being prioritized, but they would have plenty of firepower to call on as the day progressed.

With that, Craig and Frank ventured off to inspect the

Afghans on the next hill, and headed down one of the narrow paths leading into the valley about a hundred yards below them.

It was a beautiful day, with only a few cumulus clouds on the southern horizon. The air was chilly, but it would warm up into the low forties by early afternoon. It was perfect weather for blasting the Taliban and punishing their sorry asses, Craig thought. As they walked along enjoying the morning, Craig told Frank that he wanted to see about getting an AC-130 gunship to work the Taliban positions through the coming night. Bombing them around the clock would help break their morale. An AC-130, with its 105mm and 40mm cannons and multibarreled Gatling guns, would turn the night into a living hell for the Taliban.

The men crested the next hill and were greeted by Sergeant Haidar, one of the few seasoned veterans fighting with this group of Karzai's troops. That was not surprising, given that Karzai had managed to attract only about four hundred fighters to his banner. Haidar spoke limited English, but he and Craig managed to communicate well.

Craig pointed to the messy defensive positions. "Bad, yes, but men tired," said Haidar. "They say, 'Enemy running. No worry.' "

"Yes, enemy running," said Craig. "But enemy still can shoot." He raised his arms to mimic holding a weapon. "Be strong, Sergeant Haidar." He flexed his left arm, pointing at his bicep. "Strong."

Haidar was smiling and flexing his own arm. "Yes, strong." He turned and looked around him, shaking his head. He turned back to Craig and Frank, and smiled. "You like chai?" he asked, pointing to a small campfire a few feet away and a sooted pot sending out steam.

They started toward the fire when there was a shot from the hill line opposite them. Then several more shots, the sounds echoing slightly in the chilly morning air. They all stopped to look at the Taliban positions across the valley. The Afghans had stopped their activities, and slowly all were getting to their feet and moving to peer across to where the shots had been fired.

There was movement on the hilltop, and Craig could make out the figures of two, now three men dressed in black clothing and moving toward the edge of the hill closest to Craig and his men. The three stood in line, arms raised above their heads, each holding an AK-47 and shouting. The sound drifted across to them, faint and unintelligible. Then the three men stepped forward and began to move down the slope toward them. Craig pulled out his binoculars and focused on the figures. They were moving deliberately, picking up speed, following a well-worn trail down the hill. They were wearing loose-fitting black clothing and black turbans, and, on their chests, heavy black canvas web gear and ammo pouches for their weapons.

"Hard to say what nationality they are," Craig said to Frank and Haidar, "but they're not dressed in the local style."

The three men reached the level ground of the valley floor and, without breaking stride, picked up their pace until they were jogging, moving directly toward the hill where Craig and the others watched in mild confusion. What were these three guys up to? They were moving effortlessly, running about three to four feet apart, maintaining a line, looking ahead and up to where Craig and his Afghans waited.

Then, from down the line, one of the Afghans watching the three men steadily cross the open ground shouted, "Chechnya! Chechnya!" The cry was picked up by others. "Chechnya!" A wave of panic and fear, so intense that Craig could feel it physically, swept through the line of men on the hilltop.

In every battle they had fought with the Taliban, there had been rumors and reports that a group of Chechens was fighting with the Taliban. They were reported to be fanatical, fierce fighters, well trained and experts with their weapons. After one particularly tough engagement a few days earlier, a number of the dead among the Karzai forces had been found to have been killed by a single shot to the head. This was incredible to the Afghans, none of whom actually aimed their weapons but rather trusted Allah to guide their bullets. They thought that such accurate fire had to be the work of the Chechens.

Craig turned in wonder to look up and down the line of Afghans. He could see panic setting in. Sixty men, all armed, frightened by three men running toward them. He grabbed Sergeant Haidar and shouted, "Tell the men to shoot. Shoot!" He did the motions of holding a weapon and firing. Haidar seemed to shake himself into action.

Haidar turned, shouting orders to his men. Fear drove them now, and they scrambled to grab their AK-47s. There was a ripple of noise and movement as they slammed magazines home and chambered rounds. Haidar had his own AK-47 ready and had moved to the leading edge of the hilltop, looking down on the three black-clad figures jogging relentlessly toward them. He shouted another order, raised his own weapon, and opened fire. The gun bucked against his shoulder, and he worked the trigger in short bursts of three or four rounds.

The others began to fire long bursts, guns bucking skyward against the prolonged recoil, panic firing. After a few seconds the firing reached a peak, and Craig watched in amazement as the three men continued to jog forward through the hail of lead slamming the earth around them. Gouts of earth exploded as the bullets tore into the ground, kicking up dirt clods and sending small rocks flying. The three men did not alter their pace or break formation but jogged on at the same steady pace.

The firing was sustained for a few seconds, then began to taper off as the Afghans expended their thirty-round magazines. The three figures appeared untouched, and Craig shouted to Haidar for the men to continue to fire. A ragged volume of fire began as nervous hands worked full magazines into the weapons; then the firing swelled up and down the line. The noise was almost deafening, and Craig put his index fingers into his ears to save his hearing. But again the three fighters ran on untouched.

They were now nearing the base of the hill, and as silence

fell along the line of men at the top of the hill they could hear the three men shouting, "Allahu Akbar!" over and over as they ran on. It was too much for the Afghans, and again the shout of "Chechnya!" rose in the air. As if on signal, the entire group of sixty men turned and began to run from their positions. Craig was shouting for them to stop, and grabbed at one man near him. But the man jerked free, staggered, and turned to join his comrades in a headlong run down the backside of the hill.

Craig and Frank looked over the hillside at the three Chechens who were now working their way toward them. Frank said, "Those are three of the bravest men I've ever seen, or they're three crazy motherfuckers. Either way, I don't want to stay around and meet them. What about you, Craig?"

Craig turned. "Let's introduce ourselves from afar, Frank." And he started jogging down the hill, with Frank following him, then breaking into a full run to catch up with the fleeing Afghan troops. Craig and Frank joined the men of ODA-574, looking back in amused disbelief at the three Chechens standing in the position they had just abandoned.

Craig yelled to the air force tactical air controller, "Is that B-52 on station yet?"

"Yes, sir. He's doing figure eights, waiting for us to give him geocoordinates for a target."

"Well," said Craig, looking back at the three Chechens, who were now casually going through the items left by the fleeing Afghans, "why not call in the coordinates for that hilltop? We can send those three a calling card."

As the radio call was made, Craig watched the three men, who now were shouting what had to be obscenities at them. One of the men stood spread-legged and grabbed his crotch with both hands, making hip movements to emphasize his statement. Another turned and pointed his butt at them, shaking it, then turned and pointed toward them, laughing.

The tactical air controller spoke. "One two-thousand-pound bomb is"—he paused—"on the way. Count twenty-five seconds until impact."

Craig stood looking at the three men across from him. It

had been one the finest displays of bravery he had ever seen or, for that matter, heard of. Three men, running under fire across six hundred to seven hundred yards of open ground, with sixty men firing at them, and never breaking stride. Now they stood there, jeering at the men they had humiliated.

Craig was sorry for what was going to happen to them, but his men needed to be reassured; they needed to regain some of the dignity they had thrown away. Craig knew that he and Frank could have killed the three men as they worked their way up the hill. But none of his Afghans would have seen that, and there would have been no closure for the men, and perhaps there would have been some resentment toward Frank and him. This way the joke would be turned on the three Chechens.

Craig glanced at his watch. Twenty seconds. He stepped forward and raised his right arm, waving it slowly back and forth in a broad arc. One of the Chechens saw him and raised his own right arm, middle finger extended in salute. The GBU-31 exploded at that moment within feet of the Chechen standing so proudly. The hilltop exploded in a massive blast of fire and smoke. A huge cheer went up from the Afghans surrounding Craig.

For a second, Craig thought he could see a human form in the fiery heart of the blast, but it passed so quickly that he thought he must have been imagining it.

CHAPTER FORTY-TWO

The morning of 27 October brought a number of interesting cables. One was a proposal for a meeting in Dushanbe between CINC CENTCOM (U.S. Army Central Command),

General Tommy Franks, and General Fahim. This would be an opportunity for Fahim to make his case face-to-face with General Franks and to allow Fahim to review his plans for an assault on Kabul.

In addition to General Franks, Hank from the CTC would be there, as would Admiral Calland, chief of CENTCOM's Special Operations Command (SOCOM), under which the Special Forces A-Teams were operating. With General Fahim already in Dushanbe, and Engineer Aref planning to join Fahim, the timing could not have been better.

I drove out to the landing zone at Astaneh with Mumtaz to be on hand to meet with Aref before his 8:30 a.m. flight. Aref was looking forward to the proposed meeting and said he would have Mumtaz arrange for the details of the proposal to be passed to General Fahim by radio even before his helicopter would arrive in Dushanbe. Aref asked if I was going to attend. It seemed a good idea, and I told him I would try to arrange to be there. I stood well back from the swirling gray-brown dust cloud, waving at the departing helicopter, thinking how quickly things seemed to be moving.

The morning cables had reported that four of the replacements for my team had arrived in Tashkent the previous day. My replacement turned out to be an old friend whose name also happened to be Gary. Gary 2 (as Gary 1 immediately dubbed him) was also scheduled to travel with Hank to Dushanbe. I figured that Rick and I could travel to Dushanbe, attend the meeting with Franks and Fahim, then pass the baton to our replacements. Chris and Murray were to join us in Dushanbe for the rotation out.

When I got back to the compound, Murray was there and was upset. He wanted an explanation as to why he had been pulled out of Baghram. According to him, he "had the SF guys eating out of his hand, and things had been going great." I told him that Headquarters was sending in replacements for some of our team, and he and Chris had been selected to rotate back to Headquarters. He was needed here to get ready to depart.

I felt bad about the situation. I really liked Murray, and I knew he felt he had been doing work of real value, but the story of him ignoring the danger of enemy fire bothered me, and I was concerned about his safety. No one ever said that a command was easy.

At about half past nine that morning, we got a radio message from the helicopter that they were encountering high winds and heavy dust, and visibility below a couple of thousand feet was almost zero. Ed said the control tower at Dushanbe airport was reporting equally bad conditions, and he expected a decision to be made within a few minutes to close down air operations there until the dust storm blew itself out. A minute or so later, Ed was back on the radio saying he was returning to the Panjshir; the weather conditions were so bad ahead that they could not see well enough to locate an alternative airfield, let alone fly all the way to Dushanbe.

Rick and I went down to the landing zone to wait for the helicopter's arrival. It was good to see the tiny dot appear off to the northern sky. The helicopter arrived back safely. Aref followed Buck off the aircraft, and it was clear that although Aref was smiling, he was shaken. He said the flight had become rough when they hit the high winds, and the air inside the aircraft had gotten dusty. He could not see anything but a brown swirl outside the windows. Glad to be back safely in the valley, Aref said later that if he had been in a Northern Alliance helicopter, he would not have survived; those aircraft were in such bad repair that any of them would surely have crashed. We talked about his making the same trip the following day if the weather permitted. To my surprise, Aref said he would be happy to try again tomorrow.

PART ELEVEN

JAWBREAKER TEAM AND THE TRIPLE NICKEL AT BAGHRAM AIR BASE

Late October 2001

CHAPTER FORTY-THREE

Daytime Action

Stan checked his wristwatch and noted that it was almost ten o'clock. The morning had gotten away from him. He visited General Bismullah Khan's G-2 (intelligence) shop early that morning to gather information for a report on Taliban movements over the last twenty-four hours. Of course he also got an earful from Major Nanullah complaining about the lack of U.S. air strikes on Taliban targets within sight of the major's office. Stan went back to his office and drafted the reports for transmission but found he was unable to connect with Headquarters to send the messages. Pappy thought he knew what the problem was, and promised Stan he would personally visit Baghram the next day to bring a connector and a new cable that would fix it.

With nothing more to do there, Stan took a drive to the airport to visit the Triple Nickel. As his Toyota Hi-Lux pickup rounded a sharp bend in the road, the old control tower for the air base appeared through the trees. The truck pulled alongside the building and stopped, its tires raising a billow of dust. Three or four Northern Alliance soldiers, all carrying AK-47s, were standing alongside the building. They're our guards, thought Stan, except the danger was not a direct attack on the position by Taliban troops but from long-range fire from heavy machine guns or mortars. That happened frequently enough for everyone to remain alert. No one had been injured yet, but the sound of a heavy 14.5mm round smashing into the concrete wall behind which you are working was a not-so-subtle reminder that thousands of bad guys within sight were anxious to kill you.

Stan thanked his driver—a grisly veteran with heavy shrapnel scars on the entire right side of his face, his right eye a milky, fixed orb—and made hand gestures for him to wait. After climbing out of the truck, Stan walked over and shook hands with the Afghan NCO in charge and joked with him in Russian. It was always a good idea to be congenial to the enlisted men who would do the actual fighting should there be an attack on the tower.

The walls of the building were battle-scarred, pockmarked by shrapnel and hundreds of bullets. The entrance to the building—missing its door and frame—opened into a small corridor with a concrete stairway leading to the tower area. Even the walls inside the building were bullet-marked, and Stan marveled at how much damage the building had sustained yet was still erect and in use. The paint on the dirty concrete stairs had long been worn away, and the center of each step was worn from the thousands of feet that had made this same climb.

Entry into the central room was by a square opening in the floor. An iron railing had once lined three sides of the opening. The room was bright on this sunny day, and the view from the glassless windows was spectacular. But Stan felt exposed, vulnerable, as if in plain view of the thousands of Taliban troops occupying the lines facing the south side of the building.

In the center of the room, two large wooden tables pulled together were covered with maps and odds and ends of the Special Forces team's personal equipment. Several M-4 rifles, the new cut-down version of the old M-16, were on the table along with a military HF radio set, water bottles, MRE boxes, and several NVG sets. Of the eight wooden chairs in the room, four were currently occupied by Triple Nickel operators working the binoculars and large spotting scopes set up on the windowsills facing the enemy positions. Murray and one of the senior NCOs were seated at the table transferring to the map geocoordinates from the NCO's notebook of new Taliban positions spotted that morning.

Murray and the NCO exchanged greetings as Stan pulled up a chair. "How's it going?" he asked.

The master sergeant, a combat veteran from the Gulf War with whom Murray had become friends, shook his head slowly and gave Stan a wry smile. "Same as usual, Stan. More targets than a hound dog has fleas, and we'll be lucky to get two or three aircraft to respond to our requests for strikes."

"Yeah, the target deck for today is sixty-five aircraft, with targets in the Qandahar, Jalalabad, and Mazar-e Sharif areas," said Murray. "High-priority tank repair depots and warehouses down south. Secondary targets include a troop barracks and supply depot south of Kabul. We'll get the leftovers, if any are available."

Stan shook his head. "I can't understand the strategy. The enemy is just outside these windows—hundreds, thousands, of Taliban and Arab fighters. We have tanks and assembly points marked, artillery positions, and ZSU positions, and the bombing is focused on warehouses."

Suddenly there was a flurry of conversation from the men working at the windows who were talking excitedly and pointed to the southeast. Stan and Murray moved to squat behind them. The air force special tactics specialist who handled coordination between the ODA and the U.S. military aircraft flying bombing missions spotted a truck convoy carrying about 150 Taliban troops and heading toward a complex identified as an assembly point. This was a prime target.

"Call it in, Phil," said Warrant Officer D., the team's second in command. "This is too good to miss out on."

Stan picked up a spare set of binoculars and moved to a window. He focused in on the line of dust being raised by a convoy of what looked like six or seven heavy Russian transport trucks. Stan could just see the men riding in them seated and standing, the dust swirling up from the tires around them. "They really don't think we can hurt them," Stan said aloud, more to himself than making conversation.

Warrant Officer D. turned to Stan. "If we can convince the AWACS [Airborne Warning and Control System] to release a B-52 for this strike, we'll show those bastards just how much hurt we can bring down on them."

Phil made contact with the AWACS aircraft that was on station providing control for the bombing missions to be made that morning.

"This is TIGER One, Control. Request release of aircraft to conduct priority strike on heavily occupied enemy position one point five kilometers south of my position. Approximately one five zero enemy combatants and seven heavy trucks, with an unknown number of other enemy combatants at that same location."

There was a pause, then a crackle of static, then a voice. "TIGER One, this is Control. Negative on your request. Targets in today's deck are being engaged as top priority. Anticipate we will have several aircraft to release to you later this morning. Will monitor situation, and Control will contact TIGER One, if and when aircraft become available. Out."

There were groans of dismay from the group of men crouching around the open windows. Another letdown. They might get an F-16 or perhaps, if lucky, a B-52 with one heavy bomb, and they would kill a few Taliban, but nothing like the massive damage they could inflict if they had a fully committed B-52. After the puny strike, General Bismullah's radio intercept team would report the Taliban commanders laughing at how weak and ineffective the Americans are, how little damage they are causing with their occasional bomb or two. It was frustrating.

Stan set down the binoculars and turned to Murray. "I'm going back to the office to work on a message to JAW-BREAKER and Headquarters on this situation. It won't do any real good, but I want it on the record."

He turned to leave, and Murray said, "Let's go out tonight with the night shift. I'd like to work up close and personal for a change. We had better luck getting aircraft last night. Maybe we'll get lucky again tonight."

"Good idea. I'd like that too."

Night Action

Stan abandoned his tan corduroy sport coat for a Northern Alliance dark green field jacket and was putting the finishing touches on securing his canvas web gear and ammo pouches. He would be carrying his AK-47—its metal folding stock making it the envy of all the Afghan troops who saw it—and his Browning 9mm Hi-Power automatic pistol. He had on a black wool watch cap, and his face was streaked with just enough camouflage paint to break its silhouette. His NGV set hung around his neck.

The door to his room pushed open, and Murray's camouflaged face appeared. "Ten o'clock, Stan. Time to go. The vehicles are here, and Triple Nickel is saddling up."

Stan clicked off the single lightbulb dangling from the ceiling on an electrical cord and walked out the door. Murray was in front of him, heading for one of the two Toyota pickup trucks parked outside the building. Stan could see four Triple Nickel soldiers loading gear into the rear of both trucks, and he slung his small backpack onto the pile of canvas bags in the first truck in line.

Captain R., ODA Team leader, called out, "Everybody set? Let's mount up." Stan fit himself so his back rested against the equipment bags, then pulled his knees up toward his chin, holding his AK-47 between his legs, muzzle skyward. Then the engines turned over, and the trucks jerked forward and headed toward the control tower.

This was the phase of operations that Stan liked best. The men would dismount near the control tower building, then make their way along a carefully marked path toward the NA frontline positions facing the Taliban forces. The team used several locations for night operations, each offering an excellent vantage point from which to call in air strikes on the enemy positions before them. The night vision goggles were essential, because the path they walked twisted through areas of uncleared land mines and unexploded ordnance. Once in position, they would be close to the enemy. On an earlier night, they had selected a spot from which to work that turned out to be only five to six hundred yards from the Taliban. They were so close that in the still of the night they drew fire when the Taliban could hear the muffled voice of the tactical air operator calling in the enemy's geocoordinates.

Neither Stan nor Murray was required to go along on these night missions. Laser target designation was the mission of the A-Team. But this was a team effort, and that meant sharing the danger. Besides, they had been having more luck in getting aircraft to strike targets on this front at night than during daylight hours, and being part of the operation that brought down fire and destruction on the enemy was just too good to miss.

The path toward the front lines meandered through an area littered with the wreckage of Russian military aircraft, their twisted, burned, and broken airframes mute evidence of the ferocity of years of fighting that had taken place for control of this air base. Russian MiG fighters, AN-12 transport aircraft, some old twin-wing aircraft that no one on the team could identify, and even several huge IL-76 cargo aircraft lay in mock formations, row upon row of battered, blasted hulks. Stan would have loved to explore the old wrecks, but he knew that the ground was littered with unexploded ordnance, for these aircraft had been shelled and bombed repeatedly over the years, long after they were abandoned.

They passed out of the area of the dead aircraft and entered a line of small trees. The long drought had stunted their growth, but they still offered good cover for movement.

The position they would use for this evening's operation was behind a high earth berm facing the enemy. The radio equipment was set up at the base of the berm, to help muffle the sound of the communications by the tactical air controller. The three A-Team members positioned themselves along the top of the berm, each behind sandbags they had placed there some days earlier. Stan and Murray joined them, taking up what had now become their usual positions. Weapons were unslung and placed within easy reach, and the SOFLAM equipment was set up.

Earlier in the day, targets were discussed, and a priority list was made. It was not extensive; they did not expect to get more than three or four aircraft, and those would likely be U.S. Navy aircraft, whose loiter time over target would be short, given the distances they flew to and from their aircraft carrier.

Stan watched the open area between his position and the enemy. The nearest Taliban position was about five hundred yards away. He felt fairly confident that the enemy had not figured out how the team worked or how targets were identified and marked for the aircraft. Without night vision capabilities, the Taliban were blind after dark. Stan knew that he and the others were invisible to the enemy, but it still felt odd to be lying in the open so close to enemy guns.

At 11:40 p.m., the tactical air controller tapped Captain R. on the ankle and whispered that he had two navy F/A-18 Hornets inbound, due in twenty minutes. They each carried two 500-pound high-explosive guided bombs and were requesting target geocoordinates. The Hornets would try to hit four targets. Captain R. huddled with his men behind the top of the berm to figure out the best sequence of strikes to be taken by the aircraft.

The first target—observed earlier that day—was a group of mud-walled buildings serving as a troop assembly point. A second convoy of trucks was seen arriving at the complex just before darkness fell.

A T-55 tank and a nearby ZSU-23 cannon were the next target on the list. These had been in place for nearly a week, sitting in clear view of the team, and were just too good to pass up any longer.

The Taliban command post could be identified by the several antennas on its roof and the heavy personnel traffic in and out of the building. Several 14.5mm heavy machine guns were positioned to defend it. The hope was that the senior officers for this sector would be sleeping inside the building.

The fourth target was an M-30 artillery battery, two heavy cannons placed about a mile behind the front lines. These were recent emplacements, obviously put there to add fire-power to an impending attack.

The SOFLAM laser, invisible to the naked eye, reached out to touch the group of buildings making up the first target. The CAS specialist was working the radio and was now in direct contact with the pilot of the first inbound F/A-18. The noise of the aircraft was rapidly growing louder. There was a slight pause, then the CAS operator said, "Weapon away." Each man reached up and turned off his NVG set, and almost immediately there was a flash of blinding light and a shock wave swept over the battlefield. An orange-red fireball leaped into the sky, carrying with it dirt, metal, and bodies, leaving smoke and dust boiling from the wreckage of what had been the sleeping quarters for a number of Taliban fighters.

After a short interval, the SOFLAM laser was aimed at the second target. The second F/A-18 was inbound and con-firmed the target. Again there was the sound of an aircraft's twin engines roaring, and another fireball blast. This time, Stan could see the turret of the T-55 tank twisting through the air end over end as sparks of molten metal mixed with the cloud of smoke and debris that rose above the position.

The first aircraft had made a wide turn and was inbound for its second pass. The SOFLAM laser touched the com-mand post, and the CAS operator and pilot confirmed the target. The bomb fell not on but next to the building, but the blast was strong enough to blow through the side of the mud structure. A fireball lit the inside of the building and blew out the bricked-up windows.

Stunned Taliban all along the front began to fire. A ZSU-23 fired blindly into the sky as if hoping to hit the unseen air-craft. AK-47s, heavy machine guns, even pistols were ham-mering away in all directions. Stan heard the snap of rounds passing close overhead, and several bullets hit below them on the earth berm. Stan lowered himself slightly so that only the top of his head was above the berm. He just had to see the fourth target get hit.

The last 500-pound bomb detonated between the two M-30 artillery pieces, and the blast lifted them into the air, twisting them into grotesque shapes. Then there were secondary explosions as ammunition for the guns began to cook off. The air was filled with thunderclap explosions and sparking trails of flying molten metal. The firing from the Taliban lines died quickly as men ducked to cover themselves from the falling rock and metal debris.

The CAS operator thanked the two pilots for a job well done, and the men on the berm shook hands excitedly. This was the best single strike they had called in yet. Tomorrow morning, for a change, General Bismullah would be happy. Stan thought long and hard about how to write up this success on his report to the CTC to convey how effective and devastating the bombing could be on this front if the aircraft were made available.

No other aircraft were released that night for the Kabul front.

CHAPTER FORTY-FOUR

On 28 October the weather over the valley was cold and clear, and the weather watcher in the mountains gave the go-ahead for a flight over Anjuman Pass. Our pilots were ready to fly Aref to Dushanbe, pick up the four incoming team replacements and supplies waiting there, and return to the valley. The aircrew spent extra time that morning going over the aircraft to make sure there were no residual problems from the dust storm of the previous day. Mumtaz had Engineer Aref at the landing zone half an hour before scheduled take-off, and I met with him to discuss the upcoming meeting with General Franks.

I did not have to tell Aref that the meeting was an ex-

tremely important one for General Fahim and the Northern
Alliance. I explained that General Fahim must be well prepared for these discussions, because General Franks would
want to know details such as size and disposition of Fahim's
forces, the plan for the assault on Kabul, and the plans for a
breakout on the Takhar front and a push on Talaqan city. At
the same time, I said, General Fahim should be clear in exactly what he needed from General Franks in the way of air
support for his upcoming attacks and whatever supplies and
materiel he needed to bring his forces to full combat readiness. General Franks would want to know why Fahim had
not attacked the Taliban forces when Dostum and Atta were
on the offensive in the Mazar-e Sharif area and were both
making slow but steady progress. I strongly suggested that
Fahim be candid and straightforward in his responses. General Franks had to come away from this meeting with confidence in General Fahim and his ability to successfully carry
out the planned offensive.

My jeep was midway across the Panjshir River, splashing
and bouncing over the basketball-size river rocks, as the helicopter lifted off and headed north up the valley. As I watched
it become a small dot in the sky, I hoped that General Fahim
would hold his own against what was surely going to be a
high-powered group of American officers sitting across the
table from him.

An hour later, Rick, Chris, and I were sitting at the main
worktable reading the morning cable traffic when the helicopter came over the radio. Greg was on the microphone and
said they were experiencing fuel line problems—clogged
fuel filters—and would land just outside Faizabad to try to
fix the problem. He sounded calm, as though making an un-
scheduled emergency landing in the middle of nowhere was
an everyday occurrence. He signed off, saying they would
contact us as soon as they knew the extent of the problem.

This was the second serious situation with the helicopter
in two days. I could not help but think of a humorous description of a helicopter I once heard—ten thousand moving

parts trying desperately to come apart. The problem had to be dirt in the fuel that we were forced to use. The local gasoline we were burning in our generators was so dirty that despite filtering it through a sock as we filled the tank, the fuel filter would still clog quickly, sometimes once an hour, shutting down the generator and starting a string of profanity from our communication specialists, Pappy and Fred.

Buck said he would normally change fuel filters on the helicopter once every eight hours of flight time, but now he had to change them every two to three hours. Although this situation was serious, Faizabad is on the far side of the Hindu Kush, and there were ample landing areas available. None of us had asked the question, at least not out loud, of what would happen if the fuel filters clogged while in the mountains, with no place to land. I did not know that we would get a firsthand answer to that unasked question in just a few days.

Thirty minutes later, Greg called in to report that the fuel filters had been changed and the engines were running smoothly. They were again on their way to Dushanbe. They would check the helicopter carefully once in Dushanbe and planned on draining the tanks and refueling with clean fuel there. They would overnight in Dushanbe and not be back in the valley until late the next afternoon.

Late that afternoon I started feeling bad again. Well, what did I expect? It had been more than a week since I'd had any symptoms of my previous bowel problems. I went to bed early that evening, modified water bottle close at hand.

CHAPTER FORTY-FIVE

The next day, 29 October, began at 4:00 a.m. for me, with an urgent call from nature. I was surprised that my system had held off that long. I took a Cipro and drank a healthy swallow of Tagamet, then headed off to heat the water for my shower. The weather matched how I felt, with low gray clouds and a threat of rain.

A little later there was a cable from Dushanbe confirming the status of our helicopter. The fuel tanks would be cleaned this morning, and if things went well, the crew would be ready to lift off by two that afternoon. The cable also reported that my replacement, Gary 2, had arrived in Dushanbe from Tashkent the previous day. The other three team replacements would fly back to the valley this afternoon as scheduled, but Gary 2 would remain in Dushanbe to take part in the meeting with General Franks.

I was glad that Gary 2 had been selected to replace me. He had been a student of mine when I was an instructor at the Farm. He had worked Iranian operations for a number of years, and although he did not have direct experience in Afghan operations, he did speak Farsi, which would come in handy here.

Rick and I met with the three Delta Force operators who had come in with Colonel H.'s SOCCE Team. They were all younger than the other teams' Special Forces soldiers we had met so far, and none of them had any real idea of the situation on the ground in Afghanistan. Their mission was to do initial planning for how the Shelter Now hostages might be rescued, so we gave them a full briefing on all we had pulled together. Chris was especially thorough in his follow-on briefings, walking them through the structure and nature of the Taliban, and on how tribal and family ties worked here, so they could understand the negotiations taking place between Aref's officers and Taliban intelligence and prison officials on releasing the hostages. We suggested they visit the Kabul front and get a firsthand look at the front lines to see what obstacles they faced in trying to get the hostages through those defensive positions.

After their visit to the front lines and several more days of discussions, they came to us with their plan. It was another "simple plan." An element of Delta Force would stage in a small convoy of local trucks just behind NA lines opposite the "new road" to Kabul. The convoy would then drive straight down the new road toward Kabul and the prison, fighting their way through Taliban defensive positions and checkpoints. They would then battle their way into the prison, grab the hostages, and drive to a designated landing zone just outside Kabul, where U.S. military helicopters would pick them up. Needless to say, we did not write up this plan for Headquarters to consider. I think even they realized the plan was both impossible and lame, and we never heard any more from the three Delta operators on rescue plans.

At 4:00 p.m. that afternoon, our helicopter landed at Astaneh with the three replacement team members. Rick's replacement, George, was a solid officer with an excellent reputation. Between Gary 2 and George, the team would be in good hands. We welcomed them warmly. With Stan down at Baghram and Brad off in Takhar, sleeping quarters were not cramped.

After dinner we started the briefing process, bringing the new men up to speed on the situation here in the valley. We introduced them to Mumtaz and Jan Mohammad, then took them over to meet Colonel H. and his team. I told George that we would transfer responsibility for the cash the next morning. That would mean a formal hands-on count of the money, with George signing a receipt for the funds for my retention.

We sent a cable notifying Headquarters of the arrival of our replacements. I went to bed early again, still feeling rocky.

CHAPTER FORTY-SIX

Our plans called for Rick, Chris, Murray, and me to travel to Dushanbe in the early afternoon of 30 October, to be in place for the meeting between generals Fahim and Franks. That would be the first leg of our return journey back to Washington. I should have known that those plans would slip. The thirtieth dawned with heavy, low clouds over the valley, and the report from the weather watcher was that heavy snow was falling over the mountains. The forecast called for the weather front to remain in place for at least the entire day. We were stuck in the valley until tomorrow at the earliest. I knew that Hank would represent my views about how to adjust the bombing strategy to support General Fahim's Northern Alliance forces, but I wanted to be there, to add my personal observations to the equation, and perhaps help shape General Franks's decision on how best to proceed.

Little would be going on here in the valley or down on the Kabul front. The limited bombing that would normally take place would be on hold because of the weather, and without Engineer Aref we would have only minimal operational activity on our several ongoing intelligence initiatives, such as the Shelter Now hostage planning or efforts to coordinate capture operations against bin Ladin's key lieutenants.

I sat with George on the floor of the office area, and we carefully counted the money from the four large cardboard boxes. I would count a pile of cash, make a note of the amount, and pass the cash to George. He would count it and we would confirm the amount. We repeated the process with every pile. I had been keeping duplicate records of my own on all my cash disbursements, which included all the payments listed in this text, and a number of others not mentioned here. In the thirty-three days since we had arrived in the valley, I paid out $4.9 million. George signed for slightly more than $8 million in cash, and I was happy to see the responsibility pass to him.

I found Jan Mohammad and presented him with $10,000 for use in repairing and restocking the two elementary schools in the village. Both buildings, rebuilt only in the last eighteen months, lacked such essentials as windows, doors, desks, and blackboards. I had not previously mentioned my plans to give him this money, and he was shocked but pleased at the gesture. He said he would visit each school after lunch and have the teachers put together a list of the essential repairs they wanted made, as well as a list of supplies for the children. He hugged me hard and said the village would never forget our team. Tears ran down his cheeks, and I knew I had made the correct gesture to thank him for his hospitality and companionship. I asked him to get all the household staff together in the courtyard just before lunch so the team could present them with gifts of money to thank them personally. He was beaming as he walked away.

I got together all the team members who were available to join me in the presentation to the staff. Each of the cooks— we had two by then, although together they did not add up to one real cook—got $200. The young men on the staff each got $100, as did the village baker, who had made and delivered our fresh bread each day. Even the village barber got $100 for his efforts. He had come to the compound once a week for the past few weeks but hadn't accepted payment from any of us. Later I cornered Jan Mohammad alone and passed him $1,500 for his personal use. He had done so much to make our life in the valley comfortable, and had taken such personal pride in all the improvements he made to the food service and sanitation in the compound, that he deserved every penny I gave him. By the time lunch was served, we had a very happy group of Afghans working for us.

The cables from Headquarters contained gloomy news. The debate continued over the fate of Kabul and how to deal with the Northern Alliance. The lack of focus in our bombing campaign was of concern, because our efforts to date seemed to be having little impact on the Taliban forces and their willingness and ability to fight.

Rick spent some time in the afternoon on the secure phone trying to arrange for travel plans to get us back to Washington, if and when we managed to get out of the valley. With the number of U.S. military and other aircraft now flying between Washington, Frankfurt, and Tashkent, we hoped that our small group would be able to hitch a ride on one of them rather than have to travel by commercial airline.

That evening Rick and I smoked cigars on the patio, standing close to the wall to avoid the light mist of falling rain. My thoughts were on Dushanbe and the meeting getting under way there. I was feeling as gloomy as the weather, and I made an early evening of it and headed off to bed.

CHAPTER FORTY-SEVEN

Halloween dawned wet and cold, but the forecast did call for a possible break in the weather that afternoon.

I did not expect a cable from Dushanbe on the results of the meeting until early afternoon, but at about ten that morning Rick and I called Dushanbe and were able to get in touch with Hank. He was upbeat and said the meeting had gone well, but the most disappointing aspect of it was General Fahim's performance. The meeting was held in General Franks's huge U.S. Air Force C-17 cargo aircraft, reconfigured to serve as his mobile office. Hank said he thought Fahim had been overwhelmed by the setting—with General Franks and his senior staff (all general officers) and Admiral Calland arrayed around one side of the table, and Fahim, Aref, and a young Afghan translator on the other side.

General Franks pushed Fahim for an outline of his plans for an assault on Kabul and pressed him for a timetable when the attack would begin. In response, Fahim outlined his position on the Kabul front and pointed out the strengths of the Taliban and Arab defensive positions he faced. He also pointed out that he had been promised that the presence of Special Forces would bring sustained, heavy bombing down onto the Taliban. That had not happened, and the bombing continued to be limited in scope and effectiveness.

General Franks kept pushing for specific plans, a specific time line for a breakout toward Kabul and the same for the Takhar front toward Talaqan. Fahim seemed somewhat flustered by this, although he did manage to explain that his forces did not have the strength on their own to break through the Taliban and Arab defenses. If he had such strength, he would have already started his attack. He needed the promised bombing to weaken the Taliban. If the general could not promise that assistance, then Fahim would attack on his own, because they could not afford to sit out another winter in their hilltop defensive positions. Hank said that General Franks then promised to shift the bombing campaign to concentrate on the Kabul front, and requested that General Fahim coordinate his plans with the CIA and Colonel H. in the Panjshir.

Overall it was a successful meeting. Although General Franks had not been overly impressed with General Fahim, Franks did feel that he could work with him.

The agreement to shift the bombing strategy to focus on

the Taliban was indeed welcome news. It was what we had been waiting for since the bombing campaign had begun on 7 October, twenty-four days earlier. If the bombing did shift, and if we hammered the Taliban hard for three or four days, I was sure the Northern Alliance would smash through their defensive positions and be on the outskirts of Kabul in two days.

At 12:30 p.m., Mumtaz came to the office with news that the weather over the Anjuman Pass had cleared, and the clouds over the valley had lifted and the sun was peeking through. The decision was made to take off for Dushanbe as soon as we could get to the landing field and ready the helicopter to fly. The four of us who were due to depart made hasty good-byes, lugged baggage to the waiting vehicles, and headed to the landing field at Astaneh.

I was upbeat. Although we were leaving with the job un-finished, Hank's news from Dushanbe was positive. With U.S. military assistance, Fahim would have little difficulty breaking out on both key fronts. The NA forces around Mazar-e Sharif continued to slowly press the Taliban back toward the city. This was the beginning of the end for the Taliban, although they did not know it yet. Our team was in good hands. George was already getting on top of things, and Gary 2 would be here, probably on the return flight of the helicopter today, or tomorrow at the latest.

We stored our gear and I took a seat in the rear of the heli-copter, on one of the two fold-down chairs affixed to the front edge of the large clamshell cargo doors. There is a small window by each of these seats, and they are much more comfortable than the seats in the front of the aircraft. The drawback, however, was that I was sitting on a remov-able section of the aircraft, held in place by two large (and, I hoped, strong) hinges on each of the doors. Rick took the other seat, and we smiled and gave each other a thumbs-up.

The flight was routine as we climbed steadily to the north. The scenery out the window was more barren and stark than when we had flown in on 26 September, and within thirty minutes we were seeing snow on the tops of the hills. As we neared 14,500 feet at the top of the Anjuman Pass, we saw heavy snow cover below us. The pass would be closed to vehicular traffic until early summer next year. I guessed that our tanker truck with its load of helicopter fuel was stuck somewhere down there. The hills had given way to full-fledged mountains, and rocky walls and snowy crags rose above us as we climbed.

Buck moved into the cockpit area, standing behind Ed and Greg. I thought he just wanted a better view of the scenery we were passing over. As we crested the high point of the Anjuman, we were surprised to see ahead and below us a solid bank of heavy gray clouds filling the valley into which we were about to fly. The mountain peaks rose out of the clouds on both sides of the aircraft. Suddenly we were buffeted by strong headwinds, and the helicopter jerked and bumped. Then we were turning around, heading back, and the helicopter began to climb again, back up over the crest of the Anjuman. Buck came out of the cockpit area and shook his head; we were returning to the valley.

As we were getting off the helicopter, Buck said, "Man, that was a close one."

"Yeah," said Rick, "that cloud bank looked bad."

Buck shook his head. "Ed called ahead to Dushanbe, and they said the cloud cover was down to a few thousand feet. Flying through those mountains in those clouds would be like playing Russian roulette. The only thing that could be worse would be having the fuel filter lights go red. There is no alternative landing area in those mountains. I sweat bullets every time we fly this route."

At 5:00 p.m., almost as if on schedule, the low clouds over the valley opened and spilled a steady, hard rain. We had had rain several times before, but it had been hardly more than a mist. This was our first downpour, and I wondered about how the hard, sun-baked mud roofs of our buildings would hold up under this soaking. I stopped Jan Mohammad, who was busy supervising dinner preparations, and he assured me the roofs would not leak. I wanted to believe him.

The construction of the roofs on these buildings was unique, and I have seen it used only on the two buildings in our compound in Barak. It appeared that the builders had constructed the walls first, then laid timbers, all about twelve inches in diameter, on the walls to act as beams, spacing the timbers about a yard apart. On top of these beams they used wood from shipping crates to form the first layer of the roof. I could still see the Russian-language stencils on the wooden pieces. On top of this they put down a mixture of straw and mud, which dried to an almost rock-hard consistency in the hot sun. Still, mud was mud, no matter how hard, and it was pouring rain.

I returned to my room at 8:30 p.m. to relax and read, trying to avoid the tenth BBC news broadcast of the day proclaiming that the United States was failing in its bombing campaign against the Taliban. As I opened the door I was greeted by what sounded like a miniature waterfall. The light revealed a cascade of water streaming down the wall opposite me, splashing into a growing puddle on the floor.

Jan Mohammad rallied the boys, and there was a thirty-minute Chinese fire drill in and around my room. The problem was discovered to be, of all things, a tennis ball lodged in one the roof drains. Once that was removed and the standing water swept off the roof, the leak was easy to plug. Cleaning up the room was a job, but the boys seemed experienced in this procedure, and soon the room was back in order.

I went to bed but had a difficult time falling asleep, because I kept expecting to hear the sound of water splashing on the floor. I should not have worried, though, because the roofs here never leak.

PART TWELVE

THE BOMBING STEPS UP

1–4 November 2001

CHAPTER FORTY-EIGHT

The next morning, 1 November, was as wet as the previous night, and the rain showed no sign of letting up. The storm was dropping heavy snow on the Anjuman Pass and the mountains to the north. Winter was settling in rapidly. The long-range forecast called for bad weather for at least another five days.

Rick was trying to find an alternative to having to fly over the mountains to get in and out of the valley. Our airfield at Gul Bahar had been completed for more than two weeks, but we had yet to use it. Rick thought that a midsize fixed-wing aircraft, which had recently arrived in Tashkent, might be able to use the Gul Bahar airfield, flying in from the north and west, avoiding the Hindu Kush Mountains. The air operations officer and the pilots in Tashkent were willing to consider using Gul Bahar, but it would have to be surveyed and certified by our pilots. Ed and Greg agreed to fly down to Gul Bahar to complete the survey as soon as the weather permitted.

We spoke to Stan at Baghram around noon, and he reported no change in the pace or intensity of the bombing. ODA-555 was still able to get only single aircraft for strikes on the Kabul front. Brad reported the same situation from Takhar. I was beginning to suspect that the Dushanbe meeting had not been as positive as Hank had thought.

In the late afternoon, however, there was a new development in the bombing, but this took place on the Mazar-e Sharif front. ALPHA Team reported that major air strikes had taken place that day involving B-52 and B-1 bombers hitting six key Taliban positions. Northern Alliance radio intercepts of Taliban communications indicated that the Taliban had suffered losses of more than three hundred men and a senior Talib commander. The NA reported that the Taliban radio communications in the aftermath of the bombing were full of panic and fear as the full extent of the damage and the casualties became known. Additionally, NA radio intercepts detailed orders by Taliban army headquarters in Kabul to the Taliban commander at Konduz to move massive amounts of military supplies to Mazar-e Sharif. Kabul was sending seven hundred Taliban fighters to Mazar by way of Bamiyan Province, but movement was expected to be difficult because of heavy U.S. bombing in that area.

This was encouraging news. It was not what was promised in Dushanbe, but at least there was a developing focus in the bombing. The impact of sustained, heavy bombing on the inexperienced Taliban fighters was becoming apparent from the panic and fear heard in the radio exchanges around the Mazar battlefields. Several more days of this level of activity would bring clear proof of just how weak the Taliban forces really were. Although I would have preferred the test case to be the Kabul battlefields, breaking the Taliban around Mazar-e Sharif would provide the evidence that this new focus in the bombing campaign was the correct one.

A few days earlier, Pappy had discovered a stash of DVDs that he had brought with him and forgotten. He quickly set up one of our larger Sony laptops in the hallway outside the office area, and we were able to watch a selection of movies. He even rigged external speakers to the laptop so the sound quality was greatly improved.

Unfortunately, Pappy's taste in movies was not that refined. We had such gems as the *Great St. Louis Bank Robbery,* starring a very young Steve McQueen; *Hell Is for Heroes,* also with Steve McQueen; and three or four others of this caliber. How Steve McQueen's career survived those two films is beyond me. The most current movie was the second Austin Powers film. I never managed to see the entire film in one sitting but would wander by and catch a scene or two. I came to detest the film, and especially Mini-Me.

At about half past seven that evening, a few of the team were seated in the hallway watching Steve McQueen shoot a bunch of Germans when there was a loud crash and shouting from the pilots' room. I thought a fight had broken out, but it was the commotion of a leaking roof pouring water behind a wooden shelf attached to one wall and causing the shelf to give way. Another Chinese fire drill ensued, with the young Afghans scurrying around on the roof, in the pilots' room, and in the hallway, dragging out wet lumber, soaked clothing, and books.

As things calmed down, I got a cup of coffee and headed off to my room.

CHAPTER FORTY-NINE

The weather forecast of the previous day had been wrong; 2 November dawned cold but cloudless. The weather watcher radioed that the Anjuman Pass was clear. A radio check with Dushanbe told us that they had rain there, but flight operations were under way at the airport. I started to make preparations to depart, putting the clothing I had worn in the last few days back into my two duffel bags. It seemed as though it would be a leisurely morning.

That changed with an 8:00 a.m. radio call from Stan at Baghram. One of the ODA-555 soldiers had been sick for the past two days, and the Special Forces medic couldn't determine what was wrong with the soldier. He had a high temperature and a terrific headache, and even morphine did not break the pain. The medic requested that we try to medevac the soldier to the Special Forces base at Karshi Khanabad, in Uzbekistan. We responded immediately.

The flight crew headed for the airfield with Doc in tow to fly to our airfield at Gul Bahar. Stan would assist Triple Nickel personnel in moving the soldier to Gul Bahar to meet our helicopter. They would come back at Astaneh to take on the four of us slated to depart, and we would fly on to Dushanbe.

Mumtaz drove down to the landing field with the four of us to say good-bye once again. This time I thought for sure we would make it. I told him that the increased bombing around Mazar-e Sharif was a good development, one that foreshadowed similar bombings at Kabul and on the Takhar front. I am not sure he believed me, but he smiled and we shook hands warmly.

At 9:00 a.m. our helicopter swooped in from the south and landed. We clambered aboard, and Rick and I took the cargo door seats again. The soldier was on a stretcher on the right side of the front of the aircraft, with the medic sitting next to him. Doc exited the helicopter, because there was nothing he could do that the medic was not already doing. By 9:11 we were on our way.

We made the now familiar steady climb northward, heading for the Anjuman Pass. The soldier was still, his knit watch cap pulled over his eyes. Doc had said the soldier might have some form of meningitis; if so, he needed serious medical treatment quickly. Things seemed routine until, once again, I saw Buck move forward into the cockpit area. We were just cresting the Anjuman, and from what I could see out of my little window the weather seemed clear. Buck came back into the passenger area and knelt by the medic, speaking into his ear. Buck looked up at the rest of us, shook his head, and made a circular motion with his hand. We were turning around and heading back to the valley. Had the weather changed ahead of us? I knew this was a serious decision and one the pilots had not made lightly, not with the soldier in his present condition. I felt a real sense of disappointment when we began the descent and headed back to the landing field.

We exited the front door while Buck opened the cargo doors to ease the job of getting the stretcher off the helicopter. Once that was done and the soldier was moved, Ed and Greg joined us at planeside to tell us what happened. "This time it was the fuel filters. The first one went red just before we got to the top of the pass, and the second went red just as we started down the other side." Ed said he would have chanced it with one filter clogged, but not with both. He had never tested the engine's ability to fly while sucking dirty gas straight from the tank, and he didn't want to start today at 14,500 feet with no alternative landing field available.

Back at the compound we learned that Pappy had been on the radio with Task Force Dagger and reported the problems that our helicopter had experienced. Colonel Mulholland had ordered a medevac flight for his men to take off at 3:00 p.m. This medevac mission would be the first daylight flight operation conducted by Task Force Dagger.

Right at 3:00 p.m. we were notified that the flight had taken off as scheduled; however, within thirty minutes the aircraft had run into bad weather, which was likely to get worse at higher altitudes. This proved to be the case, and by 5:00 p.m. Task Force Dagger called to report that the flight was returning to base.

Outside of these concerns, the news from ALPHA continued to be positive. A predawn airdrop of ammunition and supplies had been successfully completed, with the materiel being equally divided between Dostum and Atta. Dostum had gained nearly six miles of ground that day against stiff Taliban resistance and pushed up the Shulgara river valley toward Mazar. American bombers had provided daytime tactical air support for Dostum's forces, and that support had been crucial in ensuring Dostum's successes.

We learned from Task Force Dagger that another military medevac mission was scheduled for early the following day. This time, however, two CH-53 helicopters would be flown from the Jacobabad airfield in western Pakistan. This would be a long, difficult flight over rugged terrain still firmly under Taliban control. Colonel H.'s SOCCE would handle the landing field markings, but we asked to be informed of the arrival time so we could have several team members, Doc specifically, standing by there to provide assistance if needed.

We all went to bed that night expecting a call in the early-morning hours that the CH-53s were inbound. The call never came.

CHAPTER FIFTY

We were all up early the next morning, gathered in the office area to check on incoming cable traffic for word on what had happened to the medevac mission. There was nothing in the cable queue, so Rick walked over to meet with Colonel H. to see if he had word on what had transpired.

Doc beat us all to the news by turning on the BBC. One of their news readers was reporting a story of the crash of a CH-53 helicopter some miles south of Kabul in the predawn hours that morning. Four of the eleven crew members had been injured in the crash, but all had been rescued by a second CH-53. There were rumors that the two helicopters had been on a rescue mission to bring back an injured Special Forces soldier. No mention was made as to where the injured soldier was located.

Rick returned from seeing Colonel H. with confirmation of the crash. Apparently the flight had encountered high winds and dust, and the lead aircraft had been too low and had bounced off a hilltop and crashed. The second helicopter had immediately landed and taken the other crew on board, but the mission had to be aborted. The air force was debating whether to fly in a crew to repair the downed aircraft and try to fly it back to base, or simply destroy the helicopter where it sat, to deny it to the enemy.

The pilots thought about making another flight in our helicopter over the Anjuman but finally decided that it was too windy to risk the effort, especially with the problems we were having with dirty fuel and clogged fuel filters. There was nothing to do but wait.

At 3:00 p.m. we were contacted by Task Force Dagger with word that they would fly another medevac mission that night. The Special Forces were coming for their comrade. This time two CH-47s, large twin-rotor cargo helicopters, would fly the mission, and they were scheduled to arrive at the Astaneh landing field at 2:00 a.m. (the early-morning hours of 4 November). We were also told that Hank, Gary 2, and Admiral Calland had moved from Dushanbe to Tashkent and would be on the CH-47s that night. We four departing team members would fly back on the CH-47s with the injured Special Forces soldier. For some reason I knew that we would make it out of the valley this time.

It was near freezing for the first time since we had arrived. We moved to the landing field a little before one in the morning, a hard trip for the injured soldier, even on a stretcher. According to Doc, the soldier's condition was about the same, and although he was in a lot of pain, he seemed to be holding his own.

My driver was a young man whom I had not seen before. He was dressed in Northern Alliance military clothing, with a thin field jacket for his coat. He had boots but no gloves. When I repacked earlier that day, I had found a second pair of high-quality wool gloves in the bottom of one of my duffel bags. I gave them to the young man, saying in Dari that they were a gift for him. He looked incredulous but pulled them on; he flexed his fingers, then started to cry. He shook my hand hard, thanking me, and I was embarrassed at his emotion at my simple gesture. I could only guess that he had been surprised at the gift and even more surprised at the quality of the gloves. They were undoubtedly the first pair of gloves he had ever owned. No Afghan in the valley had better gloves than he did.

At almost exactly 2:00 a.m. we heard the sound of the heavy engines of the CH-47s off to the north. Our landing lights were on, and the landing field itself was broad and flat. Even those two big helicopters could easily land there simultaneously. As they came into view and began to descend on their approach, the static electricity created by their rotating blades began to generate sparks from the dust being swirled into the air. The whirling blade tips seemed to glow, and orange spark trails circled with the blades—an eerie sight. Both helicopters touched down at the same time, and the engines were kept on. There was a scurry of activity at the rear ramp of each aircraft as crew members unloaded baggage and passengers departed.

Rick and I moved forward and found Gary 2 in the crowd. He and I shook hands, and I leaned close to speak into his ear over the noise of the turbines. I was happy to welcome him to Afghanistan but wished we had had more time for the turnover. I saw Mumtaz nearby and called him over and introduced him to my successor. I said a quick good-bye to Mumtaz—my third or fourth at least—and headed off to find Hank, who was standing with Rick. We said hello over the noise of the turning engines, and Admiral Calland came up and we shook hands with him. The crew chief of the CH-47 that we were standing near approached us and motioned for Rick and me to follow him. I looked around and could see Chris and Murray following the stretcher onto the second CH-47. We were quickly seated, then we relaxed and watched the crew go about its preparations for takeoff.

The helicopter was totally dark, and everyone was wearing night vision goggles. Two of the crew took up seats at the open rear of the helicopter, their feet dangling over the edge. Each worked a machine gun into place, allowing them to fire out of the rear of the aircraft if required. Two larger machine guns were mounted one on each side toward the front of the aircraft; they looked like multibarreled Gatling guns, capable of putting out an incredible amount of firepower. The green light cast by the night vision goggles reflected around the eyes of several of the crew members, giving them an almost alienlike appearance. We had put on our sound suppressors as we sat down, but we could still hear the noise of the two huge engines revving. There was a jerk, and then we were airborne. I looked at my watch. It was 2:20 a.m. on 4 November 2001, and we were wheels-up, leaving the Panjshir Valley.

CHAPTER FIFTY-ONE

We did not arrive in Tashkent until late afternoon on 4 November. Our CH-47s had flown into the U.S. Special Forces base at Karshi Khanabad, about a hundred miles north of Tashkent, early that morning, and we had been put in a vacant tent used as a ready area for ODA Teams preparing to enter Afghanistan. We rested on canvas cots, tired and cold, wondering when we would be discovered by the CIA group working on the base. We were finally located by Jim L., a retired SAD paramilitary officer, who had spent an hour or more looking for us. He said that there was some confusion on how to move us to Tashkent, because our CIA air operations officer there had failed to schedule a pickup flight to transfer us back to Tashkent. Things had apparently not improved in the support shop at our Tashkent office during our absence. Around three that afternoon, we finally were put on board one of our helicopters and flown down to Tashkent.

We checked into the Sheraton Hotel and marveled that the short skirts of the reception staff had gotten even skimpier in our absence. I stood in the shower with hot water cascading over me for twenty minutes, promising myself I would never again take a hot shower for granted.

We ate at the bar and I finally had a Russian Baltika No. 3. Baltika comes in nine numbers, 1 to 9, with No. 3 being a mild beer suitable for American tastes. No. 9 is obviously brewed for Cossacks; it has three times the normal alcohol content of most other beers. The Russian beer tasted cold and smooth.

The helicopter crew had told us that a G-5 (Gulfstream Five) aircraft was in Tashkent, and Rick had been on the phone with our local air operations officer several times to see if we could use it; if not, we needed to make commercial airline reservations. Finally, at 8:00 p.m., Rick got the call saying we would fly out on the G-5, and pickup would be at 7:00 a.m. the following morning. I slept like a baby that night, enjoying the feel of fresh, clean sheets.

The Gulfstream aircraft was a dream to fly home in. We re-fueled in Frankfurt, and then it was on to Dulles airport in northern Virginia. We landed at 6:30 p.m. in a light mist of rain that made the lights of the private flight service terminal and the tarmac glitter. The door was opened and we filed off—Murray first, of course. Murray's girlfriend was there to greet him, as were Rick's wife and two small children. Chris and I hung back to let the reunions take place, then we were swept up in the celebration. The children had to see "Daddy's airplane," and as they clambered on board, Murray said his good-byes.

Chris and I dragged our bags into the small brightly lit ter-minal building and used the public phones to call home. Chris was calling his father, with whom he would stay for the next several days before rejoining his wife and children at their overseas location. I called Betsy to tell her I was at Dulles and would take a taxi home. I was thrilled to hear her voice and know she was so close. Rick and his family walked by, all laughing and talking at once, and we waved good-bye again. Murray and his girlfriend had already departed.

One taxi was parked at the stand when Chris and I exited the terminal. I let Chris take that one and stood waiting for another to appear. The rain had picked up, and it was cold. After a few minutes I went back inside and asked if someone would call a taxi for me. As I waited back outside, it seemed very quiet, with the street dark, rain falling, and me standing there alone. I knew that a warm, loving homecoming was waiting for me in just forty-five minutes or so, but I could not help but think about what we had just done. I had taken a team of seven CIA officers into northern Afghanistan just days after the 9/11 attacks, the first Americans to go back into Afghanistan, striking the first blow in the newly declared war on terrorism. We had been at risk, far out on our own, with little support or backup available for weeks on end.

We had accomplished our mission. The defeat of the Taliban in the north and the capture of Kabul were still nine days in the future, but the results of our efforts were clear—victory would come. But here I stood alone, no fanfare, just me waiting for a taxi in the rain. Yet this was how it is supposed to be; this is how the CIA has always been—hard, dangerous work in difficult, dangerous places, done with pride and competence and without recognition or applause.

The taxi pulled up and the driver helped me stow my bags in the trunk. I settled into the rear seat and said, "Take me home."

PART THIRTEEN

THE FALL OF KABUL

1–14 November 2001

CHAPTER FIFTY-TWO

The early morning of 4 November found Gary 2 reviewing the situation in the north with Hank and Admiral Calland over cups of hot coffee. The 30 October meeting in Dushanbe with General Fahim had focused on the U.S. bombing strategy in the north, with Fahim pressing for massive U.S. air strikes on the Taliban front lines north of Kabul and along the Taliban lines facing Fahim's forces on the Takhar front. Fahim was upset that the United States was pounding the enemy around Mazar-e Sharif and near Konduz while ignoring the main concentration of Taliban forces at Kabul and Takhar. After much discussion and some hard questions to Fahim by General Franks about Fahim's plans for the assault on Kabul, the meeting had ended with an agreement that the United States would shift its bombing campaign to concentrate on the Kabul and Takhar fronts.

On 1 November there had been a dramatic increase in the number of bombing sorties conducted in the north, especially around Mazar and Konduz, where General Dostum and Commander Atta's forces were making slow but steady progress against the Taliban forces. There had also been major air strikes on the Takhar front, with B-52 and B-1 bombers hitting six key Talib positions and killing as many as three hundred of the enemy, including a senior Taliban military commander. Northern Alliance radio intercepts of Taliban communications indicated that conditions were deteriorating for the Konduz garrison, and the local commander was trying to move all surplus military supplies to Mazar. The good news was that the increased level of bombing was continuing in

those areas. The bad news was that there had been no change
in the level of bombing around Kabul.

Mumtaz, after he had welcomed Gary 2 on the landing
field at Astaneh that morning, had passed on the news that
General Fahim and Engineer Aref were scheduled to arrive
in the valley from Dushanbe later that day. Mumtaz said that
in his message Fahim requested a meeting with Gary 2,
Hank, and the admiral as soon as it could be arranged. It was
obvious that the first question Fahim would ask would be,
Where is the promised increase in bombing around Kabul?
There was an answer to that question, but not one that would
be acceptable to General Fahim.

The meeting later that day was indeed a difficult one.
Fahim was polite but firm. He stated that, based on the
promises made at the 30 October meeting, preparations were
under way to ready the Northern Alliance forces for an attack on the Taliban lines north of Kabul as early as 5 November. He outlined his plan, which called for a two-pronged
attack toward the south, following the two main roads leading to Kabul. He had twenty tanks, twenty Russian BMPs
(armored personnel carriers), fifty artillery pieces, and up to
twelve thousand troops ready to attack. Despite these numbers, Fahim insisted that he needed sustained, heavy U.S.
bombing to break the strong defensive positions that the
Taliban held in a line of wadis (eroded streambeds) and
small villages directly in front of the points of the planned
advance. Without that bombing, the attack would likely fail,
because his forces lacked flexibility, his armored force was
small, and the indirect-fire weapons were difficult to maneuver. Hank and Admiral Calland promised Fahim that the shift
in bombing would begin shortly.

The promise was easier to make than to keep. The issue of
bombing around Kabul was still being debated within the senior decision-making circles of the U.S. government. Combat operations in the areas to the west, around Mazar and
Konduz, were going well, and significant progress was being
made on the ground. Mazar was expected to fall to General

Dostum within the next few days. The U.S. military wanted to reinforce success by concentrating on hitting Taliban forces in those areas. If the few key roads and mountain passes could be secured by Northern Alliance forces, the Taliban routes of retreat to the south would be cut. The capture of Mazar would shake Taliban morale in the north. Then the full weight of the U.S. bombing would shift to the Takhar front, allowing the Northern Alliance forces under Bariullah Khan to break out and move to capture Talaqan, putting more pressure on Konduz and the Taliban forces in that area. Once Talaqan and Konduz were captured, the focus would shift to the Kabul front.

Although this military strategy made sense to U.S. war planners, it ignored the tremendous psychological importance that the capture of Kabul held for the Northern Alliance leadership. Kabul was the political heart of Afghanistan. Its capture by Northern Alliance forces would symbolize the inevitability of victory over the Taliban and validate the years of sacrifice and struggle that the Northern Alliance had endured. Trying to explain to General Fahim and the senior political leadership of the NA that Kabul was of secondary importance in the fight for the north was an impossible mission.

Fahim's counterargument was that the capture of Kabul would be a key event that would demoralize the Taliban across the north and hasten the collapse of Taliban forces across the region, including in and around Kabul. On the other hand, the fall of Mazar and Konduz would have little impact on the morale of the Taliban leadership and forces in Kabul, and a major battle would still have to be fought to drive the Taliban from Kabul.

Adding to the difficulty of convincing Fahim of the U.S. strategy to move on Kabul last was the recognition by Fahim and the senior Northern Alliance leadership that there were grave reservations within the senior ranks of the U.S. government over allowing the Northern Alliance to capture and occupy Kabul. Years of political dealings with the U.S. government had made it painfully clear to the Northern Alliance that there was a strong anti-Tajik lobby within the ranks of senior U.S. policy makers. At the 30 October meeting with General Franks, it had been clear that Franks and his senior officers believed that General Fahim was holding back, trying to preserve his military strength for the post-Taliban political struggle. They clearly felt that Fahim's insistence on heavy U.S. bombing of the Taliban forces he faced was to allow the United States to do the heavy lifting and make Fahim's capture of Kabul less costly. The "Kabul last" strategy seemed to fit into the Northern Alliance's fears that the U.S. government was reluctant to see the Tajiks gaining political advantage over the Pashtuns in the south.

Fahim was correct in his analysis, for despite the agreement struck at the 30 October meeting, General Franks continued to say that he had no confidence in the Northern Alliance to carry the fight to the Taliban at Kabul. The issue of who would capture and occupy Kabul continued to plague U.S. policy makers almost to the very minute of the city's fall to NA forces. There were serious reservations about allowing the Northern Alliance forces to actually take control of Kabul. Although there was no question that Fahim's forces were essential to winning the battle for the Shomali Plains, north of the city, the Principals Committee in Washington was struggling to come up with a workable plan to keep the Tajik forces out of Kabul and bring in some outside force to administer and police the city.

Policy makers in the United States continued to debate the timing of the shift in bombing to the Kabul front even as the situation on the ground began to evolve toward a resolution.

Several days following the 4 November meeting with Fahim, Hank and the admiral departed the valley and Gary 2 had settled into the, by then, well-established routine of managing JAWBREAKER.

The military situation in the west continued to go well. On 6 November, reports were received that the Taliban was desperately trying to reinforce Mazar-e Sharif. U.S. tactical air strikes were taking a high toll on Taliban forces. In a battle for a strategic village called Dara Suf, the Taliban defenders had been almost wiped out, with only twenty men able to escape. Reinforcements sent from Mazar-e Sharif to the Dara Suf area had been pounded by U.S. air strikes.

On 7 November, Gary 2 made the bone-jarring drive down the valley to meet with General Bismullah Khan at his Jabal-os-Saraj headquarters. The general reviewed the developing plan for the assault on Kabul. Sitting before the large window with the panoramic view of the Shomali battlefield, the general discussed the problems he faced in planning his attack. The Taliban had had years to harden the battlefield. Each house seen below was a virtual fort, with roofs reinforced, walls strengthened, and interlocking fields of fire established. Intensive bombing could destroy or damage many of these positions, but if the bombing was not strong or sustained, taking these positions would cost the Northern Alliance forces dearly. The situation would not get any better with time, for the Taliban were bringing in reinforcements daily.

Bismullah Khan stated that he needed three to four days of round-the-clock bombing. The small villages and wadis directly in front of his lines must be damaged heavily. Bismullah said he would be attacking on a front almost five kilometers wide, with a concentration of forces to the west on the old Kabul road, and an equally strong element attacking on the east down the new Kabul road. With strong preparation by U.S. aircraft, the initial attacks should succeed. If U.S. tactical aircraft were on call as the attacks developed over the next several days, so they could quickly react to Taliban counterattacks, the chances of overall success would be greatly increased.

On the drive back to the valley, Gary 2 reviewed the meeting in his mind. This discussion had been exactly the same as that held with General Fahim on 4 November. What these generals were saying made sense. Gary 2 believed their statements that without strong U.S. tactical air support before and during the attack on Kabul, the Northern Alliance forces were likely to fail to break through to the city. If the

NA could defeat the Taliban forces without U.S. assistance, they would have done so long before now. The question that Gary 2 pondered on the bumpy drive back to the compound was how to make the policy makers see the truth of the situation on the ground north of Kabul.

The honest answer to that question proved to be that the timing of the bombing of the front lines at Kabul and the decision of whether or not the Northern Alliance would occupy Kabul itself was determined by circumstances on the battlefields of northern Afghanistan, not in the meeting rooms of senior Washington officials.

Takhar Front
10–11 November 2001

Brad was kneeling next to Bill, the air force sergeant tactical air specialist from ODA-585, as he set up the SOFLAM equipment. Brad was running through the checklist in his mind as he watched Bill work. Brad had spent two full years training on the SOFLAM during his own time as a Green Beret ODA Team member, and he itched to use the equipment in a real combat situation. Well, he might not get that exact wish, but in just a few minutes he was going to take part in a combat operation that would bring down death and destruction on the enemy.

Word had come down late the previous night from Gary 2 and the JAWBREAKER Team back in the Panjshir Valley that the U.S. military had decided it was time to widen the bombing campaign in the north to intensify the focus on the Takhar front. The battles for Mazar-e Sharif and Konduz were going well. A breakout by General Bariullah Khan's Northern Alliance fighters at Takhar would allow them to move on Talaqan, putting a huge squeeze on the Taliban. Although they had been getting five or six sorties a day, the new strategy scheduled to begin that morning would provide dramatically higher numbers. Brad and the ODA Team members were anxious and ready.

Brad looked around and saw Jeff, one of the replacements

who had joined the CIA team in the valley, who was working at the other end of the trench line with two of the ODA NCOs. They were setting up a Mark-19 40mm grenade launcher, a modern semiautomatic version of the Vietnam-era M-79 grenade launcher. Jeff was a CIA operations officer with no prior military experience, and Brad had feared that the seasoned Special Forces soldiers would resent Jeff's lack of experience in these types of field operations. He need not have worried, for Jeff's enthusiasm and willingness to pitch in on any and all tasks, no matter how dirty or dangerous, had won over the ODA.

Jeff had joined Brad and ODA-585 on 6 November, and in the four days since his arrival he had adopted the style of dress of the Special Forces soldiers, and even their salty language. His flat-topped brown Chitrali hat was pulled rakishly over his right ear, and his white-and-black Panjshiri scarf was tied like a bandana around his head, outside his dark green L.L. Bean Gore-Tex parka. His folding-stock AK-47 was slung to hang across his back.

They were working on a hilltop on the right flank of Bari-ullah Khan's northernmost front, just a mile or so south of the border with Tajikistan. The position offered an excellent view of the Taliban positions to their front and for several miles to their left. They had been looking at these targets for days, praying for more aircraft to be released to their AOR (area of operational responsibility). Now that situation was about to change. Word the previous evening was that they would have as many as twenty aircraft at their call rotating on station throughout the day.

Jeff came over to where Brad was kneeling and hunkered down with him. "Bill said I could fire the Mark-19 if we have to return fire. That baby will reach out two thousand meters."

"Let's hope we don't have to return any fire today," said Brad. "I'd rather be delivering fire on the enemy than dodg-ing his incoming."

There was a crackle of radio static, then the ODA Team leader, Master Sergeant B., was speaking to AWACS Con-trol. Two F/A-18s were inbound and would be on station in about twenty minutes. They were each carrying two 500-pound "dumb" bombs—old-fashioned iron bombs that depended on pilot skill and excellent ground-to-air coordination. Brad thought, Well, that's what the ODA does best.

The radio was turned over to the air force tactical air operator, and the team gathered to discuss the best targets for this round of "dumb" bombs. A large bunker complex about eight hundred yards out, located on the slope of a tall hill, was the first choice. It was easy to identify (and they could paint it with a laser to assist the pilot in spotting the target), and the team could talk the bombs in to the target, providing the pilot with the exact point of impact of each bomb so he could adjust his drop point.

The second target would be a trench/bunker complex located five hundred yards south of the first. Bariullah Khan's intelligence unit reported that this was a key al-Qa'ida position, manned by Arab, Chechen, and Uzbek IMU (Islamic Movement of Uzbekistan) terrorists. Visions of the Twin Towers burning flashed in Brad's mind, and he prayed there would be some real payback on the foreign terrorists out there in those positions.

As the team members prepared to move to their positions in the trench line, Master Sergeant B. said, "Now remember, let's keep a low profile up here. Our job is to call in hurt and pain onto those bastards. We don't want to be exchanging fire with them, even though I know we would all love to make this a personal fight." He paused, then said, smiling, "I can assure you that each of us will get an opportunity to personally waste more than a few of those animals before this is over." With that the men dispersed and took up positions along the trench line. Brad noticed that Jeff moved down the trench to a position near the Mark-19 grenade launcher.

The first 500-pound bomb landed short, impacting ten yards south of the complex of buildings, exploding in what turned out to be a heavily occupied trench system. The fireball and blast of earth and smoke skyward was filled with bodies, parts of bodies, weapons, and other debris. As the shock wave reached the hilltop and the sound rolled over them, Brad could see clumps of materiel falling to earth. The smoke of the blast began to drift toward the buildings, and Brad could see a few men moving around the buildings, looking toward the impact point.

Bill, the air force controller, was talking to the pilot of the plane that had just dropped the first bomb. "This is TIGER Three. You were one zero meters short of target. We see lots of movement in and around the impact point. This is a prime target. TIGER Three will laser-mark the target for your next run."

The second bomb detonated directly on the building complex, blowing a huge cloud of fire and debris skyward, and Brad could see more human figures twisting upward in the blast. He could hardly believe how powerful the two blasts had been. These are only 500-pound bombs, he thought. Wait until we get a B-52 with 2,000-pound JDAMs (joint direct attack munitions)!

The attack on the al-Qa'ida position was even more spectacular. The first bomb impacted on the south corner of the small complex of mud structures, blowing the roof off one of the buildings and exploding out through the bricked-up windows. This target was five hundred yards farther away than the first, and Brad had to use his binoculars to see the destruction clearly. He could see flames beginning to appear inside the damaged structure, and the tiny figures of men running away from the burning building. Then there was a series of quick, sharp explosions, the flashes seen seconds before the sound rolled across to where Brad knelt. He saw more and more flashes and heard larger explosions and the sound of bullets cooking off. The al-Qa'ida had been storing ammunition in the building. Smoke was now billowing from the torn sides of the structure.

The second bomb finished off the bunkers, exploding in the center of the roof of the last building in the small complex. The fireball rose through the roof and smashed out through the window openings, sending debris skyward. There was a pause, then a second large explosion blew apart the rest of the building, sending huge chunks of rock and wood twisting and turning into the sky. Mixed into the debris cloud were long, shiny metal tubes. Brad's mind registered the objects as rockets, probably 122mm ground-to-ground rockets, favored by the Soviets and Mujahedin during the long years of the Jihad.

Brad turned to look down the trench line and saw that Jeff and the men of the ODA were smiling, hands pumping, giving one another a thumbs-up. Bill's radio crackled, and he leaned into the microphone and spoke with what Brad assumed was AWACS Control.

Bill looked up and said loud enough for all to hear, "We have a B-52 coming in from Diego Garcia loaded with two-thousand-pound JDAMs. Arrival on station estimated for three zero minutes. Then we have two B-1 bombers inbound with eighteen thousand-pound JDAMs each. They arrive in six zero minutes. Gentlemen, let's select the next target deck. This is going to be a very long and very productive day."

The Panjshir Valley
10 November 2001

Gary 2 sat across from Engineer Aref, whose face once again reflected worry, concern, and anger. Mumtaz was next to Aref, and Gary 2 noted that he was sitting particularly still. This will be a tough meeting, Gary 2 thought as he smiled across at Aref.

Aref, who had called the meeting, started the conversation. "Agha [Mister] Gary, I must speak plainly. General Fahim and the senior Northern Alliance leadership met this morning to discuss the situation. The general is disappointed. Despite promises by General Franks, Agha Hank, and the admiral, there is still no heavy bombing here on the Kabul front. Yet radio reports from General Dostum and Commander Atta, and now even from General Bariullah Khan at Takhar, say that U.S. aircraft are striking the enemy heavily in those areas." He paused, looking directly at Gary 2, then said, "What answer can I give the general as to why no serious bombing is taking place here?"

Gary 2 leaned forward, looking back at Aref. "Engineer, I know there is still only limited bombing here. But things around Mazar and Konduz are *khub-ast* [good]." Gary 2 had a habit of slipping in Dari words and phrases when speaking to Aref or Mumtaz; usually these fit the context of what Gary 2 was discussing. "Many Taliban are being killed, and Dostum is almost in Mazar. Taliban are retreating south, from Mazar and Konduz, and U.S. aircraft are pounding them. The bombing is heavy at Takhar. Things are *besiar khub-ast* [very good]."

"Yes, yes," Aref said with a dismissive tone. "I know about the successes at Mazar and around Konduz. I know the bombing has intensified on the Takhar front. But, Agha Gary, what about Kabul?"

"Engineer, I have been in contact with Hank back at CTC. As he personally explained when he was here in the valley, the U.S. military is trying to capitalize on those successes by hitting the enemy hard and often there. With Dostum and Atta moving forward so well, they want to see General Bari-ullah's forces make a breakout and drive through Takhar Province and take Talaqan. That will seal the fate of the Taliban in the north.

"Then the focus will be on Kabul and hammering the Taliban positions to allow General Bismullah Khan to attack." As Gary 2 spoke, his voice had gotten louder and louder, another of his old traits.

Aref raised his hands, palms forward, almost as if fending off Gary 2. "But why does Kabul come last in the plans? We have the largest, best-equipped group of Northern Alliance fighters in the north, ready to attack. Dostum's forces are small, as are Atta's, when compared to the army that General Fahim has assembled here. Dostum has taken weeks to move on Mazar, and then only with massive bombing by your air force. Fahim can take Kabul in two or three days with that kind of support.

"Let me ask you, Agha Gary, are there some political reasons behind this delay?" Aref quickly continued before Gary
could respond. "Dr. Abdullah's proposed visit to Washington
was rejected. The airdrop of supplies and ammunition to
General Fahim's forces here in the valley has not happened,
despite repeated reassurances. You now have a team with
Khalili in Bamiyan, and he is getting bombing support. Your
predecessor, General Gary, was candid in saying that the
Tajiks of the Panjshir are distrusted back in Washington."

"The points you make are true," said Gary 2, "but there is
no hidden message in them. Engineer, I can only say that
U.S. air support will come to the Kabul front. Hank told me
last night that if there is a successful breakout by Bariullah
Khan in Takhar, the heavy bombing will shift to Kabul.

"I spoke with Brad in Takhar just thirty minutes ago. The
bombing at the Takhar front is going well, and General Bariullah thinks he will be able to launch his major offensive as
early as this afternoon. Engineer, the bombing shift could
start here at Kabul tomorrow."

Aref leaned back in his chair and rubbed his hand through
his sparse black hair. "Yes, Agha Gary, tomorrow." He leaned
forward, hands on the edge of the table. "But please tell
Hank, tell General Franks, tell everyone, that if the bombing
does not come by tomorrow, then General Fahim will order
the offensive to begin, without U.S. air support." He looked
down at the tabletop, then back at Gary 2. "Victory at Mazar
or Konduz—or in the entire north—will be hollow if we fail
here at the Kabul front."

South of Mazar-e Sharif
Evening, 10 November 2001

R.J. and Frank were lying in the dark, prone on the top of a
large, flat rock near the crest of a tall hill overlooking what
would probably be the last Taliban effort to prevent General
Dostum's forces from breaking through and entering the city
of Mazar-e Sharif. There was enough moonlight to allow
them to see the lines that Dostum's men had established sev-

eral hundred yards below the base of the hill. A broad plain opened at the base of the hill, and R.J. could make out the Taliban defensive positions three thousand yards away.

R.J. looked at his watch and touched Frank on the shoulder. "Ten minutes to go."

Frank nodded. "Yep, this is going to be a real show. You think those boys across this plain have any idea what's in store for them?"

"No, not any more than those poor Iraqi assholes did in Desert Storm. Back then they dropped two BLU-82s on the Iraqis, both at night. The first one was set to be a ground burst, and the next night they rigged the bomb to explode in the air. They wanted to test the difference in damage between the two blasts in a desert environment. The damn things weigh fifteen thousand pounds each, and the blast is so huge that it creates a mushroom-shaped cloud, just like an atomic bomb. The Iraqis thought we'd nuked them."

Frank glanced over toward the group of Afghans gathered around General Dostum. Dostum had a pair of Russian night vision goggles dangling from his neck, courtesy of ALPHA Team, and was seated on a rock overlooking the plain. Frank could see the ODA Team hunkered down behind an outcropping of rocks beyond Dostum's group. "Well, everyone's gathered for the show. Hope this isn't a fizzle."

"I really don't think we have to worry about that," said R.J. "My worry is that they'll push the damn thing out too soon and it'll explode close to us."

"Oh, yeah, nice thought. Thanks," Frank said with a laugh.

R.J. heard the faint drone of the engine on the MC-130 aircraft, and looked to his right, scanning high in the sky. He could see nothing, even with the moonlight and the stars, but he knew it was the plane carrying the first BLU-82. As the plane drew nearer, R.J.'s mind played out what was happening above him. He knew that the aircrew was busy getting ready to push a large pallet carrying the bomb out of the rear of the aircraft. The MC-130 would actually jerk upward as it was freed of the weight of its cargo.

R.J. knew the sequence of events after the bundle left the

aircraft. The heavy wooden pallet would separate and fall away, twisting and turning, as the heavy cylinder, the BLU-82, continued its plunge earthward. A drag parachute would deploy from the rear of the bomb, slowing its descent, the heavy weapon jerking and swaying under the small canopy in a pendulumlike movement. R.J. tried to anticipate when the bomb would strike, and found himself holding his breath, his eyes now fixed on the enemy lines across the valley.

Seconds later there was a tremendous flash, and a visible shock wave rocketed outward from the detonation of fifteen thousand pounds of high explosives. The noise followed almost simultaneously, and as R.J. dropped his head to the rock face and covered his head with his hands, the shock wave struck with crushing power. He was shoved violently backward off the rock, hitting on his heels and slamming over backward to bang and bounce off the hard-packed dirt. A rush of wind moved back toward the blast to fill the vacuum that the massive blast had created. R.J.'s ears were ringing, and the sounds of men shouting came to him as if from a distance. He looked over at Frank, who was lying flat on his back, arms sprawled and body relaxed in unconsciousness. Damn thing knocked him out, R.J. thought as he rolled over to kneel next to Frank. He ran his hands over Frank's upper body. A touch to the rear of Frank's head disclosed a growing bump and some blood from where he had struck the ground. It did not appear serious.

R.J. pulled himself to his feet and almost staggered backward in awe of the sight he faced across the plain. A huge, boiling, mushroom-shaped cloud was growing from the impact site, its base several hundred yards across. It looked exactly like every photo or film he had ever seen of a nuclear explosion, and a jolt of primeval fear shot through him. The air was rumbling, the hills echoing the thunder of the massive explosion. My God, he thought. We were a mile away from the blast and it beat the crap out of us. What was it like out there on the Taliban lines?

R.J. knelt back down by Frank, wet his handkerchief with water from his canteen, and wiped Frank's face. Frank began to stir, groaning, his face grimacing in pain. "Ugh . . . oh, man. . . ."

"Relax, Frank. You banged your head. It knocked you out, but I think you're going to be fine." R.J. stopped talking because he could hear the drone of aircraft engines.

"Oh, crap, here comes the second plane with another BLU-82 surprise for the Taliban." R.J. raised Frank slightly and pushed his small backpack under Frank's head, putting the damp handkerchief on the bump as he lowered Frank's head to rest on the soft pack.

He stretched out next to Frank. "I think I'll pass on watching the second bomb hit. Once is enough for me."

The second blast was as powerful as the first, the shock wave slamming into the hillside where they lay behind the large rock. The thunderous noise rocked R.J., and he closed his eyes and tried to relax as the ground beneath him shuddered as if in pain. All he could think was, Those poor fuckers out there. They're getting an early look at what hell will be like.

Mazar-e Sharif fell to Dostum's forces that night.

The Kabul Front
11 November 2001

Gary 2 was up early reviewing the excellent news of the previous night. The fighting in the north around Mazar-e Sharif and Konduz was going well, with thousands of Taliban fighters retreating south from Mazar toward Kabul or to the east toward Konduz, where the airfield remained in Taliban control. Commander Sayid Jafari, one of Atta's senior subcommanders, was advancing on a key bridge in the Nahrin District, Pol-e Khomri, trying to cut off one of the main routes south. He had taken three thousand Taliban prisoners that day. Commander Khalili was to attack Bamiyan city later on 11 November; if he was successful, he would cut off another key route to the south. Northern Alliance radio intercepts indicated that the Taliban commander at Talaqan, Mullah Daduallah, had informed the Taliban leadership in Kabul that the situation north of Talaqan was hopeless and he was abandoning the city. He and at least fifteen other senior Taliban commanders would retreat to Konduz.

Late in the afternoon of 10 November, General Bariullah Khan's forces had launched a full-scale offensive along the Takhar front. Fighting had been fierce, but the bombing campaign of the past few days had weakened the command and control structure of the Taliban forces. Taliban resistance there had collapsed, and by the morning of 11 November Bariullah's forces were poised to move rapidly toward Talaqan, following thousands of retreating Taliban fighters. Bariullah expected to take the city later that day. He had established contact with two of the key local Taliban leaders who remained in the city, Abdullah Qard and Shabir Ahmad, and negotiations were under way to buy their defection.

Late on 10 November, Gary 2 had spoken with Hank from the CTC. Hank reported that the long-promised increase in bombing at Kabul would start on the morning of the eleventh. Gary 2 had immediately met with Colonel H., who had received the same excellent news from Task Force Dagger, and they discussed strategy on how they should maneuver to ensure that ODA-555 and JAWBREAKER could provide maximum support to General Bismullah's forces when the offensive against Kabul began.

In a radio exchange down at the Kabul front, Stan reviewed with Gary 2 General Bismullah's two-pronged attack plan, and he explained that ODA-555 and Stan's CIA element would split into two groups. "We're supposed to be getting twenty-five sorties today," said Stan. "One of our groups will work on targets on the western end of Taliban lines, above the old Kabul road. Doc will be with that group. A couple of small villages there—Agbelak and Estalef—are going to be tough nuts to crack. The general is trying to convince the commander of that section to defect, but he may need a lot of convincing. I'll be with the group working targets on the east end of the Taliban lines, above the new Kabul road. The wadis there are heavily defended. Our focus today is to break those defenses, to allow General Bismullah to attack as early as tomorrow morning.

"Once the attack is launched, both our groups will stay as close to the frontline fighting as possible so we can call in CAS to react to any stiff resistance we run into."

"You guys shouldn't get too close to the frontline fighting," said Gary 2, knowing full well they would ignore his warning. "In the meantime, I'm going to meet with Aref to arrange for JAWBREAKER to move forward. Apparently there were plans made back in October, when the bombing campaign first started, to shift the team to Jabal-os-Saraj. Mumtaz says that a small compound was identified back then that we can use. We want to be close to Bismullah so we can coordinate any shifts in his overall battlefield strategy with you. We'll call you both just before we break down the equipment for the move. It'll take about four hours for us to shift south and get set up in our new location."

"Sounds good to me. Oh, and don't worry about us, Gary. We're not planning to be too close to the fighting. But I don't doubt that there will be pressure from the team to be within rifle range as things get hot."

"Just remember that your job is to help the Northern Alliance carry the fight to the Taliban, not for you guys to take on the Taliban yourselves."

"Yes, sir," said Stan. "You can count on that."

Gary 2 thought he could hear a snicker in Stan's voice as he broke the connection.

12 November 2001

Noises of movement around him brought Stan out of his light sleep. He looked at his wristwatch—4:30 a.m. He had slept four hours. The predawn darkness seemed heavy and somber. He knew that thousands of men out there in the dark were stirring from sleep—nervous, tired, dirty, cold, and stiff—worried that today was perhaps their last. For many, it would be. The five Triple Nickel team members were moving about, pulling their gear together. Stan rolled out of his sleeping bag, rubbed his face, and ran his hands through his hair. Well, he thought today is the big day.

The previous day had had spectacular successes. Protected by a small group of Northern Alliance commanded by Captain Amir Mohammad, the Triple Nickel had worked the front lines all day and well into early evening. Aircraft had been plentiful and the targets too numerous to count. The earth had shook, rocked, and shuddered from the impact of heavy bombs exploding. Fortified buildings, dug-in tank positions, masses of dug-in troops, command bunkers and artillery, and ZSU-23 positions had been struck and pulverized. The radio intercepts of Taliban communications were filled with screams and the sounds of confusion, pain, and fear. The Taliban troops had never experienced anything like the destruction being rained down upon them. After the first several air strikes, the pace and intensity of the bombing began to increase in tempo, and there was no indiscriminate return fire. Huge blasts hit targets with amazing accuracy, sending towers of earth, metal, and bodies skyward. The men out on that plain could only press themselves into the earth, twisting themselves into the smallest shape they could manage, and pray that somehow they would survive the day—a day that seemed would never end.

Word from Gary 2 last night, calling from the team's new headquarters in Jabal-os-Saraj, was that Talaqan had fallen to General Bariullah's forces in the early evening of 11 November. Thousands of Taliban troops had been caught in the open, retreating to the south, or moving toward Konduz, and casualties had been heavy. Konduz was surrounded, and negotiations were to start the next day to try to get the defenders to surrender. The spirit had been beaten from the majority of the Taliban fighters, although there were pockets of strong resistance from groups of Arab, Chechen, Uzbek, and Pakistani fighters. Bamiyan city was ready to fall to Commander Khalili. Word was that Ismail Khan was having success around Herat, and Northern Alliance commander Ebreham Ali was on the move in Ghowr Province. Things looked good all across the north.

*   *   *

Stan was drinking a cup of instant coffee, sitting with the rest of the team and discussing what was going to happen later that day, when Captain Amir arrived. Amir was a short, stocky bear of a man whose uniform seemed a size or two too small for his body. He wore a full beard and always had his white-and-black scarf wrapped several times around his neck, giving the appearance that his head rested directly on his shoulders.

"Gentlemen," Amir said in greeting, "today is a big day! General Bismullah has given orders for the attack to begin at seven-thirty"—he paused, looking at his watch—"in two hours, as soon as it is full light. He would like you to work close to the front, overlooking the Taliban defenses in the line of wadis guarding the highway. I will lead you to the overlook we have selected as soon as you have finished your morning meal."

The men stood up almost as one, and Captain R., the Triple Nickel's commanding officer, said, "Captain, breakfast is over. We'll pack our gear and be ready in five minutes to move out." He turned to survey his team, then smiled and said, "Let's go send more of those sorry bastards to paradise." There was a round of happy noises as they set about cleaning up the area.

Stan was exhausted. It was dark now, and his ears rang from a day filled with the sounds of exploding bombs, machine-gun fire, mortar rounds going off nearby, and men dying. There had been thirty sorties available that day, and the Triple Nickel had used them as close support for Bismullah Khan's attacking troops. That had put the team moving forward just behind the attacking troops, monitoring the battle and bringing in bomb strikes on pockets of stiff resistance that developed. It also put the team under continuous fire from the enemy virtually all day.

The attack on the wadis above the old Kabul road had kicked off a little late in order to have several 2,000-pound smart bombs dropped on the forward Taliban positions—"to wake the devils," as Captain Amir had said.

The first elements of the Northern Alliance forces hit the wadis hard, moving in even before the smoke and dust of the explosions had cleared. The battle was intense, and it took five hours of close-in fighting, hand to hand at times, with pauses only long enough to call in bombs to pound enemy positions from the air and smash their defenses. Again it had been the foreign fighters—the Arabs, Pakistanis, and Chechens—who offered the strongest resistance.

But once through those defensive lines at the wadis, the Northern Alliance was able to advance quickly. Taliban forces began breaking and retreating, or surrendering, leaving pockets of foreign fighters to stand and oppose the NA advance. Those pockets were the prime targets of the Triple Nickel and U.S. air strikes. Progress down Highway 1 was slow but steady, and Stan and the team had moved forward with the advance elements.

They learned from Captain Amir that the attack on the eastern end of the Taliban lines had been much easier. After the pounding inflicted on the key villages of Agbelak and Estalef the previous day, the Taliban commander in Agbelak had contacted the NA commander opposite him and opened negotiations to surrender his forces. General Bismullah Khan had monitored the negotiations, but as the 7:30 a.m. time for the attack drew near that morning, he became convinced that the negotiations were a delaying tactic. His forces drove into Agbelak and took it with little resistance, then immediately attacked Estalef, with similar results. Movement south along Highway 2 had been steady, with the only strong resistance coming from foreign fighters.

Captain R. sat down next to Stan and offered him a bottle of water. "Have a drink, Stan. Wash out the taste of battle."

"Thanks," he said, taking the bottle. "How do things look for tomorrow?"

"Captain Amir reports that General Bismullah says there'll be some heavy fighting on the Shomali Plains on both fronts; there are still strong pockets of the enemy out there. Mostly foreigners, though. They're picking up radio intercepts that say the Taliban leadership is beginning to leave the city, heading south and east."

"When General Babajan stopped by earlier, he told me that Professor Sayyaf was moving with four thousand of his men toward Jalalabad, to head off the retreat in that direction." Babajan was one of General Bismullah's division commanders who was running this wing of the NA forces.

"Damn good news," said Captain R. "Things keep on like this tomorrow, we'll be in Kabul by day after tomorrow."

Stan drank deeply, then said, "I called JAWBREAKER a few minutes ago. Gary says that things in the rest of the north are moving well. Konduz is the only place there's still strong resistance. Again, it's the foreign fighters who are willing to stand and die."

Captain R. stood. "We need to move forward a little. The guys have spotted a good place to hunker down for the night. We'll shift and then grab something to eat. It'll be another long day tomorrow."

13 November 2001

It was 5:30 a.m., and Gary 2 was sitting across from General Bismullah Khan and Mumtaz in what passed for JAWBREAKER's office space in the new compound in Jabal-os-Saraj. Late the previous night, the general had called Mumtaz to ask for a meeting with Gary 2 early the next morning. A pot of Starbucks coffee was brewing on a table nearby as the three men discussed the situation on the battlefield.

"Agha Gary," said the general, "things went very well yesterday. Your men and the Special Forces soldiers did outstanding work. The enemy fought hard here at Highway One, and the air strikes your team was able to call in proved decisive. Please forward my thanks to your men."

"Thank you, General. I'll tell them of your kind words. But how will you fight today?"

"Most of the Taliban forces have retreated. The Arab fighters and other foreigners have rallied some units, and there are strong pockets of the enemy who will fight hard to keep us out of Kabul. On the east, at Highway Two, we will be able to push deep toward Kabul. Highway One will be more difficult. But with the help of Allah and the help of your men and your aircraft, we will be at the gates of Kabul tonight.

"Now, Agha Gary, that brings me to my real question. Will the U.S. government support my moving my troops into Kabul itself?" The general paused, taking a sip of coffee.

Gary 2 had been expecting this question. "General, let me be very honest with you. There is still some concern back in Washington that there will be a wave of revenge killings by your forces if they move into Kabul. I have tried to assure Washington that that will not happen, but the Pakistanis continue to complain to Washington about what will happen if the Northern Alliance takes Kabul."

The general shook his head. "Agha Gary, the Pakistanis would have us wait until a Pashtun force can be assembled to formally occupy Kabul. That would take months." He paused, looked toward the corner of the room as if collecting his thoughts.

"There will be no revenge killings. Of that I can personally assure you. We have reports—radio intercepts and human reporting—that many from the Taliban leadership have already fled the city, many leaving throughout last night. Yes, there are many within my forces whose families have suffered at the hands of those men. But"—he paused and looked squarely at Gary 2—"I have given strict orders that no killings, no brutality will take place—on pain of death.

"I want you to pass that assurance on to Washington. But also tell the leaders there that by tonight Kabul will be open to me. The city will be empty of Taliban defenders by tomorrow morning."

"But how can you be sure they won't fight for the city?"

"Agha Gary, this is Afghanistan. The Taliban leadership in Kabul has watched their army be ground into dust. Thousands and thousands of Taliban have died in the past ten days. They are beaten. They will flee to the south and to the east, toward their friends in Pakistan. Believe me, this is my country, I know."

Gary nodded. "General, I'll send a message to Washington as soon as we finish this meeting. However, I'm not sure what the NSC's position will be on the Northern Alliance entering Kabul."

The general finished his coffee and placed the cup on the table. "Agha Gary, I say this to you in all candor. I am going into Kabul regardless of what your NSC decides. I must move to protect the innocent citizens there. Now, please excuse me. I must see to today's battle preparations."

The men rose and shook hands, and the general turned and hurried out of the room. Mumtaz moved to follow him, then paused. "Gary, we must plan for a move into Kabul tomorrow. You will want to have your team in Kabul as soon as General Bismullah moves his forces into the city. You will need to be there to ensure that Washington has the correct information as to what happens there when we 'devil Tajiks' recapture the city."

It was late in the afternoon by the time the three-vehicle convoy arrived at General Bismullah Khan's building that served as his headquarters compound in Charikar, some five miles south of Jabal-os-Saraj. As the vehicles turned off the main road, the old Kabul road, Gary 2—riding in the front passenger seat of the second vehicle—could see that the small walled compound was situated on the southern edge of the city, built on a ridgeline that offered a commanding view of the Shomali Plains spreading out toward Kabul. In the distance were the bright flashes of shells exploding, their sound like distant thunder. Reminds me of a summer thunderstorm that swept over and is now moving away, thought Gary 2. Only there are no puddles of rainwater standing here and no fresh, clean smell in the air. Just destruction, dust, debris, twisted metal, and dead men left in its wake.

There was the usual round of confusion as the men climbed out of the vehicles and ordered themselves by their rank and status. Gary 2 and Mumtaz moved to the front of the small group as they walked toward the open gate before them. The gate led to a small but beautiful garden, the last light from the setting sun painting the apple trees and rosebushes with a pinkish tinge. The air seemed fragrant, and the rumble of battle was almost silenced. They moved quickly across the garden on the gravel path, and entered the main building through the open door.

General Bismullah appeared from a large room on the right and walked toward Gary 2 with his hand outstretched. "Welcome, Agha Gary," he said, grabbing Gary's hand and pumping it. "Please, come." He motioned toward the room from which he had exited. "There is much to talk about."

After tea and coffee had been served, Bismullah leaned back in his chair and took a long sip from his cup. Gary 2 thought he looked tired, and he noticed that the general's clothing was dirt-stained and his boots were dusty and scuffed. It had been a long, hard day.

"General, I met with Engineer Aref just before coming here. He says the battle was hard fought but you were successful across the entire front. Kabul is close to your hand."

The general's eyes crinkled in a smile over the rim of the teacup, and he nodded as he set down the cup. "Yes, Agha Gary, things went very well today. We are only fifteen kilometers from Kabul here on Highway One and perhaps twenty kilometers away on Highway Two." He ran his hand across his face, pressing his fingers together on the bridge of his nose and rubbing the corners of his eyes.

"For the most part, the Taliban forces are beaten. Those that remain on the plain are those standing with foreign fighters. My commanders in the forwardmost units attacking the enemy report that the prisoners they have taken say the foreigners are pledged to fight to the death." He shook his head, his mouth pursed.

"It is a senseless fight to make. If they were Afghans, we could convince them to surrender, for that is our way. But these foreign devils, they all want to become martyrs. Well, they will get their wish, for tomorrow I will send all of them to hell."

"General, how long do you think it will take to smash the resistance you face on the plains?"

"Agha Gary, my men will be in Kabul by late tomorrow afternoon. We have reports that senior Taliban leaders are already fleeing the city. The forces we face will fight hard and will undoubtedly die well. But if you continue to help with your incredible bombs and with the spirit of my men, we will crush them before nightfall."

"General, I assure you that you will receive the same level of support from our side as you have these past few days. With your permission, tomorrow morning, before dawn, I will personally join Stan and the Special Forces team here on Highway One. I want to be with them as your men make the final fight for Kabul."

The general's smile broadened. "Yes, Agha Gary, join your men. It will be a good fight." He paused, then said, "In fact I would welcome your entire team moving into Kabul as soon as we can secure the city and ensure your safety. I want to have you and the Special Forces soldiers on hand to monitor the situation as my forces take control and bring order and security to the city. Washington will believe your reports—much more than any assurances I can give them—on how my men behave."

"Of course, General," said Gary 2. "I was going to ask when we could move into Kabul. In fact, Engineer Aref and I were discussing that topic. It seems he has a location in mind where we—the entire team—can be housed. He said there was a hotel near the old American Embassy that would be perfect."

Mumtaz broke in to explain to the general the details of the hotel that Aref had mentioned. Gary 2 missed a lot of the exchange between the two, because they spoke in rapid-fire Dari, but he caught the gist of Mumtaz's explanation. The hotel was a large two-story structure that had served as a VIP guesthouse for the Northern Alliance during the 1992–96 time frame and then served the same purpose for the Taliban. It was only about a mile from the American Embassy, and although it suffered damage at the hands of the Taliban, it would be an excellent temporary base of operations.

The general turned to Gary 2. "I agree with Engineer Aref. I will provide a squad of soldiers to secure the hotel as my forces enter the city. They will ensure that it is clear of Taliban and no surprises were left behind. It will be your headquarters, at least for the first few days."

The general leaned back and looked thoughtfully at Gary 2. "So, from your plans to move into Kabul with my forces, I assume that Washington is happy with my plans to occupy the city."

Gary 2 smiled. "Well, to be honest, General, I don't know what Washington thinks of your plan. But the reality is that you command on the battlefield, and the fighting tomorrow will certainly result in your capturing the city. The situation on the ground always dictates the actions we take in the field, regardless of all the planning and hand-wringing done back in Washington. General, I will see you in Kabul tomorrow evening."

14 November 2001

Gary 2 stood next to Stan in a circle of Triple Nickel soldiers, each man sipping a cup of hot Starbucks coffee. Gary 2 had arrived at the team's location at 5:30 a.m. with two large plastic thermos jugs of freshly brewed coffee, a treat that the men on the front lines had not enjoyed in a number of days.

Gary 2 looked around at the men. All were dirty—clothing dusty and mud stained, beards unkempt, fingernails dirt-rimmed. Only a little water was available for washing, and a swipe of the face and a rinse of the hands was all that any of the men could manage. Yet they were excited, happy to be where the action was. "The pointy end of the spear," as Captain R. liked to say. The morning was cold and the coffee was steaming, and their breath clouded as they drank and talked about the coming events of the day.

"Captain Amir was by just before you arrived," Stan commented to Gary, "and said the attack will kick off at six-thirty."

"That's when the first sortie will be on station," added the air force CAS specialist. "We're promised all the aircraft we can handle today."

Gary 2 smiled. "Yeah, isn't it strange how fast things can change." Addressing Captain R., he asked, "What does it look like we're facing today?"

Captain R. turned slightly to face the battlefield. He pointed toward what appeared to be a group of low mud buildings on a small rise of land about a mile away. "That's the first objective for today. The Arabs have moved a couple of hundred men in and around that bunker complex. They have at least one ZSU-23 and a number of 14.5mm machine guns in place." He took a long sip from his cup and looked back at Gary 2. "I think the situation calls for a kinetic solution. Four five-hundred-pound iron bombs or perhaps a single two-thousand-pound smart bomb should do the job. We'll see what we have first on deck."

Stan looked out at the battlefield. "Ah, what a way to start the day! Reminds me of Robert Duval in *Apocalypse Now*."

As one, the entire group said, "I love the smell of burning napalm in the morning!" All laughed loudly, smiling and slapping one another on the back. Gary 2 thought of his high school football team just before the start of the second half in a game they were winning handily. Happy, cocky, confident, totally enjoying themselves.

Captain R. turned to Gary 2. "We thank you for your kindness in providing us a well-appreciated taste of home. But I think it's time to saddle up and start the day."

Gary 2 looked out toward the bunker complex. "Let's start the day with a bang. Good luck, gentlemen."

It was 5:30 p.m., and darkness was only an hour away. Gary 2 stood in the small VIP parking lot next to the main terminal building at Kabul airport listening to the sounds of a firefight drifting toward them from the city. He looked around him. The main terminal building was empty, the exterior blasted and pockmarked and the windows without glass looking out at the destruction left by twenty-plus years of war. He did a slow 360-degree turn, looking back north at the ground that had been so strongly defended by the enemy, columns of smoke rising here and there across the expanse of the plain. In the foreground as he turned, the grassy areas beyond the single broad concrete runway were littered with collapsed buildings, what remained of their walls rising out of rubble, and surrounded by the crumpled wreckage of smashed aircraft. The runway was strewn with debris—rocks and rubble, twisted pieces of metal, and what looked like at least one dead body half concealed by the weeds at the edge of the runway across from where he stood.

He turned to look at the city. The beginnings of the slums on the northern edge of Kabul were only several hundred yards away, and the city proper began less than a mile from where he was standing. He had studied the old map of Kabul that he had brought with him from Headquarters, and he knew that the American Embassy was only two miles south, just barely out of view.

Gary 2, Stan, and the men of ODA-555 had followed General Bismullah's forces across the last ten miles of the Shomali Plains for most of the day, calling in aircraft to strike the enemy whenever they paused to form a defensive position. The fighting was fierce at times, but when the bombs struck with such incredible accuracy and unbelievable force, the outcome of the battle was never in doubt.

The movement toward Kabul had been slow and dangerous. They drove in Toyota pickup trucks and an SUV, staying for the most part on the highway. The roadside was littered with the debris of battle—smoking tank hulks, their heavy steel bodies blasted and twisted, the corpses of their crews scattered in grotesque poses around the wreckage. Mud-walled buildings that had been turned into defensive bunkers were smashed open, dust and smoke still rising from their interiors, dead bodies draped in twisted clumps here and there in the rubble. The men had to pause a number of times to help bring in fire on stubborn pockets of Taliban and foreign fighters. Stray rounds hit around the vehicles or passed with sharp cracks overhead. Miraculously, the small convoy was untouched.

They had passed through miles of total destruction. The Shomali Plains had once been the garden spot of Kabul, the fields rich with grapevines, olive trees, apple trees, melon patches, and cornfields. Irrigation canals had crisscrossed the fields; brimming with water that had turned the plains into a sea of lush green. Then, in the early 1980s, the Soviet army had destroyed most of the trees and vines to remove the Mujahedin fighters' cover, who made the lives of the Soviets hell with ambushes and improvised explosives. The destruction continued after the Soviets left Afghanistan in 1989, with the communist Najibullah regime leveling buildings and constructing defensive positions to try to maintain its hold on the city. There had been some progress in rebuilding the plains after Najibullah fell in 1992, but the Taliban reversed that in 1996. They went even further by having the irrigation canals filled in, as punishment for resistance to their "enlightened" rule. The massive bombing and intense fighting of the past few days had completed the destruction.

The vehicles had passed entire villages flattened and churned to rubble. They had to ford two streams, bouncing down the rocky banks, splashing through the shallow streambeds, and scrambling up the other side. The bridges had been destroyed and lay awkwardly twisted off their concrete foundations. The dead lay sprawled in single, soiled clumps or in groupings of twisted arms, legs, and weapons. Gary 2 had thought more than once that this was like passing through hell.

They had arrived at Kabul airport at 5:10 p.m. and were waiting for the rest of the JAWBREAKER Team to join them from Jabal-os-Saraj. Stan looked around. "Not all this destruction is old. We blew those IL-76s back in October. The air force was anxious to eliminate any and all Taliban aircraft, and we coordinated the bombing from Baghram. I think they took out maybe ten or twelve aircraft that one night."

Gary 2 shook his head. "It's impossible to tell what's new damage and what are old wrecks from the 1980s. Everything out there is blown to hell."

There was a swell of sound from the city, with a tank firing, explosions, and heavy machine guns firing. Gary 2 looked off toward the city, trying to pinpoint the source of the fighting. Smoke was rising from three or four locations, but then an explosion lifted a churning cloud of smoke and debris into the air.

"That's a couple of miles from here," he said. "Sounds like things are heating up. That can't last much longer."

Just then an SUV bounced into view, kicking up a trail of dust, coming from the direction of the city. As the truck pulled up to them, Gary 2 could see Mumtaz in the front passenger seat. He had gone into the city with Captain Amir to check out the hotel that would serve as the temporary safe site for the team and ODA-555 while the city was being secured.

Mumtaz was smiling and approached them with hand extended. "Agha Gary," he said, shaking his hand, "things are going well. The last large pocket of resistance is under attack, and General Babajan says he is confident the fight will be over in the next thirty minutes.

"In the meantime, the hotel we have discussed is secured, as General Bismullah promised. You will like it. It appears to be in decent condition, although those Taliban pigs have fouled the bathrooms and used several rooms to stable goats. We will begin cleaning tomorrow. Come, it is only about five kilometers from here—very near your embassy."

Gary 2 removed his hand from Mumtaz's grip. "What about my team? They have not yet arrived from Jabal-os-Saraj."

"Don't worry, Agha Gary, we will radio Hafiz, who is leading them into the city. He knows the hotel very well. He will bring the team straight to the hotel. We have some of our soldiers on duty to provide perimeter security. Aref has al-.

ready coordinated that. Come, let's get everyone together and I will lead you to the hotel."

Gary 2 looked at his wristwatch. It was 6:00 p.m. on 14 November as the convoy drove past the American Embassy compound. He had asked Mumtaz to have the convoy slow so they could get a glimpse of the embassy. It struck him that they were the first Americans back in Kabul in many, many years. Gary 2 had time to get a good look at the embassy building, a white marble structure, now gray-brown from years of dust and neglect. The tall black iron picket fence looked rust stained but solid, and he knew that the Afghan staff that had worked at the embassy back in 1988 when the embassy had closed had remained on the payroll all those years since and had worked to maintain the compound and the buildings.

Gary 2 sat back and reflected on the events of the past ten days. He had arrived on 4 November with the situation still uncertain. No one had any idea how the fighting in the north would evolve, or if the Taliban would make a strong defense of Kabul and the other cities of the north. Now, ten days later, he was leading his team into a liberated Kabul, and all the major cities in the north except Konduz were in Northern Alliance hands.

There was much work to be done over the coming weeks, but right now there was time to relax and reflect on the victory in the north. He saw a sign ahead marking the hotel they were to occupy. Our first night in Kabul, he thought. Man, who would have believed this even a week ago?

The skyline ahead was suddenly lit with the bright flash of an explosion. Tank fire. The general was cleaning up the last resistance. The sound of gunfire came from the direction of the explosion and rose to a crescendo, then died down, ending in the faint sound of several single shots being fired.

Stan leaned forward from the backseat. "I think we can officially declare that Kabul is in Northern Alliance hands as of"—he paused to get the time—"six-thirty p.m., 14 November 2001."

AFTERWORD

On the morning of 9 October 2004, I sat in the office of the director of the Afghan intelligence organization, Amrullah Saleh, discussing the national presidential election taking place across Afghanistan as we spoke. More than eight million men and women were braving threats of violence by the Taliban and al-Qa'ida, long lines, and foul weather—low temperatures and dust storms across the southern half of the nation, rain and snow in the northern areas—to cast their ballots in the first ever, free, democratic election to choose who would be their national leader.

Director Saleh is a longtime friend. I have known him since my September 1996 visit to Kabul to meet Ahmad Shah Masood. Saleh was a trusted protégé of Masood's and became chief of the Northern Alliance office in Dushanbe, Tajikistan, in 1997. During the years that followed, the CIA maintained contact with Masood primarily through Saleh's Dushanbe office. In late October 2001, Saleh, then only thirty years old, was summoned to the Panjshir Valley to join Engineer Aref as his special assistant in managing the Northern Alliance intelligence organization. His duties kept his contact with my JAWBREAKER Team to a minimum, but that changed with the fall of Kabul. When the victorious Northern Alliance forces occupied the city on 14 November 2001, Engineer Aref and his team assumed control of the remnants of the previous national intelligence organization, renaming it the National Directorate of Security (NDS). Saleh became head of Department One, in charge of liaison with the CIA.

As we sat in Director Saleh's office, with his TV set carrying live election coverage from around the country, he and I reflected on the changes that had taken place in Afghanistan since the first CIA team entered the country in September 2001. I recalled to him that on the night of 9 October 2001, Rick and I stood together in the yard of the compound in Barak, smoking cigars under the shelter of a mulberry tree, cold rain falling, discussing the situation we faced. The U.S. bombing campaign had begun two nights earlier and the initial results were disappointing. There were no U.S. military personnel in the country, and we had no idea when the first Special Forces ODA team would arrive. The weather was already deteriorating in the mountains in the north, promising an early winter. It would be an understatement to say that things looked bleak. Yet here we sat, Saleh now the director of the NDS, watching the election process unfold peacefully across Afghanistan.

Saleh told me that he had taken his place at his neighborhood precinct at 6:00 a.m., rather than at the VIP polling station established for senior government officials, to stand with his neighbors to vote for the first time. He was so obviously excited and proud of casting his vote that I was embarrassed at my own rather blasé attitude toward participation in past U.S. elections.

This was a significant day in the history of modern Afghanistan, one that demonstrated just how much progress had been made in rebuilding the country after more than twenty-five years of war. It also served to highlight just how much more remains to be accomplished, and to point out the obstacles that must be overcome if that war-ravaged nation is to achieve economic and political stability, and never again to be used as a sanctuary for terrorists.

I spent the month of October 2004 in Kabul, my fourth visit to Afghanistan since departing the Panjshir Valley in the predawn hours of 4 November 2001. Those visits over the three years provide a basis of comparison for me, as I examine the current situation in the country and speculate on its future.

Critics claim that the effort to impose a Western-style democracy on a nation so ethnically divided as Afghanistan, whose basic infrastructure—roads, electric power system, irrigation network, and educational system—is virtually nonexistent, where so much of the population is illiterate, and where for twenty-five years the rule of law has been replaced by an "AK-47 culture," is doomed to failure. Those critics may ultimately be proven correct, but the experiment started in early 2002 following the Bonn Agreement, which established the framework for an Afghan interim government and for the creation of a national constitution, and set the timetable for democratic elections, is an experiment the Western democracies owe the Afghan people, and is one that should be given every chance to succeed. The successful, peaceful election on 9 October, which placed Hamid Karzai in the presidency, is testimony to the fact that the majority of the Afghan people believe in the experiment.

The road ahead for Afghanistan is not an easy one. The problems facing President Karzai and his government are many, and there are no quick or easy solutions available. I am certainly no political expert, and do not pose as one here, but I would like to touch on a few of the key issues facing the Afghan government, discuss some of the pitfalls that lie ahead, and talk about what the United States might do to assist.

Historically, the central governments ruling in Kabul have been weak, hampered by a lack of a significant, reliable financial base, which hindered those governments' ability to raise, maintain, and field an army capable of projecting military power into the provinces. Other than a relatively small gemstone mining industry centered in the Tajik areas in the northeast, there have been only two reliable national sources of income: taxes collected on the movement of goods across Afghanistan's borders and along its internal road network; and monies collected from the illegal opium trade and smuggling. Strong tribal leaders in the country's border provinces have easily usurped the collection of the majority of these funds.

The billions of dollars that poured into the country during the 1980s only worsened this situation, as those funds went to regional commanders and political figures in the outer provinces, allowing them to strengthen their influence. Opium production continued throughout the years of fighting, and has increased dramatically in the three years since the defeat of the Taliban. Regional leaders have always profited from the drug trafficking, either by direct involvement in the shipment of drugs or by taxing their movement through their areas of control. This wealth continues to enrich a handful of regional leaders and allows them to fund their own strong, armed militias. This has left the central government in Kabul perpetually dependent on the handouts of foreign governments and international financial institutions, and unable to afford to build a true national army that could impose its will on the powerful regional leaders.

Karzai and the Afghan Interim Government (AIG) found itself in the same situation as earlier central governments when they assumed power in early 2002. After a January 2002 conference in Tokyo, there was hope of economic assistance coming. Led by the United States, the participating nations promised to provide $5 billion in aid and reconstruction financing for Afghanistan. However, little in the way of funding materialized from those pledges. The United States provided only around $750,000 the following year, and the majority of those funds were for humanitarian assistance, rather than reconstruction.

Ismail Khan in Herat, General Dostum in Mazar-e Sharif, and the forces of General Fahim Khan on the border with Tajikistan, as well as numerous smaller regional commanders in the eastern provinces, quickly grabbed the opportunity to assume the collection of customs' duties and road taxes, allowing them to further strengthen their powerful militias, and encouraging them to resist cooperation with the government in Kabul. The AIG was faced with the problem of building a national army from the ground up, while hampered by a lack of funds, and it could do nothing to effectively oppose these developments. The decision by the U.S. policy makers that the U.S. military not be utilized to support the AIG against Afghan regional leaders further hindered the Karzai government during this period.

Over the past three years, things have slowly improved for the Kabul government. Training for the Afghan National Army (ANA) is moving forward. There is an internationally supported effort to disarm, deactivate, and reintegrate the regional militias, although progress is hindered by the regional leaders who control those forces.

In mid-2004, Karzai began taking on the powerful regional leaders. Ismail Khan and General Dostum were removed from their self-assumed roles as governors of their respective provinces. As the October national election approached, Karzai then fired his vice president, Marshal Fahim Khan. Fahim was replaced on the Karzai ticket by one of Ahmad Shah Masood's brothers, Ahmad Zia. This move served as a slap to Fahim and his inner circle of Panjshiri Tajik colleagues, who could hardly oppose the inclusion of Masood's brother, even at the expense of Fahim. Karzai went on to win the presidency in a fair, honest process, and the seventeen other candidates, including Ismail Khan, Dostum, and Yunis Qanooni, a Panjshiri from Fahim's inner circle, reluctantly accepted the results.

International monetary donations have grown over the past three years, and the United States has significantly increased its funding for the national reconstruction program. The U.S. military has fielded a number of provincial reconstruction teams (PRTs) around the nation, to provide small-scale assistance, new school buildings, new wells, irrigation projects, and road repair directly to villages in the local areas. Much more in the way of financial assistance and support is needed, but the progress is encouraging.

However, the power of the regional leaders remains a potentially serious threat to the stability of the central government, even after the successful presidential election. Ismail

Khan remains a powerful, locally popular, political and military force in the west, and his close ties to the Iranian government and the financial resources he still controls make him a force to be dealt with. Dostum, who is probably the most devious political figure among the regional leaders, is also a serious potential threat to the Karzai government. Dostum maintains close ties to the Uzbek government, which would like to see Dostum in control of the Afghan provinces bordering Uzbekistan, to serve as a buffer against Islamic fundamentalist groups to the south. The most serious potential threat to stability, however, is Marshal Fahim and his Panjshiri tribals. With perhaps twelve thousand fighters under his command, Fahim and his militia are the single most powerful military force in the country (not counting the more than twenty thousand U.S. soldiers stationed there).

Another problem the Karzai government has faced in the past three years was Engineer Aref and the National Directorate of Security (NDS). Despite his performance in running Masood's intelligence organization for years, and an impressive start in the first six to eight months of 2002, Aref simply proved unable to adapt to the task of moving the NDS toward becoming a broad-based, ethnically mixed, professional organization. Through 2003, it became increasingly clear to Karzai, and to the CIA, that Aref was stuck in the past, using the NDS for the benefit of his own ethnic and personal interests, often working behind the scenes against Karzai and the government. In January 2004, Karzai removed Aref as director of the NDS, "promoting" him to a newly created position as special adviser to the president on intelligence matters—a position with no duties or responsibilities.

In February 2004, Karzai selected Amrullah Saleh as the new director of the NDS. Saleh had done an outstanding job as chief of Department One, but his support for real reform within the NDS earned him the enmity of Engineer Aref. In late 2003, Aref removed Saleh from his position, demoting him to a low-level job of no importance. Saleh toughed it out, continuing to work from within the NDS to bring about positive change.

His appointment as director of the NDS is a bright spot for the future of the organization. He is a Panjshiri Tajik and he's cut from the same mold as Ahmad Shah Masood. Saleh looks beyond his ethnic background and tribal affiliations to a broader vision of Afghanistan, to a democratic nation, governed by the rule of law, wherein all ethnic groups are treated equally. In his first nine months as NDS director, he has had a real impact on the organization, moving it forward with reorganization and restructuring, instituting training at all levels, establishing a recruitment program based on talent rather than ethnic or family background, and dramatically improving morale and performance. It was due to the excellent work of the NDS that the election was held in such a peaceful and orderly manner. Much remains to be accomplished within the NDS, but Director Saleh is moving the organization on the right path.

The developments outlined above are encouraging. With luck, and with the United States and other nations increasing monetary support for reconstruction efforts, and concentrating on the establishment of the Afghan National Army, there is hope that this experiment in democracy will succeed. But the increase in financial assistance, and the renewed commitment to ensure that President Karzai and his new government receive the level of support needed to tackle the problems they face, will require the United States to refocus some of its attention back to Afghanistan and away from Iraq.

Iraq has been the primary focus of the U.S. administration since mid-2002. As Afghanistan began to take a backseat to Iraq in the allocation of financial and personnel resources, it became difficult to fit discussions of Afghan issues into the schedule of the NCS. Aid and assistance were significantly cut, and any suggested new initiatives received short shrift from the policy makers. In order for this newly elected

Afghan government to succeed, the amount of economic assistance provided over the next three to four years by the United States must increase significantly, to perhaps $3 or $4 billion a year, with appropriate advice and guidance from the United States. This would have a tremendous impact on the ability of the Karzai government to break the hold of the regional leaders and accelerate the national reconstruction progress.

You cannot buy an Afghan's loyalty, but you can rent it. After so many years of warfare, death, and destruction, the Afghan people desperately want peace and an opportunity to build a secure life for themselves and their families. A central government with financial resources and a plan for nationwide recovery could bring direct benefits to provincial populations in a way that undermines the influence of the provincial tribal leaders and warlords. Traditionally, loyalties in Afghanistan shift when individuals see that their benefits and rewards will increase. Financial and social rewards from a central government, one able to provide military protection from rapacious warlords and their militias, would be welcomed throughout the nation.

The impact of United States' focus on Iraq is most seriously felt in the war on terrorism being fought along the eastern border of Afghanistan and Pakistan. In early 2002, in the immediate aftermath of the battle at Tora Bora and the subsequent escape of Usama bin Ladin and his chief lieutenant, Ayman al-Zawahari, CIA and specially trained U.S. military Special Operations units began to organize teams in the provincial areas east and southeast of Kabul along Afghanistan's border with Pakistan. These teams, relatively small and mobile, operated out of temporary compounds protected by local commanders, who provided manpower, intelligence, and firepower as the teams tracked down terrorist elements in the area. Initial results were promising.

However, as early as March 2002, the U.S. military began to withdraw many of the key units involved in this effort, in order to allow them to regroup and train in preparation for the coming war with Iraq. These special units were replaced, for the most part, with members of conventional U.S. military forces, such as the 10th Mountain Division and the 25th Infantry Division. While staffed with excellent, brave soldiers, these forces lacked the training and the agility in guerrilla warfare of the Special Operations units. At the same time, the focus on Iraq also began to increase within the CIA, and it became a magnet that drew away personnel and resources, making it increasingly difficult to staff the CIA teams in Afghanistan with experienced paramilitary officers. The complexion of border area operations started to change.

Over the next eighteen months, operational bases in the border areas slowly grew in size, taking on the aspect of permanency, and operations tended to focus less on sending out small teams and more on attempting larger sweeping operations through an area, to locate terrorist suspects, weapons, and ammunition. More often than not, these sweeps resulted in the alienation of the local tribal populations in the area, who deeply resented the destructive searches of their homes and the frightening of women and children.

In late 2003 there was public discussion in the media of a spring military offensive in the Afghan border regions to root out bin Ladin. Spring came and went with no offensive. The U.S. military and the CIA were unable to shift the additional manpower resources required to conduct the operation—the demands of Iraq simply did not allow it.

Finally, there is the problem of Pakistan. For our military efforts in eastern Afghanistan to succeed, we need the full cooperation of Pakistan's military forces. Given the rugged terrain along the border between the two countries, the only way to execute effective combat operations against terrorists hiding there is to have military forces on both sides of the border working together as hammer and anvil. That is, one side attacking while the other side holds firm, trapping the enemy. U.S. forces can move freely throughout the border areas inside Afghanistan; but on the other side, the "anvil," the Pakistani military is restrained from operating in the tribal areas of their country, a strip of land that's more than two thousand miles long and runs the length of Pakistan's border with Afghanistan. In a tradition that extends back to the time of British rule of the region, the fierce tribes that inhabit those areas would rather fight than allow any outside force, even the Pakistani government, access to their homelands, and this state of affairs is not likely to change anytime soon.

As outlined in the text of my narrative, Pakistan has long been viewed within the U.S. government as the "bad boy" of South Asia. Pakistan's efforts to develop nuclear weapons and long-range ballistic missiles have been a source of diplomatic irritation between the two countries since the 1980s. The Pakistani government has long supported the militant Muslims in occupied Kashmir in their guerrilla war against India. These militant Kashmiri fighters are viewed as freedom fighters by Pakistan, while the U.S. government considers them terrorists. The interference with internal events in Afghanistan between April 1992 and September 2001, with the Pakistanis supporting first the Mujahedin fundamentalists and then the Taliban in their civil wars to gain control of the country, further cemented Pakistan's reputation as a troublemaker and a danger to peace and stability in the region. As a result, the United States imposed sanctions against Pakistan for decades. Even today, there is almost always a knee-jerk reaction in the U.S. Congress to any proposal for an improvement in our diplomatic relationship with Pakistan, although Pakistan has proved to be our most important ally in the war on terrorism.

In the immediate aftermath of 11 September 2001, the Pakistani government was faced with a harsh decision: cooperate with the United States in its war on terrorism or be considered an enemy in the coming fight. The Pakistanis made the decision to side with the United States. Pakistan's intelligence organization, the Interservices Intelligence Directorate (ISID), has proved to be an effective partner in assisting the CIA in the arrest of hundreds of al-Qa'ida members inside Pakistan. These include some of the most senior al-Qa'ida operatives yet captured, such as Khalid Sheik Mohammad, the principal planner of the 9/11 attacks. That cooperation continues today, but the Pakistani government is paying a serious internal political cost for their efforts.

During the 1980s and the early 1990s, the ISID arranged for Kashmiri militants and their Pakistani supporters to be trained in camps in Afghanistan, alongside foreign volunteers who had come to take part in the Jihad against the Soviets. Many of those foreigners were al-Qa'ida members, and bonds of friendship and common cause were formed among those training together. Since early 2002, whenever a raid has been conducted in Pakistan against an al-Qa'ida safehouse, al-Qa'ida members are found being hosted by militant Pakistanis, primarily from the Lashkar-e Tayyiba or the Jaish-e Mohammad groups, supporters of the Kashmir insurgency. Those groups deeply resent Pakistani government cooperation with the United States and publicly blame Pakistani president Parviz Musharraf for that cooperation. He has been the target of several assassination attempts by these groups.

Facing this pressure from internal militants, the Pakistani government and military were reluctant, up until late summer 2004, to move into the tribal areas to cooperate in the task of crushing the al-Qa'ida and other foreign elements hiding there. These are the most religiously conservative areas of the country, with thousands of small religious schools teaching the most radical versions of Islam to their students. Under strong pressure from the U.S. government, the Pakistani military forces moved into the tribal area of Waziristan, south of Peshawar, facing strong armed resistance and taking heavy casualties in clashes with the tribes there. This military action only added more political pressure on Musharraf and the Pakistani military.

Despite this costly cooperation, the U.S. government has resisted proposals to provide the Pakistani government with any substantial diplomatic or economic incentives. As of late 2004, Pakistan's military establishment fully backed Musharraf in the fight against al-Qa'ida, but there was growing resentment within the senior ranks of the army at the lack of gratitude and tangible rewards on the part of the United States for the sacrifices made and risks taken by Pakistan in this effort.

If we are to succeed in convincing Pakistan to cooperate fully in an effort to clear the border areas of terrorists, to take the political risks and bear the costs of operating in the tribal areas, then there must be a shift in the U.S. diplomatic stance with Pakistan. We need to revitalize diplomatic relations with Pakistan, provide substantial aid and an assistance program for the Musharraf government to better address the pressing social and economic problems facing the country. We need to reward Pakistan's military, perhaps by allowing significant military sales to Pakistan and addressing such issues as the F-16s purchased and paid for years ago by Pakistan's air force but held by the United States as part of the sanctions program. The fight in Waziristan has cost the Pakistan army millions of dollars and the lives of hundreds of soldiers. To tackle the tribal areas along the length of the border will be even more costly. There must be some payback, some substantial reward, for that effort.

Usama bin Ladin and Ayman al-Zawahiri are hiding somewhere in the tribal areas of Pakistan. They are undoubtedly being assisted by tribal leaders who dislike the Pakistani government and who enjoy the financial rewards bin Ladin brings to them. Winning full Pakistani military cooperation, refocusing military strategy by U.S. forces on the Afghan side of the border, bringing back Special Operations units, and beefing up the number of CIA teams in the border areas would allow for coordinated military operations on both sides of the border. This is the only way to locate and eliminate bin Ladin, al-Zawahiri, and their al-Qa'ida followers.

While there are positive developments taking place in Afghanistan, progress rests on a shaky foundation. Given the lead the United States has taken in Afghanistan since September 2001, moving forward to ensure that the progress already made continues lies with the U.S. government. To make the changes necessary to press forward, this administration must make some serious, difficult choices. Iraq is a problem for which no clear solution exists. The United States is continuing to pour billions of dollars and sacrifice the lives of American soldiers in order to bring peace and democracy to Iraq. This is being done at the expense of Afghanistan, a country where our efforts since September 2001 have already achieved the real prospect for peace and democracy, and the hope of scoring a significant blow in the war on terrorism.

The U.S. policy makers need to step back and reevaluate our plans and programs for Afghanistan, so as to be able to take advantage of the present-day situation that exists in that country. We need to increase financial assistance to the Karzai government, to allow it to develop a nationwide reconstruction program and build an effective national army. The regional tribal leaders, and the powerful warlords, need to be disarmed and their militias reintegrated into the civilian workforce.

The most significant area of unfinished business in the war on terrorism is centered in the border areas between Afghanistan and Pakistan. Our current mode of operations and the structure of our military and CIA forces in those border areas are ineffective in bringing the fight to the enemy hiding in those mountains. The strategy should be reconsidered and U.S. military Special Forces units returned to the area, along with seasoned CIA SAD paramilitary officers.

At the same time, U.S. diplomatic policy toward Pakistan should be reviewed and reconsidered, with the aim of strengthening the Pakistani government's, and their military leadership's, resolve to press hard to root out terrorist strongholds and hiding places in the tribal areas.

The shadow of Iraq falls over this region, and it will be difficult for this administration to shift away from Iraq, even in the small degree that the above changes would require. The money needed to fund the discussed changes for one year would probably amount to less than the cost of one week of U.S. military operations now taking place in Iraq.

Given the total preoccupation with Iraq, I am not confident that the U.S. government will make the policy adjustments necessary to improve conditions for the success of the democratic experiment in Afghanistan, or refocus diplomatic and military efforts back to the South Asia region in order to capture Usama bin Ladin and defeat al-Qa'ida. The opportunity to make these changes exists now; if we fail in these efforts, we do so at our peril.

—Gary C. Schroen
Reno, Nevada
Thanksgiving Day 2004

INDEX